1. summary of Model in OSS
   each will do what

2. User / what shall be considered
      regarding the used
   from design   to implementat. of OSI

3. how do you define OSS

4. where are 3 phes of decision making

You have been asked to
design a OOS for

BUILDING DECISION SUPPORT SYSTEMS

BUILDING DECISION SUPPORT SYSTEMS

John L. Bennett, editor
IBM Research Laboratory
San Jose, California

ADDISON-WESLEY PUBLISHING COMPANY
Reading, Massachusetts • Menlo Park, California
London • Amsterdam • Don Mills, Ontario • Sydney

ADDISON-WESLEY SERIES ON DECISION SUPPORT

Consulting Editors
Peter G. W. Keen
Charles B. Stabell

Decision Support Systems: An Organizational Perspective
Peter G. W. Keen and Michael S. Scott Morton

*Decision Support Systems: Current Practice
and Continuing Challenges*
Steven L. Alter

Electronic Meetings: Technical Alternatives and Social Choices
Robert Johansen, Jacques Vallee, and Kathleen Spangler

*Computers and Profits: Quantifying Financial
Benefits of Information*
Jack P. C. Kleijnen

Measurement for Management Decision
Richard O. Mason and E. Burton Swanson

Building Decision Support Systems
John L. Bennett

Library of Congress Cataloging in Publication Data

Main entry under title:

Building decision support systems.

(Addison-Wesley series on decision support systems)
Includes bibliographical references.

1. Decision-making—Data processing. 2. Management
—Data processing. 3. Management information systems.
I. Bennett, John L.   II. Series.
HD30.23.B84   658.4'03'02854   82–1632
ISBN 0–201–00563–8   AACR2

ISBN 0–201–00563–8
ABCDEFGHIJ–MA–898765432

SERIES FOREWORD

This is the fifth book in the Addison-Wesley Series on Decision Support and the one most specifically focused on building decision support systems. To some extent, it is a taking stock of where we stand in terms of clear, articulable principles for the design and development of decision support systems. An important feature of the book is that the authors (or at least one of the coauthors) of almost every article have been working in the DSS field from its inception. They have been influenced by its early concepts and claims; the process of building DSS has provided continuing tests of those concepts.

The outcome of that experience has been some distinctive techniques for DSS development. Decision support research has largely been a net importer of ideas from other fields. Research-based DSS practice may be a net exporter in terms of understanding how to build interactive systems for nontechnical users, how to evolve complex systems out of simple components, and how to use prototypes as the base for joint user-designed learning. Anyone interested in the craft of system development should find the articles on the topic in this book practical and useful.

Taking stock involves looking at unresolved or new issues as well as consolidating what has been learned so far. It seems clear that future research on decision support will increasingly draw from artificial intelligence in order to meet its goals of helping managers improve their effectiveness. It is also apparent that we know far less, in terms of proven practice rather than just assertions, about exploiting emerging capabilities in the area of data base management than we do about modeling languages. One of the continuing challenges for decision support is to learn how to apply new technologies to achieve the end of better decision making.

The term DSS has moved from being a somewhat recherché concept put forward by only a few academics and practitioners (1975–78) to being a cliché, loosely applied to almost any interactive system for managers. Software vendors label their products DSS, and their competitors criticize the concept of DSS as a way of attacking the products. This book would compound the problem if it focused only on building systems, for that is only one facet of DSS.

The other is decision making. While many of the arguments and techniques in the book have general applicability (to office technology especially), they derive from the experience of building systems to support management decision making. There will always be a tension—ideally a creative one—in the DSS field between Decision and System. The link is Support. The quality of the support we can provide managers depends on our understanding of both decision making and system building.

Peter G. W. Keen

CONTENTS

John L. Bennett

CHAPTER 1

INTRODUCTION

This book is focused on building Decision Support Systems (DSS). It brings together accounts of experience, told in the words of those involved in the development of DSS. It covers the full cycle of DSS evolution—the initial gleam of an idea in the mind's eye, the resulting system that contains the function needed to support people in making decisions, and the redesign phase based on what has been learned. As used here, the term "building" includes planning, design, development, testing, and incorporation into the user's work.

Within the Addison-Wesley Series on Decision Support, this book is the first to emphasize managing the detail of the human interface to the DSS and allocating the computer resources required to build a system. Throughout the book the reader can observe a human focus; our user is a real person rather than an abstraction. The authors chose techniques responsive to the human limitations of the decision maker. In addition, each chapter is an implicit (and sometimes explicit) commentary on the human limitations of DSS developers as they seek to understand and respond to the needs of users. Thus though the authors work from a base of technology, and though the results of their work are embodied in technology, the human dimension plays an important role in what has been achieved and what remains to be done.

Before proceeding to some comments on the chapters, it is important to outline the definition of DSS that colors the interpretation used here. We adapt the words of Keen and Scott Morton, which appeared in the first book in the series [1]. A DSS is a coherent system of computer-based technology (hardware, software, and supporting documentation) used by managers as an aid to their decision making in semistructured decision tasks. We stress *supporting* rather than *replacing* managerial judgments. We focus on improving the *effectiveness* of decision making rather than on merely improving its *efficiency*. For the purposes of this book we need to elaborate on each of these concepts.

Numerous papers have been devoted to all aspects of structured, semistructured, and unstructured decisions. In fact, the concept has been so influential that almost all authors felt compelled to give in the introduction to their chapter their own account of its influence on their work. For our purposes we adopt the definition of Stabell [2].

A task is unstructured when:

1. Objectives are ambiguous and nonoperational, or objectives are relatively operational but numerous and conflicting;

2. It is difficult to determine the cause (after the fact) of changes in decision outcomes and to predict (in advance) the effect on decision outcomes of the actions taken by the decision maker; and

3. It is uncertain what actions taken by the decision maker might affect decision outcomes.

Note that the focus is on objectives and that Stabell distinguishes between outcome (goal achievement) and actions (steps taken to achieve the goal). The missing link is the inability in unstructured tasks to connect in any deterministic way the user actions (procedures) with favorable decision outcomes. Thus we know that the decision maker will act to obtain and use information, but we cannot prove that any particular action has an essential link to the quality of the decision which follows.

The distinction between effectiveness of decision making and efficiency in decision making is crucial for understanding the impact (actual and potential) for DSS. We again adapt the work of Keen and Scott Morton [1] as influenced by Stabell.

Effectiveness in decision making requires us to address the process of identifying *what* should be done. Effective decision making requires consideration of the criteria influencing the decision. Thus, in this view, we need to discover the decision maker's perception of the decision situation in order to increase the decision maker's effectiveness. This is fully as important as identifying the surface "facts" of the situation. It is often the case that the "facts" which initially appear important when working within a semistructured or unstructured decision situation are not the ones that, after they are explored by the decision maker, turn out to be the most influential in affecting decision outcome.

Efficiency in decision making addresses the means for performing a given defined task in order to achieve outputs as well as possible, relative to some predefined performance criteria. The definition of efficiency used here is closely related to the term's use in physics and engineering: an output value divided by a value for the input resources used to obtain that output.

Compared with effectiveness, efficiency implies a narrowing of focus in order to get a specific job done. Typically, it takes the form of minimizing time, cost, or effort to complete a given activity. Stabell in Chapter 10 of this book gives examples of how an analysis can focus unduly on initial parameters, leading to "lots of numbers but not much insight." Effectiveness, on the other hand, implies a broadening of focus in order to find out what set of activities should be considered. It requires defining and searching a decision space to become more confident that the goal itself is relevant and appropriate.

Thus, to support decision making, we must move beyond merely seeking the efficient means necessary for achieving a given end. The added requirement is the decision maker's need to look for a clear definition of the goal, and in this book we first focus on ways to assist the decision maker in being efficient in the pursuit of a goal that in itself is effective. Effectiveness requires the decision makers to adapt and learn, to make a responsive adjustment to changes in the environment for and within which they make decisions. Again, to paraphrase Keen and Scott Morton [1], decision makers need to be concerned with effectiveness in unstructured processes; efficiency in structured processes, where the goal is already set, can be programmed and delegated. Stabell reinforces this idea. Effective behavior maximizes *goal* attainment for a given set of resources used. It includes a scanning of opportunities; it implies a larger frame of reference. Efficient behavior minimizes the resources used to achieve a given level of decision outcome; it implies (once the context is frozen) a system closed with respect to a shift in goals.

From this perspective it is easy to see why all the authors in this book emphasize the design of the interface between the decision maker and the computer. The purpose of a DSS cannot be achieved without impact on the *process* of decision making, on the behavior of the decision maker. In decision support we seek to increase the decision maker's ability to deal with complexity and uncertainty. From this perspective we can also point out a growing recognition of the link between DSS use and management learning. Discovering how to be more effective requires "divergent" thinking as the decision maker is stimulated to expand the set of open decision possibilities. Discovering how to be more efficient requires "convergent" thinking as the decision maker uses tools to achieve results in reduced time or at reduced cost.

The physical realization of a particular DSS—the tangible qualities of computer display screens, terminal input keyboards, and printers—forms the decision maker's interface to the system. But, as can be seen in the following chapters, we take these physical elements of the DSS to be "given" for the most part. We instead direct our attention to the design of the software which shapes the content appearing on the screen, interprets the user action at the keyboard, and formats the printed output. The reference material describing the function and the operation of the system is also part of the user interface. This supporting documentation is, however, merely a means to achieve the goal of productive use. Thus we note the amount of developer energy that goes into making the operation of the DSS "obvious" to users, so that the quantity of needed documentation can be reduced.

This book maintains a focus on design and implementation strategies that differ markedly from those of more customary data processing techniques. The latter lead to systems that deliver factual information, but the *process* of obtaining that information does not in itself directly contribute to a change in decision-maker perceptions. The emphasis in this book on decision-maker participation in DSS use arises from the essential dynamics of the information assimilation process. This process is personal to the decision maker during goal exploration. It then becomes an explicit goal of DSS construction to facilitate and direct this decision-maker learning.

PURPOSE OF THIS BOOK

The primary purpose of this book is to serve readers who want to develop a personal, mental model of what it means to build a DSS. Such a model is needed in order for them to understand and assimilate the information that they will read in the literature on DSS design and development.

Some readers will actually be responsible for constructing a DSS. These readers seek guidance concerning trade-off decisions appropriate for their own specific working environment. They will read each chapter in order to sharpen their judgment for making design decisions and for managing the resources necessary in constructing a computer-based DSS. For these readers DSS design is particularly challenging because of the paramount importance in decision making of the human (the managerial user) and because of the need to influence the organizational environment in which the DSS will be used. Thus, in building a DSS, needed shifts in the decision process (related to effectiveness) must be planned and managed. This aspect of construction is in addition to the planning for and management of computer resources (related to technological efficiency) and to the revision of organizational procedures needed to accommodate the DSS.

Other readers will be looking for general background to help them understand the place of DSS in the general milieu of computer applications on the one hand and the emphasis on support of office work on the other. For example, computer applications have led to the capture of operational data from manufacturing, service, and distribution activities. The authors in this book suggest how the data can be extracted, subsetted, and aggregated to support decision making in the management of physical resources. By analogy, the use of computers in the office (for word processing, text processing, and communication) is leading to the capture of operational data from offices throughout many enterprises. Given an appropriate point of view, it may become possible to see how ideas tested in current DSS can be adapted to include support of decision making in the management of personnel resources.

DSS use, like the use of an office workstation by a professional, is discretionary. What has been learned about DSS built around workstations targeted for management users also offers insight on how professionals use office workstations. As Keen has suggested to me in conversations, the DSS experience can serve as a learning curve for management use of office workstations.

To support this variety of reader purposes, the authors were invited to submit chapters on the bases of their known interests and their current projects relevant to building DSS. Each chapter was developed independently; but because of the communication within the community of DSS workers, many authors were aware of the ideas used in other projects. As editor I have made suggestions to avoid overlap, but some repetition of ideas is inevitable. In fact, the reader should realize that those elements appearing in several chapters are the ones that are important in any DSS work.

The authors have aimed to give the reader as much technical content and practical insight as they can within the framework of the series. A different approach to a book on building DSS would be to focus on the concrete, specific details necessary for the complete description of a system. This could be immediately useful to the reader who happens to have the same working environment and very similar computer resources and who is seeking to solve the very problem addressed by the author. However, such an approach does not generalize well at this stage of our understanding. There is not much theory to guide the reader in distinguishing between trivial differences that can safely be ignored (e.g., specific programming language used) and fundamental differences in the decision situation (e.g., delegated use versus personal use of the DSS) that can make specific results (effectively) nonapplicable to the reader's situation. The nature of the work in this field of DSS development requires a creativity on the part of the reader looking for solutions. This *can* be stimulated by the reader's interpretation of broad experience. It is the purpose of this book to offer such a reader a cross section of approaches and a start on the framework needed for interpreting these approaches.

SCOPE AND COVERAGE OF THE CONTENT

The authors have been asked to address the following six questions in the development of their chapters:

1. Why is the chapter topic important to the DSS designer and developer?

2. With respect to the topic, what are the *key* issues for building a system?

3. Which of these issues in the shaping of technology are particularly important for DSS?

4. What contingencies, trade-offs, and bases for compromise exist during design?

5. In contrast with other computer systems, what special considerations apply to DSS?

6. What is the likely direction of future development?

Each chapter states propositions and then works them out to achieve a reasonably unified whole. Each author or author team makes explicit observations about the bases for trade-offs and gives reasons *why* conclusions are reached. In this way they try to:

1. Suggest how experience gained from development of other interactive systems transfers to DSS, and

2. Emphasize what is unique about DSS.

The intent in asking each author or team to reveal a framework was to ensure that readers gain a better understanding. Creative analogy drawing on the part of the reader will be necessary. The value of the book lies in its power to assist readers in the process of creating personal models of what it means to build a DSS.

Readers will probably find this book valuable at several levels. For a first reading a rapid scan is helpful for picking up a general overview of approaches and for observing the style that DSS development seems to dictate. Those who have read the first book in the series [1] are well prepared to do this. A second level involves study of the point of view presented in individual chapters. One can see how the experience of the individual authors has shaped both the topics they chose to emphasize and the targets they set for themselves. The third level of reading requires a critical awareness of what is covered and what is omitted. It should be possible for the thoughtful reader to understand what lies behind author statements, how the details relate to statements made by other authors, and whether the observations appear to hold generally or to be explained by the particular circumstances. This book is in this sense unique so far in the series because the combination of authors enables the reader to see in juxtaposition the different interpretations of similar situations.

As a result of studying this book, readers should be able to:

1. Relate the ideas presented in each chapter to their particular situations,

2. Make practical use of the specific techniques described in a chapter in order to manage the particular trade-offs found necessary in their own work, and

3. See how ideas from various chapters may be tied together in a personal synthesis.

Each reader, whether a student or a designer, must perform such a creative synthesis when considering the impact of, or construction of, DSS.

All of the authors in this book are also students of DSS design. In a field as challenging as DSS development, one tends to focus energy on a particular approach as one becomes involved in a particular situation. Even we experts make working assumptions about what is important in order to filter and interpret an otherwise unmanageable mass of conflicting information. We make progress as a result of this focusing. This book offers us an opportunity to share with the reader what we have done. And from the perspective of the book as a whole, we may observe some unexamined or forgotten assumptions. The book offers us an opportunity to defocus, unfreeze, and form a new synthesis. Through this shift we are able to interpret the facts from a new perspective. As fellow students we share this learning experience with the reader.

A COMMENTARY ON THE CHAPTERS

The chapters in this book should be read with an understanding that DSS are still quite new. While the potential for computers to aid decision makers was recognized almost at the start of the computer age, numerous barriers have hindered development. A first impediment has been the lack of a basis for establishing the value of DSS results. Even in those cases where DSS were constructed (see Carlson, Chapter 2 of this book) using the available technology, lack of appreciation for their impact made it hard to justify continued expenditure. This is related to the issue of effectiveness. Because of the unstructured nature of the problems attacked with DSS, value has had to be demonstrated through multiple instances of DSS used in a variety of settings. It is true that recent developments in low-cost mini- and micro-computers have stimulated research and development. However, even earlier the cost of computer resources was not the central problem.

Second, it has taken several years to build up a body of information on how to use computer resources to support effective and efficient decision making. The remarkable growth of computer science literature bears witness to the increase in theoretical and practical knowledge. However, much of this work has been centered on the computer technology rather than on end-user support. Even less work has been directed to decision support. At the moment we do not have a detailed understanding either of management decisions or of the role that individual decision-maker perceptions play in making them. So our insight on how to apply current technology to decision support lags far behind the availability of that technology.

The third barrier to DSS has been the lack of knowledge about how to provide a manager-computer interface that would be judged effective by critical and demanding users. The advent of visually attractive terminals with two-dimensional surfaces for both display of and interaction with information has given us a technical basis for growth. We are now learning to use this capability for DSS.

The set of chapters included must therefore be recognized as expositions of what can be said with confidence at this point. The book serves as a means for taking stock; it is not intended to be "complete" or "the last word." Given the available experience, this is a good time to synthesize, to review where we are in an area of rapid technological development, and to ponder the far-reaching shifts in the way that people use computers. The cross section of DSS work reported is one view of the scene. There is no generally accepted closed set of topics that should be covered in a discussion of DSS design and development. As with any emerging, cross-disciplinary field, the central topics are still in definition.

One of the problems for the reader when authors present their own experiences in their own words is the fact that they often use vocabulary with special meaning in their own community. As an aid to the reader I have asked each author team to define clearly those concepts key to their work. Nonetheless, the reader must be alert to meanings particular to some environments. In some cases what appears to be an insignificant terminological difference actually represents a fundamentally different concept. For example, the term "implementation" is often used in DSS papers to mean "to put into decision-making practice" without special emphasis on the technical tools used to bring about needed change. In the computer industry, in contrast with the academic community, the term "implementation" is often used to mean "construction of the computer-based tool"—the writing of the programs and the acquisition of the equipment. In this latter use of the term the computer resources are but a "means" to the "end" implied by the academic meaning. However, as noted above, the hard facts of the computer system can lead to goal displacement from the "ends" (decision-making effectiveness) to the "means" (building the physical DSS).

Even within the DSS field there may be different meanings associated with the use of the same term. It is significant that those working on DSS theory often chide their colleagues in industry for their limited focus on building the DSS rather than on influencing the nature of decisions. Thus the term "implementation" tends to have a narrower meaning in industry than it does in academic circles. However, the industry emphasis on "system products" tends to have potential for broader impact than does the development of a DSS for a specific application. On the other hand, the designer of a DSS for general application must be concerned about recovering the investment costs in a broad marketplace, which the designer does not control and cannot manage. The developer of a *specific* DSS may find it easier to manage resources in its more limited environment.

With respect to the concept of implementation and its relation to the system, the work of Hurst *et al.* (Chapter 6) represents one form of DSS evolution. The Keen and Gambino (Chapter 7) description of a "system product" intended for a community of users at different locations represents a second kind of evolution in a DSS. Because the market seems to be so hard to predict, because system development seems to require so much practitioner judgment, and because the widespread importance of DSS has not yet become an article of marketplace faith, the counterpart evolution in computer industry DSS "system products" has not yet taken place. We are, however, beginning to see application generators and end-user languages being used as the base for DSS. This is particularly marked in the area of personal computing. With this warning we will continue to use the term "implementation" in its broader sense of both *building* the DSS and its subsequent *use* in decision support. Understanding how to fit specific implementations (in the narrower sense) into the larger evolution is one of the tasks that we all face, both designers and readers.

The original outline for this book sent to the authors concentrated on *building* the DSS. The chapters as they appear have much more emphasis on implementation in the broad sense than was originally envisioned. Hurst *et al.* (Chapter 6), Keen and Gambino (Chapter 7), and Moore and Chang (Chapter 8) illustrate the strong interaction between building and using the DSS. This is a fact of the authors' experience reported at this stage in the evolution of DSS. We expect that a direct focus on building DSS, the provision of a comprehensive technological tool kit or technology catalog, may become appropriate as our understanding evolves.

Carlson (Chapter 2) looks into the issue of how managers will perceive the decision support resources made available to them. The framework he presents of *representations* for conveying information to the user, *operations* for manipulating data displayed as representations, aids for user *memory*, and aids for user *control* provides conceptual categories to help bridge from theory to practice. This theme of an overall architecture needed for a successful DSS appears in several chapters. Keen and Gambino (Chapter 7) cite the work of Brooks [3] on architecture, "the complete and detailed specification of the user interface." Emphasis is rightfully placed on the critical aspects of the DSS that show through to the user. These are precisely the parts of the DSS that have to be described to the decision maker before the tool can achieve its purpose. It is therefore necessary to include in the materials used for teaching all that the user must consult in order to use the power of the system effectively.

The issue then becomes a question of what constitutes an architecture. How do we know when an architecture is complete and whether or not it is adequate? In particular, Brooks [3] stresses the role of "conceptual integrity" in designing a "good" system. This can be measured operationally in terms of user learning time, speed of use, user error rate, and user attitude toward continued use. We do not yet have a generally accepted answer to questions about architecture and conceptual integrity even though they are central for building a DSS. The concepts presented by Carlson (Chapter 2) are useful guides for interpretation.

An architecture can also give us guidance as we establish the building blocks from which we construct DSS. As in the architecture of buildings, the shape and size of the structure can suggest the nature of the elements needed for its construction. Carlson (Chapter 4) gives us an idea of what might eventually find its way into a "parts catalog" suitable for engineering a DSS. He asserts that much of computer science *can* be adapted to building DSS. Gorry and Krumland (Chapter 9) make similar points about the applicability of computer languages developed for exploration of Artificial Intelligence (AI) issues. Perhaps the availability of "off the shelf" system components as technological building blocks will be necessary before DSS can become widely installed. Hurst *et al.* (Chapter 6) reinforce this point through an analogy with the engineer who builds on the work of others. The ability to do this can free the DSS builder from excessive attention to computer-oriented detail. The creative energy of the builder can then be directed to assisting the users to clarify their decision processes.

It is clear that conversational user-computer interaction has a central role in DSS. Keen and Gambino (Chapter 7) emphasize the amount of time they spent on design and refinement of the Interactive Support System for Policy Analysts (ISSPA) user interface. Carlson (Chapter 4) cites studies showing that typically 60 percent of the software for interactive applications is devoted to code related to the user interface. Bennett (Chapter 3), in response to this, outlines issues both in "ease of use" (or usability) and in engineering the approaches needed to manage the quality of the user interface during DSS development. His guiding questions

1.   What does the user *see*?

2.   What must the user *know*? and

3.   What can the user *do* at each interaction point?

are clearly related to the framework suggested by Carlson. All of the user interface work is directed to the need to support the decision maker in finding data relevant to decisions, in developing proposed alternatives, and in making choices between alternatives.

Access to data is central to DSS. The extensive literature of data management contains a wealth of ideas, which is characteristic of a fast-moving field. What would be ideal, for our purposes here, would be a review of data base technology and an interpretation (based on examples derived from experience) to show the impact of data management on DSS practice. Such a consolidation is difficult to achieve at this time. We are missing the depth of experience needed to make sound statements. Books by Martin [4] and Date [5] provide source readings in data management and data base concepts. But readers must provide a "DSS filter" (the kind of mental model which we hope they can build for themselves through study of this book) in order to select the needed concepts and to synthesize the required understanding. Articles such as those by Carlson [6] on extraction and aggregation of data from operational files and Clemons [7] on techniques for recalculation of derived data on a schedule consistent with DSS performance needs are solid contributions to the catalog of techniques needed to build DSS. However, it is still necessary that the reader know how to interpret and apply such articles.

In addition, we stress the need for readers to sort out from the literature ideas which are attractive in concept but not yet well executed. For example, the concept of an end-user query language included as part of a data base package is good, but the designs of many actual implementations are not acceptable to the demanding DSS end user in practice. The chapters in this book by developers Hurst *et al.* (Chapter 6), Keen and Gambino (Chapter 7), and Moore and Chang (Chapter 9) show how ideas must be adapted in the face of practical computer limitations.

Models are central for applying analytic theory and methods to practical decision support. Indeed, some would say that a system is not a DSS if it does not include some sort of model representation. There is justification for this viewpoint, especially if a model is seen as an embodiment of the decision maker's own evolving view of those elements thought to be important for the decision under consideration. In this context the means offered by the DSS for representing, understanding, and modifying a model become key in maintaining the focus on decision-making effectiveness. Dyer and Mulvey (Chapter 5) discuss their experience in choosing models to meet user needs. Their emphasis is on the model selection decision and on the trade-offs necessary to fit effectively within a DSS environment. Many of the books addressing models could be reviewed from the perspective of appropriateness for and adaptation to particular DSS situations. An outstanding source of background on models applied to marketing, for example, is contained in Montgomery and Urban [8]. Because many of the models are based on work in operations research, reference to the standard text by Wagner [9] is appropriate.

In summary, data access and models are both important in DSS. DSS are a natural fusion of Management Information Systems (data and reports) and Management Science (modeling and analysis). The architectures discussed by our authors support the finding of answers to both "what is" and "what if" questions.

The reporting of experience by DSS developers associated with the Wharton School, the Sloan School at MIT, and the Stanford School of Business is central to the book. Each group of authors relates experience to some aspect of theory. Each chapter indicates how the course of development is swayed by the available computer technology, personal interaction with intended DSS users, and organizational realities.

Hurst *et al.* (Chapter 6) use an analogy with truck farming to indicate how some conditions for the growth of a DSS to maturity can be beyond the developers' control. The Alpha, Beta, and Gamma case studies show how the middle-out approach has been applied to construction of practical DSS.

Keen and Gambino (Chapter 7) offer perhaps the most comprehensive account of a DSS project. The explicit linking to the system development experience reported by Brooks [3] allows for comparison and contrast of DSS with other computer-based systems. The analysis of the school-funding decision environment allows us to understand why some of the trade-off design decisions were made. The difficulties they report in moving from a system *application* to a system *product* are a precursor of what other developers will face as the field matures.

While several authors mention incorporating a DSS into the working environment of the decision maker, no one focuses on the methodology for handling this key "socialization" process. The choice and application of resources is clearly situation-dependent. Moore and Chang (Chapter 8) illustrate how crucial for DSS survival is the adoption of the DSS concept by the organization.

Current DSS are far from being "complete" systems. Since managerial work is so heavily oriented toward personal, verbal contact (face to face and by telephone), which is not well supported by any current DSS, each DSS is likely to continue to be used as "one tool among many." This suggests a need for much more study addressing the process of incorporation of DSS into the work habits of the individual decision maker.

The terminal through which the DSS function is offered to the user has a strong influence on the user interface. Much of the relative emphasis that Keen and Gambino (Chapter 7) place on a "verb-oriented" approach can be attributed to the fact that ISSPA was originally used through a typewriter terminal. In such a case the listing of past interactions serves as an important source of "representations" (Carlson, Chapter 2) against which current user commands can operate. Carlson (Chapter 2) and Bennett (Chapter 3) suggest, in contrast to the approach of Keen and Gambino, a design framework explicitly directed to support of a DSS user working at a display terminal. On a display terminal no record of past interactions automatically appears in front of the user to serve as a representation. Thus the user at a display terminal must be able to construct (or reconstruct) a context to which to apply specific commands (abstracted by Carlson as generic "operations").

At a deeper level of analysis the apparent contradiction between the Carlson chapters and Bennett's observations on the one hand and the Keen and Gambino principles on the other hand can be resolved. Indeed, we can recognize that decision makers do speak in terms of actions (verbs) and that these actions always operate on representations (objects). We notice how the different views of the decision process can be seen as part of the same whole. Keen and Gambino are very sensitive to what managers *say*; Carlson and Bennett develop a theory of how managers can be supported in their *thinking*; and the "decision research" focus of Stabell (Chapter 10) addresses the prescriptive aspects of what managers *should do*. This is an example of the kind of careful interpretation that the reader will have to perform in order to understand what may otherwise appear to be direct contradictions throughout the book.

Much more needs to be said about the role of terminals in DSS. We are currently observing a rapid shift in the range, cost, and quality of display stations suitable for managerial use. To a large extent our understanding of DSS design has been gained through the use of terminals with far less function than those that will soon be available. For example, the intense activity in low-cost graphics displays, time-series animation, and dynamic review of model sensitivity offers dramatic increases in the understanding of phenomena important to management decision making. A report on the experience base which will be built on such capability would be a suitable topic for a subsequent volume.

We explicitly sought a chapter on the use of "natural" language at the system interface. Many have stated that the real impact of computer tools will be seen only when managers can "converse" through the user-computer interface. A number of systems have emphasized the use of natural language in the interface; see, for example, Davis [10]. However, the size of "knowledge base" resources currently required and the difficulty of constructing the dialog manager have precluded widespread use of natural language techniques.

Gorry and Krumland (Chapter 9) present the only extensive discussion of Artificial Intelligence (AI) techniques in the book. The idea behind the request for the chapter was to ask workers knowledgeable in both DSS and AI to interpret how AI developments might be applied to DSS work. It is significant that this takes the form of an essay rather than an analysis of an existing DSS applying the techniques. Once again, we have not yet had the experience using these techniques in the number of applications necessary to form a reliable base of knowledge.

Similarly, as the field of computational linguistics continues to evolve, it may be worthwhile to plan a review of this field to see how ideas developed there might be applicable to DSS construction. Our recognition of the contributions to building DSS potentially available from natural language studies, artificial intelligence techniques, and computational linguistics practice emphasizes the "opportunistic" (in the best sense) nature of our work. The methods described by the authors are influenced by many sources. But it is also clear that merely having an idea is not enough. Our authors have actually applied the ideas as a means of sorting the "good" ones which may not be practical from the techniques of seasoned value.

I was unsuccessful in finding an author for a chapter explicitly focused on the economic issues in building DSS. This topic is closely linked to the topic of evaluation. The cost of the resources necessary to build a DSS is visible and accountable. On the other hand, the less visible nature of the broadening of the decision maker's effectiveness in handling unstructured decisions makes it hard to apply accounting methods to the benefits. Hurst *et al.* (Chapter 6) explicitly address this issue in one section, and other authors allude to the difficulties of evaluation.

As is common with emerging technology, the current focus falls on building and installing. The issue is often how to make the DSS work at a reasonable cost (both technically and organizationally) rather than how to make it work well. General questions about evaluation can be asked of all authors. As editor I have often urged authors to explain *why* the points they make are important and to be explicit about their interpretations of their experience. In spite of this emphasis on my part, the reader can pose many questions that could only be answered by close examination of the particular DSS. Probably the best approach toward evaluation (determining how well we have done on a variety of dimensions) is found in Chapter 8 of Keen and Scott Morton [1]. The chapter title, "A Smorgasbord of Methods," is a reminder that we are lacking an accepted method for the evaluation of effectiveness. This brings us full circle to our opening discussion of effectiveness and efficiency.

Throughout the book the perceptive reader will note how practical facts of implementation can influence the thinking of developers engaged in battle as they shape the technology upon which they must construct the DSS. Stabell (Chapter 10), in a closing critique and in the description of how he applies "decision research" concepts in DSS practice, returns us to our earlier theme by reminding us of the need to keep a focus on *decisions* in DSS analysis, design, and evaluation. Without such a warning, it is all too easy for us as designers, with our own limited cognitive capacity and limited personal energy resources, to be swamped with the day-to-day details of the computer "means" and lose (temporarily) a clear view of the decision-making "ends."

We are now ready to turn to the words of the several authors. It is clear that the concepts and techniques used to construct DSS have many years of evolution ahead. This book can be thought of as a snapshot to show one view of the current state of the art.

ACKNOWLEDGMENTS

All the authors had an opportunity to respond to the structure and content of this introductory chapter. I am particularly indebted to P. Keen, G. Hurst, and E. Carlson for time spent in contributing clarifying comments.

REFERENCES

1. Keen, P. G. W., and M. S. Scott Morton. *Decision Support Systems: An Organizational Perspective.* Reading, Mass.: Addison-Wesley, 1978.

2. Stabell, C. B. *Decision Research: A Description and Diagnosis of Decision Making in Organizations.* Bergen, Norway: Norwegian School of Economics and Business Administration, Working Paper A79.006, June, 1979.

3. Brooks, Jr., F. P. *The Mythical Man-Month. Essays on Software Engineering.* Reading, Mass.: Addison-Wesley, 1975.

4. Martin, J. *Computer Data Base Organization.* 2nd ed. Englewood Cliffs, N.J.: Prentice-Hall, 1977.

5. Date, C. J. *An Introduction to Database Systems.* 2nd ed. Reading, Mass.: Addison-Wesley, 1977.

6. Carlson, E. D. "Using Large Data Bases for Interactive Problem Solving." *Proceedings of the International Conference on Very Large Data Bases*, Association for Computing Machinery, 1976, pp. 499–501.

7. Clemons, E. K. "Data Base Design for Decision Support." *Proceedings of the Fourteenth Hawaii International Conference on System Sciences*, North Hollywood, Calif.: Western Periodicals, January, 1981. pp. 580–88.

8. Montgomery, D., and G. L. Urban. *Management Science in Marketing.* Englewood Cliffs, N.J.: Prentice-Hall, 1969.

9. Wagner, H. M. *Principles of Operations Research with Application to Managerial Decisions.* 2nd ed. Englewood Cliffs, N.J.: Prentice-Hall, 1975.

10. Davis, R. "A DSS for Diagnosis and Therapy." *Data Base*, 8:3 (Winter 1977), pp. 58–72.

AN APPROACH FOR DESIGNING
DECISION SUPPORT SYSTEMS

Eric D. Carlson

CHAPTER 2

INTRODUCTION

Studies of specific decisions and general studies of decision making have indicated the potential benefits of computer support for decision making. These potential benefits can be divided into two categories: displaced cost and added value. Displaced cost results from reduced costs for data gathering, computation, and data presentation in support of decision making. In these mechanical tasks the dollar value of computer support is measurable. Added value results from investigating more alternatives, doing more sophisticated analyses of alternatives, using better methods of comparing alternatives, making quicker decisions, etc. Often it is difficult to identify the added value because it does not occur on a routine basis. Measuring added value is complicated by the difficulty of linking increased profits or other monetary measures to a change in the decision-making process, such as considering more alternatives. Small improvements in decision making can result in high added value. For example, one airline's computer-supported decision to redeploy aircraft on one route is reported to have increased profit by $300,000 in one month [31]. Such potential benefits continue to stimulate management's interest in computer support for decision making [10].

Computer hardware and software vendors also have an interest in the development of computer support for decision making because such support can help justify large data bases, data base management systems, additional computing power, new programming languages, time sharing, and terminals [5]. Computer support for decision making can encourage customer executives to take a per-

---

A version of this chapter originally appeared in "Proceedings of Eleventh Annual Hawaii International Conference on Systems Sciences," 1978, published by Western Periodicals, North Hollywood, California. Used by permission.

sonal interest in computers and can help the computer salesperson to encourage management involvement in data processing.

The use of computers in decision making can be described in terms of various types of decisions. Following the ideas of Anthony [3], decisions can be classified as:

Strategic planning: decisions related to setting policies, choosing objectives, and selecting resources

Management control: decisions related to assuring effectiveness in acquisition and use of resources

Operational control: decisions related to assuring effectiveness in performing operations

Operational performance: decisions that are made while performing the operations

Simon [29] classifies decisions as structured (programmable) or unstructured (nonprogrammable) depending on whether or not the decision-making process can be described in detail before the decision is made. A decision may be unstructured as a result of novelty, time constraints, lack of knowledge, large search space, need for nonquantifiable data, etc. Gorry and Scott Morton [17] combine Anthony's and Simon's categories, and their combination can be extended as shown in Figure 2.1.

FIGURE 2.1 *Different Types of Decisions and Degree of Decision Structure (Adapted from Gorry and Scott Morton [17])*

	Operational Performance	Operational Control	Management Control	Strategic Planning
Structured	Payroll Production	Accounts Receivable	Budget Analysis	Tanker Fleet Mix
	Airline Reservations	Inventory Control	Short Term Forecasts	Site Location
	Dispatching	Production Scheduling	Long Term Forecasts	Mergers
Unstructured	Solving A Crime	Cash Management	Budget Preparation	Product Planning

Gorry and Scott Morton claim that most existing computer support for decision making is for structured decisions, that some progress has been made in supporting semi-structured decisions, and that almost no computer support is used for unstructured decisions. They argue that the semi-structured and unstructured decisions (especially management control and strategic planning) are of the greatest concern to decision makers. They call systems intended to support these types of decisions Decision Support Systems (DSS). Thus DSS are a subset of Management Information Systems (MIS), since MIS include all systems which support any management decision making.

Because DSS have high potential value for both users and suppliers of computer services, one would expect to find many DSS in use. Yet the literature on the applications of computers in government and business indicates very little use of DSS. The lack of use is apparent even though there have been many attempts to develop such systems.

One survey of fifty-six DSS divided them into two general categories: data-oriented systems and model-oriented systems [2]. Data-oriented systems provide functions for data retrieval, analysis, and presentation. Both generalized and special-purpose software packages are included in this category. Systems in this category are usually developed by persons with data processing or computer science backgrounds. Model-oriented systems provide accounting, simulation, or optimization models to help make decisions. These systems are usually developed by persons with management science backgrounds. There are many opinions on why data-oriented systems and model-oriented systems have not had much success in supporting decision making. In general, the main problem seems to be a mismatch between DSS design or performance and the requirements of decision makers or decision making. The causes of the mismatch may be technical (e.g., poor response times) or nontechnical (e.g., different personal preferences). Because of the mismatch many systems which are developed cease to be used or are used for routine report generation rather than for direct support of decision makers.

This chapter proposes a framework for designing DSS which is intended to help reduce the differences between the requirements of decision making and decision makers and the capabilities of the DSS. The framework is based on a review of case studies of decision making and of DSS and on five years of experience with the design, implementation, and evaluation of a prototype DSS used in 16 applications with over 200 users [7, 18].

REQUIREMENTS FOR DSS

In order to understand DSS, we attempted to analyze the decisions and users for which such systems are intended. In particular, we reviewed and performed case studies of decision making to identify specific requirements of decision making and decision makers. There are many possible interpretations of these studies. The observations presented here are those we have found useful in the design of DSS.

Paradigms of Decision Making

Three examples of paradigms of decision making illustrate the variety of decision-making processes. The first example is the rational (economic) paradigm, which postulates that decision processes attempt to maximize the expected value of a

Allison Model

satisficing

decision by determining payoffs, costs, and risks for alternatives [11]. A second paradigm asserts that the decision-making process is one of finding the first cost-effective alternative by using simple heuristics rather than optimal search techniques [12]. A third paradigm describes decision making as a process of successive limited comparisons in order to reach a consensus on one alternative [20].

Additional evidence of the variety of decision-making processes can be found in studies of decision making. Gordon, Miller, and Mintzberg [16] identified forty processes in looking at nine types of decisions. Mintzberg, Raisinghani, and Théorêt [25] analyzed twenty-five decisions and identified seven basic processes with many variations. Carlson, Grace, and Sutton [8] observed different processes among individuals working on the same decision. Because of the variety of decision-making processes we conclude that a DSS is more likely to be used and to be cost-effective if it supports multiple processes.

Another observation on decision making which we have found useful is that different types of decisions have different data processing requirements [17]. That is, a structured, operational control decision has different requirements than a semi-structured one, and so on. For example, strategic planning decisions tend to require more varied, more aggregated, and more qualitative data than do management control decisions. And structured decisions tend to utilize more data transformations than do unstructured decisions. A specific decision may be of a different type in different organizations at different times or for different decision makers. If a DSS is designed for a specific type of decision, any change in the type of decision requires a change in the DSS to accommodate changes in data processing requirements. Therefore we conclude that designing a DSS for a specific type of decision reduces the number of decisions it can support and leads to increased cost if there is a change in the type of decision it is intended to support.

Observations on Decision-Maker Activities

Studies of decision makers have ranged from recording their daily activities to observing their use of DSS. Five observations from such studies are important in our analysis of existing DSS and in our approach to DSS design.

First, decision makers have trouble describing a decision-making process, but they do seem to rely on conceptualizations, such as pictures or charts, when making or explaining a decision [8]. In some cases the conceptualizations are not physically represented, but we can infer that they exist as a basis for verbal communication (e.g., "bottom line," "payoff curve," and "quick ratio"). Thus a DSS should not require that a decision maker be able to describe the decision-making process before the DSS is built, and a DSS should help a decision maker conceptualize a problem.

Second, decision makers' activities can be categorized even though the decision-making processes may be difficult to explain. Simon has used three categories for describing decision-making activities: Intelligence, Design, and Choice

[29]. Intelligence, or problem finding, includes activities such as comparisons of current status with goals or standards, exception reporting, preliminary computations, etc. Design encompasses activities related to development of alternatives. Choice covers activities related to evaluating and selecting from the alternatives. Studies of decision making which use this paradigm indicate that Intelligence, Design, and Choice activities are interleaved and iterative, but that these activities can be identified [27]. Identifying Intelligence, Design, and Choice activities should be a useful method for selecting operations to be provided in a DSS. However, one must be careful not to assume that these activities, and therefore the operations, will always be carried out in the same sequence.

A third observation is that decision makers need memory aids [26]. These memory aids may be physical, such as scratch paper, memos, or reports. They may be mental rules that a decision maker applies. Or they may be reminders from a decision maker's staff. By observing the memory aids used by decision makers we can identify those which DSS should provide to be compatible with the needs of decision makers. A DSS may also provide additional memory aids or faster memory aids.

The fourth common observation about decision makers is that there are differences in their styles, skills, and knowledge [23]. One possible explanation of the wide variety of decision-making processes is that the variety results from these differences. Therefore, if a DSS is designed to support a particular process, it would probably support particular styles, skills, and knowledge rather than supporting the variety which is observed to exist. Decision makers would have to conform to the style, skills, and knowledge assumed by the DSS. Another approach is to try to design the DSS to match a specific decision maker's style, skill, and knowledge. Because of the variety among decision makers, this approach is likely to require that the DSS be redesigned (or tailorable) for each decision maker and that there be techniques for characterizing a decision maker's style, skills, and knowledge. Such techniques are not yet reliable or well known [30]. Thus we conclude that, if a DSS is to support varying styles, skills, and knowledge, it should not attempt to enforce or to capture a particular pattern. Rather, the DSS should help decision makers use and develop their own styles, skills, and knowledge. If this requirement can be met, the cost-effectiveness of DSS should improve because several decision makers could make effective use of the same DSS.

Finally, a fifth observation is that decision makers expect to exercise direct, personal control over their support system [13, 24]. This observation suggests that the decision maker should be able to personally control what the DSS does. This requirement does not necessarily imply that the decision maker personally needs to operate the DSS [18]. It implies that the decision maker must understand what the DSS can do and be able to interpret its outputs. With such an understanding the decision maker can direct and evaluate the operation of a DSS and can integrate the information provided by the DSS with information from other sources.

ANALYSIS OF DSS

In the preceding section we made a series of observations about decision making and decision makers in order to specify requirements for DSS.

Decision making

1. There are a variety of decision-making processes, so a DSS should support multiple processes.

2. Different types of decisions have different data processing requirements, so a DSS needs to be flexible in order to support different types of decisions.

Decision makers

1. Decision makers rely on conceptualizations in making a decision, and a DSS should provide familiar representations (e.g., charts and graphs) to assist in conceptualization.

2. Decision makers perform Intelligence, Design, and Choice activities while making a decision, so a DSS should provide operations which support these activities.

3. Decision makers need memory aids, so a DSS should provide memory aids which help carry out the decision-making process.

4. Decision makers exhibit a variety of skills, styles, and knowledge, so a DSS should help decision makers work in their own idiosyncratic ways.

5. Decision makers expect to control their decision support, so a DSS should provide control aids which help decision makers exercise direct, personal control.

The more unstructured the decision, the more likely it is that these observations will be valid. For example, there is more likely to be a variety of processes for making an unstructured decision than for making a structured decision. Or the decision maker is more likely to want to control unstructured decision making. Similarly, the observations are more likely to be valid in strategic planning and management control decisions than in operational control or performance decisions. Thus these observations seem to characterize exactly those decisions for which DSS are intended.

The observations lead us to several conclusions about the design of any DSS. Rather than designing a DSS to support a specific decision-making process, one should design it to provide specific representations which are used in conceptualizing a variety of decision-making processes. Rather than designing a DSS to provide operations for a specific type of decision, one should design it to provide operations needed to support activities which are found in many types of decisions. Representations will provide a frame of reference for using the operations. Representations and the Intelligence, Design, and Choice categories will help in selection of the operations to be included in the DSS. To make effective use of the representations and the associated operations, the decision maker will need memory aids and assistance in controlling the DSS. Rather than designing a DSS to reduce individual differences among decision makers and to replace the memory and control aids to which decision makers are accustomed, one should provide memory and control aids that support individual differences.

The framework for DSS design which emerged from these conclusions consists of four basic components:

1. Specific representations (e.g., graphs, tables, and pictures) to assist in conceptualization and to provide a frame of reference for using the DSS,

2. Operations on the representations to support Intelligence, Design, and Choice activities in decision making,

3. Memory aids to support the use of the representations and operations, and

4. Control aids to help the decision maker control the representations, operations, and memory aids.

The correspondence between our observations on the requirements of decision makers and the proposed DSS components is shown in Figure 2.2. There are important parallels between the observed requirements (left column) and the proposed DSS components (right column). The requirements indicate characteristics of decision makers and decision making which can be observed (and recorded) in a "systems analysis" preceding the design of a DSS. The DSS components identify the computer support that can be provided for each of these characteristics. Note the expected differences between the requirements and the components, which are illustrated by the examples under each of the four parallel headings (e.g., a map outline contains less information than a city map). There are two reasons for the expected differences. First, a DSS will be only one of many alternatives for providing support for decision makers. Second, technology and costs limit the support that a DSS can provide. For these reasons the DSS representations will not be as detailed as the decision makers' conceptualizations; the DSS operations will support only some of the decision-making activities; the DSS memory aids will be activated differently than those to which the decision maker is accustomed; and using the DSS control aids will require learning new skills, making some changes in styles, and adding to the decision makers' knowledge base.

We postulated earlier that the lack of use of DSS was caused by a mismatch between the requirements of decision makers and decision making and the support provided by DSS. The mismatch can be analyzed and illustrated using the parallels shown in Fig. 2.2. For example, in our analysis of existing DSS, such as the fifty-six described by Alter [2], we identified the following problems:

1. Existing DSS do not provide decision makers with familiar representations which support conceptualization. In addition, the decision maker is often forced to deal with concepts (e.g., flow charts) and representations (e.g., printouts) which are unfamiliar and have little to do with the way the decision maker usually conceptualizes the decision.

FIGURE 2.2 *Decision Makers' Requirements and Proposed DSS Components*

Decision Makers Use	DSS Provides
1. Conceptualizations ● A city map ● Relationship between assets and liabilities	1. Representations ● A map outline ● A scatterplot of assets vs. liabilities
2. Different Decision Making Processes and Decision Types, All Involving Activities for Intelligence, Design, and Choice ● Gather data on customers ● Create alternative customer assignments for salespeople ● Compare alternatives	2. Operations for Intelligence, Design, and Choice ● Query the data base ● Update list to show assignments ● Print summary statistics on each alternative
3. A Variety of Memory Aids ● List of customers ● Summary sheets on customers ● Table showing salespeople and their customer assignments ● File drawer with old tables ● Scratch paper ● Staff reminders	3. Automated Memory Aids ● Extracted data on customers ● Views of customer data ● Workspace for developing assignment tables ● Library for saving tables ● Temporary storage ● DSS messages
4. A Variety of Styles, Skills, and Knowledge Applied Via Direct, Personal Control ● Accepted conventions for interpersonal communication ● Orders to staff ● Standard operating procedures ● Revise orders or procedures	4. Aids to Direct, Personal Control ● Conventions for user-computer communication ● Training and explanation in how to give orders to the DSS ● Procedures formed from DSS operations ● Override DSS defaults or procedures

2. (a) Existing DSS tend to segment Intelligence, Design, and Choice activities, whereas decision makers tend to integrate them. For example, Alter's data-oriented systems primarily support Intelligence activities, but not Design or Choice, and the model-oriented systems primarily support Design or Choice and assume Intelligence has been completed.

   (b) Existing DSS tend to support a single decision-making process.

3. (a) Existing DSS provide long-term memory aids (i.e., a data base) but do not provide short-term memory aids. For example, the scratch paper and staff reminders to which a decision maker is accustomed are not available in most DSS.

   (b) Existing DSS impose additional memory requirements, such as learning the names of the data in the DSS, and often the DSS does not provide memory aids to support these requirements.

4. (a) Existing DSS do not provide enough control aids to help the decision maker learn the new skills (e.g., signing onto a computer terminal), styles (e.g., automated support rather than manual), and knowledge base (e.g., learning what the operations do) which a DSS introduces.

    (b) Existing DSS replace direct control with indirect control, where one or more intermediaries interpret the DSS capabilities and outputs for the decision maker. This type of control introduces well-known communication problems [13, 22].

The proposed framework for DSS design is intended to help overcome these problems. The parallels in Fig. 2.2 indicate where support is needed and highlight the design challenges inherent in providing support which reduces the expected differences between the requirements of decision makers and the capabilities of the DSS. By using the framework we do not expect to overcome all the differences or to totally replace manual support with automated support. We do expect to be able to reduce the differences to an acceptable level and to provide support which results in displaced cost or added value.

A DSS DESIGN FRAMEWORK

This section describes the four components in the proposed framework for designing DSS and gives specific examples for each of the four.

Representations as a Focus for DSS Design

Any activity in a decision-making process takes place in the context of some conceptualization of the information used in the activity. The conceptualization may be a chart, a picture, a few numbers, an equation, etc. The conceptualization may be mental, but in most cases it is physically represented on scratch paper, blackboards, graph paper, foils, etc. A physical representation is particularly important when the decision maker wants to communicate some aspect of the decision to another person. Figure 2.3 gives examples of representations associated with some Intelligence, Design, and Choice operations used in analyzing bad debts. Figure 2.4 gives examples of Intelligence, Design, and Choice operations associated with a graph representation. Figure 2.5 lists instances of representations.

Representations provide a context in which users can interpret DSS outputs and invoke DSS operations. Representations also can be used to supply parameters for DSS operations. For example, a point selected on a graph or locations on a map can identify a key value, which will be used to retrieve detailed information. Or subdividing a list of employees or reconnecting groups on an organization chart can serve as an input mechanism for personnel scheduling algorithm.

FIGURE 2.3   *Representations for Analyzing Bad Debts*

Intelligence
- A *list* of customers with bad debts
- A *graph* of bad debts over time
- *Cross tabulation* statistics on attributes of customers

Design
- A *scatter plot* of customers by two attributes associated with bad debts used to partition customers into risk groups

Choice
- A *pie chart* of percentage of loans by customer risk groups used to evaluate the partition
- A *report* on simulated bad debt losses for each alternative risk group partition

FIGURE 2.4   *Operations Associated with a Graph Representation*

Intelligence
- *Identify* data to be graphed
- *Scale* the graph
- *Plot* data on graph

Design
- *Draw* polygons to partition the lines on the graph
- *Forecast* future data based on each partition

Choice
- *Print* summary statistics for each partition
- *Display* each partition on the graph

FIGURE 2.5   *Instances of Representations*

Histograms	Balance sheets
Scatter plots	Spread sheets
Line graphs	Schedule boards
Maps	Engineering drawings
Surfaces	Architectural drawings
Pert charts	Aerial photographs
Organization charts	Seismic plots
Data entry forms	Scratch paper
Tabular reports	Memos

Operations for Intelligence, Design, and Choice

As described previously, Intelligence, Design, and Choice [29] form a well-known paradigm, which can help classify the operations used in decision making. The three categories are "complete" in that all decision-making operations can be classified into one or more of these categories. Scott Morton [28] used these categories to describe a specific decision-making process before and after introduction of a DSS. Gerrity [15] illustrated how Intelligence, Design, and Choice could be used to analyze existing and proposed decision-making processes and to identify operations for a DSS.

FIGURE 2.6   General Decision-Making Operations for Intelligence, Design, and Choice

Intelligence
- Gather data
- Identify objectives
- Diagnose problem
- Validate data
- Structure problem

Design
- Gather data
- Manipulate data
- Quantify objectives
- Generate reports
- Generate alternatives
- Assign risks or values to alternatives

Choice
- Generate statistics on alternatives
- Simulate results of alternatives
- Explain alternatives
- Choose among alternatives
- Explain choice

Figure 2.6 lists some general decision-making operations usually associated with Intelligence, Design, and Choice. Figure 2.7 illustrates the use of the categories to describe the operations of a specific decision-making process for allocating police officers to areas of a city [8]. Note that an operation may be used in more than one activity and that there is no prespecified ordering of the opera-

FIGURE 2.7   Intelligence, Design, and Choice Operations in a Police Personnel Allocation Decision

Intelligence
- Gather data on calls for police service
- Divide city into small geographic zones
- Select subset of data
- Aggregate subset by zones
- Validate data by checking familiar zones
- Plot data values on map of zones

Design
- Set objectives for combining zones into police beats
- Develop quantitative measures for some of the objectives
- Plot data values on map of zones
- Combine zones into police beats based on objectives

Choice
- Print summary statistics on each police beat alternative
- Plot aggregate data on maps of police beat alternatives
- Modify alternatives
- Select an alternative
- Plot data on map for chosen alternative to explain choice to others

tions. The operations may involve complicated decision aids, such as simulation models or forecasting algorithms.

Memory Aids

Several types of memory aids can be provided in a DSS to support the use of representations and operations. For example:

1. A *data base* extracted from sources internal and external to the organization,

2. *Views (aggregations and subsets)* of the extracted data base,

3. *Workspaces* for displaying the representations and for preserving intermediate results as they are produced by the operations,

4. *Libraries* for saving workspace contents for later use,

5. *Links* for remembering data from one workspace or library that is needed as a reference when operating on the contents of another workspace,

6. *Triggers* to remind a decision maker that certain operations may need to be performed, and

7. *Profiles* to store default and status data.

An extracted data base is a memory for data compiled from sources the decision maker thinks may be relevant to the decision (see Carlson [6] for a detailed discussion of extracted data bases).

Views are memory aids containing specifications for partitions (groupings), subsets, or aggregations of data in the extracted data base which may be relevant to the decision alternatives. A decision often can be represented as a view. For example, a personnel allocation decision can be represented as a partition of a personnel data base where each group in the partition is allocated to a particular task. A hiring decision can be represented as a subset of an applicant data base where the subset is the list of those applicants to be hired.

Workspaces act as transient memory aids which provide a vehicle for accumulating results of the operations on the representations. For example, a "spread sheet" workspace could be used to develop product plans.

A library associated with each workspace provides long-term memory for useful intermediate or final results created in the workspace. Many times information from one workspace or library may be needed in another workspace or library. For example, a customer list may be used to identify a customer for whom the decision maker wants a graph of assets over time. Or a starting point on a map may be needed as an input to an algorithm that performs a districting operation on the map.

Links are memory aids for information needed to make such associations. When a user identifies a customer's record in a list or a point on a map, the link memory preserves the relevant data (i.e., customer identification number or the xy coordinates of the point) for later use.

Triggers are memory aids used to invoke operations automatically or to remind the user to invoke operations. A trigger may be a message telling the user that before a profit-forecasting operation can be invoked, rates of return must be assigned to various projects. Or a trigger may be a message displayed quarterly reminding the user to invoke the profit-forecasting operation.

Profiles store initial defaults for using the DSS, such as the axes labeling for a graph or the number of columns in a report. These defaults may be user-specific to help personalize use of the DSS for a decision maker. A "log" used to record a user's actions for backup or replay can be considered to be a profile memory.

Control Aids

The representations, operations, and memories of a DSS are intended to support a variety of decision-making processes and a variety of types of decisions. The DSS control aids are intended to help decision makers use representations, operations, and memories to synthesize a decision-making process based on their individual styles, skills, and knowledge. The control aids may be crucial to the success of the DSS because they help the decision maker direct the use of the DSS and because they must allow the decision maker to acquire the new styles, skills, and knowledge needed to make effective use of the DSS.

A variety of control aids can be helpful. One type facilitates the mechanics of using the DSS. Examples are menus or function keys for operation selection, standard conventions for user-system interactions (such as editing or accessing libraries) which are enforced across representations and operations, and use of representations as the context for operation selection. A second type includes aids to support training and explanation for using the DSS. These aids help the decision maker learn how to control the DSS. Natural language error messages, "help" commands, and a training method which permits the decision maker to "learn by doing" are examples of this type of control aid [19]. Decision maker control of the DSS can also be supported with aids to combine operations associated with one or more representations into procedures. A "procedure construction language" for combining DSS operations using standard programming language control techniques, such as iteration and case statements, is one example of this type of control aid. Procedure construction is also a mechanism for adding new operations. Another type of control aid is any operation that helps the decision maker change the results of other operations, such as the ability to edit results of a forecasting model. Finally, control aids can include operations for changing any DSS default values. For example, a DSS that provides operations to automatically draw a graph with a default scale and axes-labeling conventions should provide operations to change these defaults.

USING THE DESIGN FRAMEWORK

The DSS design framework is a tool for focusing the systems analysis (of decision making) preceding the design of the DSS and for structuring the actual DSS design. We will assume an interactive graphics environment in describing the use of representations, operations, memory aids, and control aids as a DSS design framework, but such an environment is not required. Both interactive systems and computer graphics expand the options available to the DSS designer. Interactive graphics should help provide control aids because user-system communication options are enhanced. Interactive graphics also allows a wide range of

FIGURE 2.8   *Analysis of an Investment Decision Using a Flow Chart*

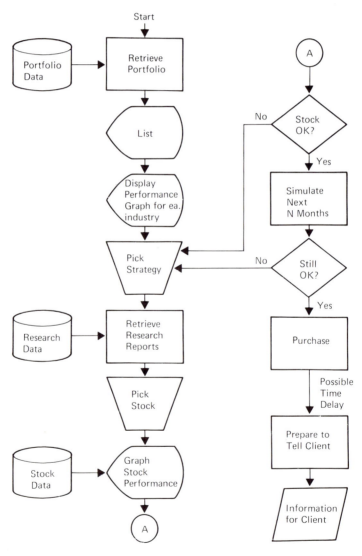

representations to be used in the DSS. Gerrity [15] and Scott Morton [28] present arguments for the use of interactive graphics for DSS.

In Systems Analysis

Figure 2.8 illustrates the results of a hypothetical analysis for a DSS for investment decision making in which a flow chart of the existing or desired decision process is used as a tool for analysis. The focus is on the decision-making process, particularly the inputs, operations, and outputs of each task. For different decision-making processes the flow charts would be different. The same set of inputs, operations, and outputs might appear, but their relationships would be different. If the flow chart (or any other tool focusing on the process) is used as a framework for the DSS design, the resulting DSS is likely to mimic the process captured in the flow chart. That is, the DSS is likely to impose a sequencing of tasks. If the decision-making process changes, the DSS has to be changed. Or if different decision makers who have different processes want to use the DSS, they will have to conform.

Figure 2.9 illustrates a schematic resulting from using the proposed DSS framework to analyze the same investment decision as in Fig. 2.8. The representations and operations are chosen as in the process-oriented analysis, but they become

FIGURE 2.9   DSS Schematic Resulting from Using the DSS Design Framework to Analyze an Investment Decision

Representations

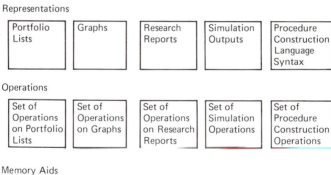

| Portfolio Lists | Graphs | Research Reports | Simulation Outputs | Procedure Construction Language Syntax |

Operations

| Set of Operations on Portfolio Lists | Set of Operations on Graphs | Set of Operations on Research Reports | Set of Simulation Operations | Set of Procedure Construction Operations |

Memory Aids

- Work space for each representation
- Library for each representation
- Data bases: portfolio data
              research data
              stock data

Control Aids

- Use menus to display operations
- Provide a training manual giving examples of how to use the system to make a decision

the basis for the DSS structure. The representation-based approach attempts to make the DSS into a decision-making scratch pad, which decision makers can use for a variety of decision-making processes. In the representation-based DSS design, the memory and control aids help the user develop the decision-making process. If the decision maker wants to follow a specific process, such as the one flowcharted in Fig. 2.8, this process can be "programmed" in the procedure construction language and executed under the decision maker's control.

Thus a DSS design based on Fig. 2.9 is more general than one based on Fig. 2.8 because it can support a variety of decision-making processes. The DSS designed using Fig. 2.9 might also be useful for other decisions, such as mergers and acquisitions, where the same representations and operations are used but the processes differ. The cost of the generality is that the DSS designed using Fig. 2.9 may be more difficult to use than one designed using Fig. 2.8 because the user must learn to develop a process with the DSS. The memory and control aids are intended to help reduce this difficulty.

In Developing a DSS Design with a Single Representation

To show how the four components in the framework fit together, a design using one representation, a scatterplot, is shown in Fig. 2.10. Results of operations on the scatterplot are displayed in the workspace. These results may be a scatterplot of data, a scatterplot of data filtered through a view, or transformations of a scatterplot (e.g., scaling). The scatterplot can be displayed and modified in the workspace by using the operations. The operations are commands the user selects, such as draw plot, label axes, scale, print summary statistics, etc. Intelligence, Design, and Choice activities identified in the systems analysis for the DSS could serve as a guide in selection of the operations to be provided. Intelligence operations might include displaying data using a scatterplot and identifying the "keys" and numeric values of points on it. Design operations might include creating groups of points on the scatterplot and making temporary ("what if") changes in values of points on the scatterplot. Choice operations might include fitting a regression curve to the scatterplot and computing ratios based on values of points selected from the scatterplot. Another method of identifying operations is to list possible transformations of the scatterplot representation—for example, plot points, label axes, scale axes, plot regression line, identify points on plot, compute ratios for a point on the plot, and save plot.

A library allows the user to name, save, and retrieve the contents of a workspace. Thus an interesting scatterplot can be named, saved, and retrieved using the library facilities. A procedure library, which is associated with a representation (e.g., an alphanumeric syntax used to construct procedures), can be accessed to execute macro-operations which may or may not be associated with the scatterplot. For example, a sequence of labeling, scaling, and drawing operations which produces a scatterplot may become a procedure. Or there might be a procedure which aggregates data for use in displaying a scatterplot.

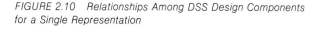

FIGURE 2.10   Relationships Among DSS Design Components
for a Single Representation

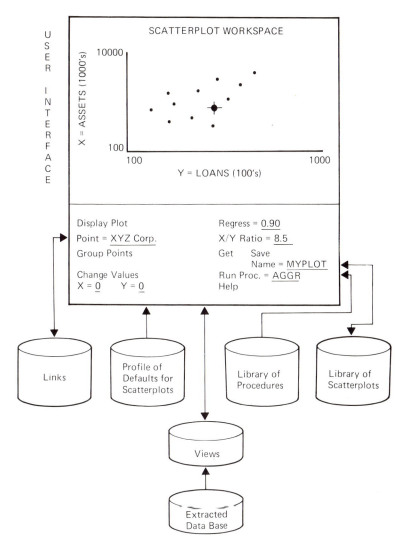

The extracted data base contains the data which can be accessed for a scatter-plot, and the view memory stores specifications for subsets (e.g., customers with over $100,000 in loans) and aggregations (e.g., combine domestic and foreign customers). The link memory is used to store data which might be useful with another representation. For example, the customer identification number asso-ciated with a point on the scatterplot could be stored in the link memory for use in retrieval of a summary report about that customer. The profile memory contains initial defaults for the scatterplot workspace, such as axes labeling and scaling, scatterplot colors, or symbols used in the scatterplot. Defaults are required when the user wants a new scatterplot but forgets to specify some parameters.

Specific control aids include the menus which present the set of operations available to a user and a "help" operation for learning how to use other operations. Note that the memory aids often serve as control aids. For example, the procedure library can serve as a control aid for invoking a sequence of operations to create a scatterplot. The default memory can help reduce the time and effort needed to display a scatterplot (by providing axes scaling and labeling for a draw scatterplot command). The workspace and library memories make it easier to re-create a scatterplot.

The representation (as displayed in the workspace) is the context in which operations are used, and the memory and control aids help the decision maker invoke the operations and use the results of the operations. If the parallels shown in Fig. 2.2 are valid, it is the combination of the four components which will help the decision maker make effective use of the DSS. That is, if any one of the four components is to help improve decision making, the other three components seem to be necessary.

In Designing a DSS with Multiple Representations

It seems likely that every DSS will require more than one representation. Figure 2.11 shows a DSS design framework consisting of four representations: tables, graphs, maps, and a procedure construction language. Each representation has operations for Intelligence, Design, and Choice and an associated workspace for presenting the results of applying the operations to the representations. For each representation there are workspace, library, and profile memory aids. The operations in each representation can access an extracted data base, possibly through a view. Views can be constructed using a representation (e.g., select points on a graph to specify subsetting) or via the procedure language. With multiple representations, link memory is very important. Information presented on a graph may lead to questions best answered using a map (e.g., "Where is that high crime area?") or using a table (e.g., "Give me a list of total crimes for each zone."). Links can help the user transfer data among representations. Control aids are provided by modules that give error messages and provide training sequences and by user-system communication conventions. Note that the control aids cover all representations, operations, and memory aids.

Every DSS will have a specific set of representations, operations, memory aids, and control aids. The generality of the DSS will depend on the skill of the designers in selecting these elements based on the analysis preceding the DSS design. The framework can provide a guide for selecting useful elements and for combining them into a DSS. Our experience with one DSS indicates that one set of representations, operations, memories, and control components can support a variety of users, decisions, and decision-making processes [7, 8, 18].

FIGURE 2.11   Relationships Among DSS Design Components
for Multiple Representations

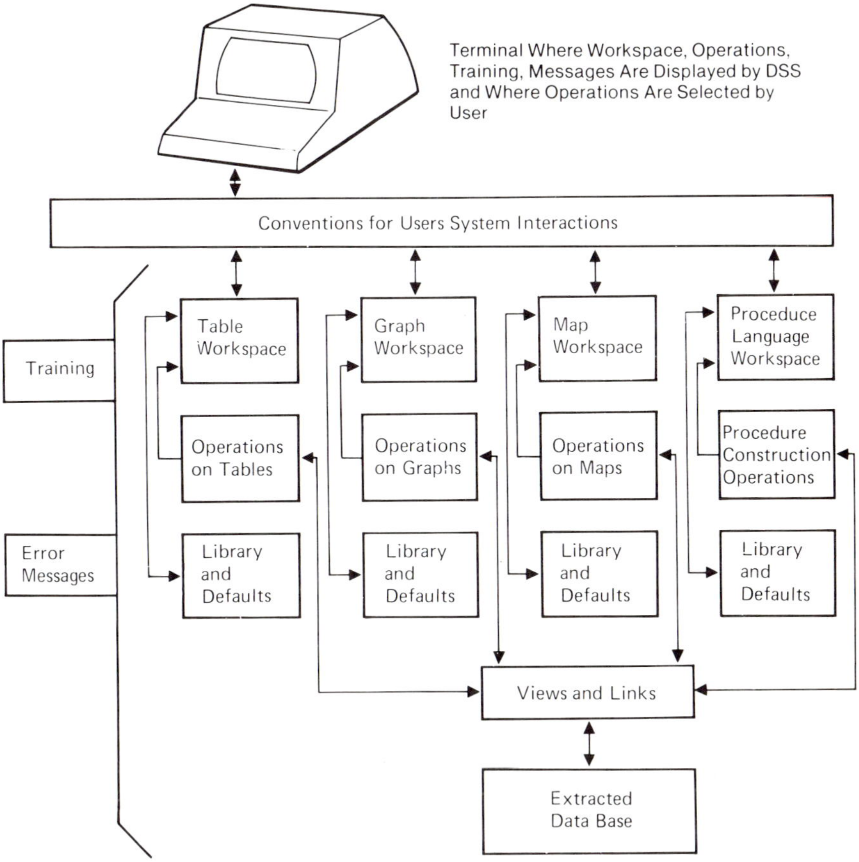

In Designing the User Interface

A detailed example of the use of the framework is provided by the design of the user interface for an interactive DSS to draw scatterplots. Figure 2.12 shows a process-oriented interface ("twenty questions") for a scatterplot. The interface leads the user through all operations possible for this representation. Each time a scatterplot is drawn the same process must be followed. The interaction requires that the decision maker have a mental picture of what is going to appear (e.g., "What is the x-axis? Do the data need to be scaled?"). Once the scatterplot is drawn, the procedural interaction must be repeated in order to make any changes. Figure 2.13 shows the same set of operations presented in the context of the scatterplot representation and supported by a set of memory and control aids. The representation makes it convenient for the user to respond only to those of

FIGURE 2.12   *Process-Oriented Interface for Creating a Scatterplot*

System:	*Choose function*	*1 = Table, 2 = Graphs, 3 = Plots*
User:	3	
System:	*Do you want a tutorial?*	*(Y or N)*
User:	N	
System:	*Enter data name for X axis*	
User:	$ LIABILITIES	
System:	*Enter data name for Y axis*	
User:	$ ASSETS	
System:	*Do you want default scaling?*	*(Y or N)*
User	Y	
System:	*Do you want default labels?*	*(Y or N)*
User:	Y	
System:	*Do you want descriptive statistics?*	*(Y or N)*
User:	Y	
System:	*Select stats*	*1 = Mean, 2 = Median, 3 = Range,*
		4 = Std. Dev., 5 = Var.
User:	1 3 4	
System:	*Do you want to execute a procedure?*	*(Y or N)*
User:	N	
System:	*Do you want to save results?*	*(Y or N)*
User:	N	

System then erases display screen and draws scatterplot

the "twenty questions" which are relevant, does not require that changes to answers be made in a particular order, does not require that all questions be answered each time the scatterplot is drawn, and presents the parameters (i.e., the questions) with the scatterplot (i.e., the result of the answers to the questions).

Exactly the same capabilities (inputs, operations, and outputs) are provided in each interface. The process-oriented interface is based on the assumption that leading the user through a process makes the capabilities easier to use. The representation-oriented interface is based on the assumption that context makes the capabilities easier to use.

In a Case Study of DSS

A comparison of a DSS containing the four proposed components with a data-oriented and a model-oriented DSS was made in a case study of DSS for a police

FIGURE 2.13   Representation-Oriented Interface for
Creating a Scatterplot

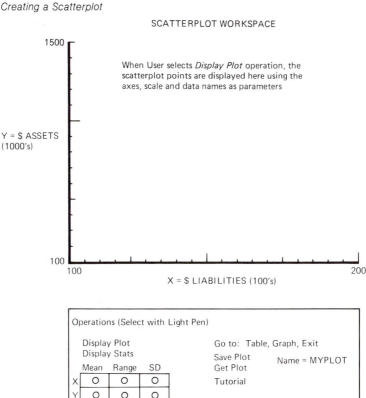

SCATTERPLOT WORKSPACE

personnel allocation decision [8]. The problem was to decide on a scheme for allocating police officers to areas (beats) of a city.

The decision was first attempted using a data-oriented DSS. Reports on calls-for-service, workload, response times, etc., were generated. The relevant data were plotted manually on maps, and police management used the maps to develop and evaluate alternative decisions. The result was an allocation plan which was more expensive and farther from the quantitative objectives (e.g., balanced workload) than the existing plan. Next, a consultant was asked to help make the decision using a model-oriented DSS to determine an "optimal" plan. The consultant interviewed decision makers, developed objective functions, collected the "relevant" data, developed an allocation model, and ran the model to make the decision. The resulting plan was rejected by police management because it violated several qualitative objectives which could not be incorporated into the model. A DSS with a design similar to the one shown in Fig. 2.11 was provided for the decision makers. The DSS was used by the decision makers to develop a personnel allocation plan, a variation of which is still in use. This plan required fewer police officers and was closer to the objectives (quantitative and qualitative) than the plans produced with the data-oriented and model-oriented DSS.

Obviously, we cannot prove that the DSS design framework caused one DSS to be more successful than the other two. However, in follow-up interviews with the police officers who used the DSS, each of the four components was referred to in some way by each officer as being a reason why this DSS was used and why it was valuable.

CONCLUDING ARGUMENTS

In spite of the current problems in developing DSS, the isolated successes and the potential for displaced cost and added value from DSS indicate that high payoffs are possible if the design problems can be solved. Our observations from studies of decision making and decision makers indicated four major problems in the designs of existing DSS:

1. Existing DSS do not provide the representations which decision makers need for semi-structured and unstructured decisions.

2. Existing DSS usually support only one or two of the three basic activities (Intelligence, Design, and Choice) of decision making.

3. Existing DSS do not provide enough support (and do introduce additional requirements) for conceptualization and memory, two areas where decision makers need help.

4. Existing DSS require specification of the decision-making process in advance, do not support a variety of styles, skills, and knowledge, and thus do not help decision makers exercise the personal control to which they are accustomed when making semi-structured or unstructured decisions.

To overcome these problems we propose that DSS be designed to provide:

1. representations as the context for system use;

2. operations on the representations to support Intelligence, Design, and Choice activities;

3. a variety of memory aids to support use of the representations and operations; and

4. aids for controlling the representations, operations, and memories.

At this stage we cannot prove that this approach is more useful or more cost-effective than other approaches. We can, however, provide arguments as to why we believe the proposed approach is better. It is easier for a DSS designer to identify the representations and the associated operations used in decision making than to identify all possible decision-making processes.

Instead of being designed as a set of operations which result in representations, the DSS should be designed as a set of representations with associated operations. The operations-based approach is more likely to impose a sequencing of the operations (i.e., a process) on the decision maker, and yet we see that to support a variety of processes, a large number of possible sequencings must be provided. The representation-based approach is more likely to let the decision maker select the sequencing of the operations, and a new sequencing (i.e., a new process) is less likely to require programming modifications to the DSS. Moreover, one set of representations and operations can support a variety of decision-making processes, because the differences among processes are more in the sequencing of operations and the decision maker's interpretation of representations than in the set of representations or operations to be used in the process. The representations also may help DSS designers and users segment the decision problem and identify the relevant Intelligence, Design, and Choice operations. Providing operations for Intelligence, Design, and Choice activities helps the DSS support the entire decision-making process and makes it easier for the decision maker to integrate these activities.

The different types of memory aids act as note pads or file drawers for decision makers. They make it possible to retrieve useful results without having to repeat the operations which produced the results. They reduce the memory load on the decision maker, reduce the complexity of using representations and operations so that the decision maker can concentrate on interpretation, help personalize the use of the DSS, and help the DSS support a variety of decision-making processes. Providing control aids helps the decision makers direct the use of the representations, operations, and memory aids according to their own styles, skills, and knowledge.

User involvement is often cited as an objective for successful DSS design and use. All four components of the proposed approach for DSS design are intended to encourage user involvement. The representations provide a familiar frame of reference for designing and using the DSS. Operations for Intelligence, Design, and Choice provide support for common decision-making activities. Memory aids help develop and store useful results. Control aids help the decision maker personally direct the use of the DSS.

Further research is needed to substantiate the preceding arguments. Yet the success of a prototype system with the four components [7] and of systems having similar components [15, 28] indicates the potential value of using the proposed approach for DSS design.

ACKNOWLEDGMENTS

This chapter represents the author's synthesis of ideas developed by members of the Decision Support Systems project in the IBM Research Laboratory in San Jose. John Bennett and Jim Sutton provided many useful suggestions based on early versions.

REFERENCES

1. Ackoff, R. L. "Management Misinformation Systems," *Management Science 14*, 4 (December 1967), B147–B156.

2. Alter, S. L. *Decision Support Systems: Current Practice and Continuing Challenge.* Reading, Mass.: Addison-Wesley, 1980.

3. Anthony, R. N. *Planning and Control Systems: A Framework for Analysis.* Boston, Mass.: Graduate School of Business Administration, Harvard University, 1965.

4. Brady, R. H. "Computers in Top-level Decision Making," *Harvard Business Review*, July–August 1967, 67–76.

5. Canning, R. G. (ed.). "APL and Decision Support Systems," *EDP Analyzer 14*, 5 (May 1976), 1–12.

6. Carlson, E. D. "Using Large Data Bases for Interactive Problem Solving," *Proceedings of the International Conference on Very Large Data Bases 1*, 1. New York: ACM, 1976, 499–501.

7. Carlson, E. D., Bennett, J. L., Giddings, G. M., and Mantey, P. E. "The Design and Evaluation of an Interactive Geo-data Analysis and Display System," *Information Processing 74.* Amsterdam: North Holland, 1974, 1057–61.

8. Carlson, E. D., Grace, B. F., and Sutton, J. A. "Case Studies of End User Requirements for Interactive Problem Solving," *Management Information System Quarterly 1*, 1 (March 1977), 51–63.

9. Churchill, N. C., Kempster, J. H., and Uretsky, M. *Computer-Based Information Systems for Management: A Survey.* New York: National Association of Accountants, 1969.

10. "Corporate War Rooms Plug into the Computer," *Business Week*, August 23, 1976, 65–66.

11. Cyert, R. M., and March, J. G. *A Behavioral Theory of the Firm.* Englewood Cliffs, N.J.: Prentice-Hall, 1963.

12. Cyert, R. M., Simon, H. A., and Trow, D. B. "Observation of a Business Decision," *Journal of Business 29* (1956), 237–248.

13. Eason, K. D. "Understanding the Naive Computer User," *The Computer Journal 19*, 1 (February 1976), 3–7.

14. Emery, J. C. "An Overview of Management Information Systems," *Data Base 5*, 2–4 (December 1973), 1–11.

15. Gerrity, Jr., T. P. "Design of Man-Machine Decision Systems: An Application to Portfolio Management," *Sloan Management Review 14* (Winter 1971), 59–75.

16. Gordon, L. A., Miller, D., and Mintzberg, H. *Normative Models in Managerial Decision Making.* New York: National Association of Accountants, 1975.

17. Gorry, G. A., and Scott Morton, M. S. "A Framework for Management Information Systems," *Sloan Management Review 13* (Fall 1971), 55–70.

18. Grace, B. F. "A Case Study of Man/Computer Problem-Solving: Observations on Interactive Formulation of School Attendance Boundaries," IBM Research Report RJ 1483. San Jose, Ca.: IBM Research Division, February 1975.

19. Grace, B. F. "Training Users of a Decision Support System," *Data Base 8*, 3 (Winter 1977), 30–36.

20. Lindblom, C. E. "The Science of Muddling Through," *Public Administration Review 19* (1959), 79–88.

21. Little, J. D. C. "Models and Managers: The Concept of a Decision Calculus," *Management Science 16*, 8 (April 1970), B466–B485.

22. Lucas, H. C. *Why Information Systems Fail.* New York: Columbia University Press, 1975.

23. McKenney, J. L., and Keen, P. G. W. "How Manager's Minds Work," *Harvard Business Review*, May–June 1974, 79–90.

24. Mintzberg, H. *The Nature of Managerial Work.* New York: Harper and Row, 1973.

25. Mintzberg, H., Raisinghani, D., and Théorêt, A. "The Structure of 'Unstructured' Decision Processes," *Administrative Science Quarterly 21* (June 1976), 246–275.

26. Newell, A., and Simon, H. A. *Human Problem Solving.* Englewood Cliffs, N.J.: Prentice-Hall, 1972.

27. Nickerson, R. S., and Feehrer, C. E. *Decision Making and Training.* BBN Report No. 2982. Cambridge, Mass.: Bolt Beranek and Newman, Inc., July 1975.

28. Scott Morton, M. S. *Management Decision Systems.* Boston, Mass.: Graduate School of Business Administration, Harvard University, 1971.

29. Simon, H. A. *The New Science of Management Decisions.* New York: Harper and Row, 1960.

30. Stabell, C. B. "Individual Differences in Managerial Decision Making Processes." Unpublished Ph.D. dissertation, M.I.T. Sloan School of Management, September 1974.

31. Time Sharing Information Services, Inc. "American Airlines Information Management System: Development, History, and Return on Investment," *Time Sharing Today 3*, 4–5 (July–August 1972), 1–15.

ANALYSIS AND DESIGN OF THE USER INTERFACE FOR DECISION SUPPORT SYSTEMS

John L. Bennett

CHAPTER 3

INTRODUCTION

Levels of Knowledge Needed to Use Computers

As with any technological innovation, the initial users of the computer were the designers in the laboratory who first constructed their invention. This user community was small and carefully selected. Each person knew the capabilities of the machine and knew through personal experience the information that was necessary to use the computer effectively. Typically, the user was able to visualize the flow of data through physical components such as AND and OR gates. As computers evolved, so did our ways of visualizing their operation. We learned to teach higher-level abstractions—registers, words, memory locations, and computer logical instructions—which enabled users to develop computer programs even though they did not know internal details of the physical machine. They did, however, have to be specially trained (as programmers) to learn how the abstractions could be used and how to form the special procedures (programs) which the computer required to accomplish useful work. These earlier designers and programmers were *committed users,* as a result of either personal interest or job requirements. Now a new class of people is becoming interested in using com-

Chapter adapted, with permission, from "User-Oriented Graphics Systems for Decision Support in Unstructured Tasks" by John L. Bennett, published in "User-Oriented Design of Interactive Graphics Systems" based on ACM SIGGRAPH Workshop, October 1976. Copyright 1977, Association for Computing Machinery, Inc.

puters. *Discretionary users* work with computers by choice. For example, managers have access to many sources of information and have many tools available for data manipulation. To capture their interest and to support their application of their judgment in deriving results, we must provide presentations directly relevant to managers and give them active control over interaction.

Display terminals showing information on a screen and responding to user input at a conversational pace can provide a level of service attractive to discretionary users. Immediate feedback gives a sense of presence, user involvement, and participation not often found with typewriter terminals. While responsive action can be obtained at alphanumeric displays, their limitation to textual characters and their lack of graphic input restrict communication between human and computer. In contrast, graphics terminals create a visual context for action by allowing direct display of instantly meaningful pictures rather than less meaningful abstractions. Pictures can be shown dynamically (through animation) in two dimensions and in color. Users can see and interact with representations familiar to them—spread sheets, maps of geographic areas, and graphs. These representations, constructed by the computer, can stimulate user recall of knowledge, can lead to creation of solutions, and can serve as a basis for user choice between alternatives.

Though the new level of support for discretionary users made possible by display terminals is becoming technically and economically feasible, current systems often require users to be knowledgeable about underlying computer-oriented details. These systems are suitable for people who are committed to computer use for work (designers, programmers, and transaction clerks) or for amusement (computer hobbyists). But discretionary users are not, and do not intend to become, computer professionals. Thus direct interactive use of computer power by managers depends upon designer ability to provide interfaces which these people are willing to use.

Decision Support Systems

The name Decision Support Systems (DSS) emphasizes the role which these computer-based aids play with respect to users. DSS provide high-level operations for retrieving data, generating alternative solutions, storing and retrieving alternatives, and evaluating alternatives. The relatively unstructured nature of the problems being attacked precludes a directed decision-making (rather than decision support) system approach.

Typical decision support system applications are computer-aided stock portfolio management, budget preparation, and allocation of personnel to service areas. In these applications the decision maker (DM) normally uses data presented in the form of tables, graphs, and pictures while analyzing a problem, designing and choosing solutions, and selling the proposed solution to the affected parties (a client, fellow managers, or other employees). The manager carrying out these tasks is accustomed to working with ideas presented orally and in a written form on paper, view foils, and slides. If we want to design computer-based tools which will indeed support the DM in these tasks, we must consider the characteristics of the intended user and the nature of the tasks carried out. Managers are experienced professionals with knowledge of their problem areas. Their recognized skills have advanced them to responsible positions. But they are often naïve in their personal use of computer systems. Graphic formats (tables, charts, and pictures) are natural to their work, but they are accustomed to having the information prepared by staff.

Data relevant to the solution of problems in these application areas may already exist in the computerized data bases used in day-to-day operation of a business. However, there are few cases in which the data are already available in the required form—with the flexibility of access, at the time needed, and at a reasonable cost—for use in managing a business.

Scope of This Chapter

We focus on the design of DSS to be accessed by managers through a graphics terminal. We realize there are many instances of highly effective computer-based DSS that are used only through a typewriter terminal. However, we seek ways to utilize the power of the graphics terminal to create a visual context.

In this chapter we discuss three principles which we have followed in our project work and which appear to be applicable to design of other systems. The principles are a cross section of those needed for a complete system; their exposition shows a point of view we can take concerning user-oriented design. By discovering which parts of our experience are of general validity, we can begin to formulate design principles useful in developing better systems. The design principles, with their emphasis on creating two-dimensional, reconstructable contexts for work on a screen, would have to be adapted for use with a typewriter terminal. The key difference is that when the computer is writing to a typewriter terminal, it has no way of determining which previous output line is currently the focus of DM attention. The DM must use a command to re-create a context for the computer rather than relying on the computer to explicitly create a context for current work. In contrast, when the computer creates a display on the screen of a graphics terminal (in response to actions of the DM), then the computer system has a record of what is displayed and can respond *in this context* to the next action.

We need to make one working assumption explicit. In an ideal DSS the computer would take an active role in leading the DM to a problem solution. This would require the computer to have an "understanding" of what the DM is seeking to do. In such a "knowledge-based" system (in the sense used by Gorry and Krumland in Chapter 9 of this book), the DM and the computer would share responsibility for arriving at a "mutually satisfying" solution. In this idealized case the DSS would take an active role in directing the DM toward optimized decisions. Instead, this chapter is directed toward design of DSS which have no "understanding" of the DM environment. In such a DSS the computer is "passive" with respect to improving decision quality. Because we do not know how to guide the DM to more effective decisions, the focus must be on making the mechanics of system operation easy for the DM to understand and to use.

In some procedures the computer may be used to *direct* the DM in steps to be followed, but these procedures will typically be computer-oriented in their results. For example, the DSS may lead the DM through a structured process necessary to construct a data base extracted to order from an operational file. In this case the DSS does have "knowledge" about the requirements of its own problem domain and can take an active role in gathering the data needed for it to provide the requested support.

The DSS we describe becomes a general-purpose tool for the user, a framework for presenting, analyzing, and manipulating information during decision making. Carlson has outlined (Chapter 2 of this book) the role of representations, operations, memory, and control in shaping a DSS design. Problem-specific models and knowledge-based facilities can be inserted in a productive way within this framework. Thus the design principles presented here are an interim approach which can lead toward a "DSS as a consultant" ideal (Gorry and Krumland, Chapter 9). Our approach concentrates on providing currently feasible support for the DM without precluding the later addition of active mechanisms needed to guide the DM toward more effective decisions.

The design challenge becomes one of providing a computer interface which the DM can interpret easily and control effectively to achieve results which are valuable. The mechanics of operation must be made smooth and error-free so that the DM faced with responsibility for *both* the decision result *and* navigation through DSS functions can concentrate on decision content. We need to enable a DM to transfer personal problem-solving skills, developed in the context of work experience, to the computer interface. If a manager perceives that time spent at a computer terminal during development of a solution is not worthwhile, the use of the terminal will be delegated. But the unstructured nature of the decision problem may prevent a clerk or operator from gaining the same kind of insight or acting on information developed during interaction in the same way as would the manager. Such a surrogate user does not have the appropriate managerial perspective.

The examples and the discussion in this chapter are oriented toward raising the level of the language which the DM uses while interacting with the DSS. We assume that in unstructured tasks control over active system use must currently lie with the DM. Thus the usability of the DSS will continue to be a necessary but not sufficient condition for the DSS to play an active role in the decision-making process.

In this chapter we introduce a set of questions we have found useful to ask during our design process. This is followed by a description of usability and how it may be measured. This exposition provides a necessary background for understanding the design principles. The remainder of the chapter presents the principles along with examples of their application to design.

THE USER-COMPUTER INTERFACE

Figure 3.1 shows a schematic representation of a user interface. Information (visual and audio) presented at a terminal passes across the interface. The "processor" within the user operates on the observed content in order to formulate an action plan. The plan must then be translated into actions accepted by the terminal. User understanding of the displayed information is influenced by both the work being done and knowledge of the computer system. In Fig. 3.1 "thought" refers to user interpretation of the displayed data. "Action plan" refers to changes the user wants to see in the displayed representation. This is, of course, influenced by what the user *expects* it is possible to do with the system. "Translate for system" refers to any steps the user must take to transform desired direct actions into actions which will be accepted by the system. For example, the user may wish to command the system by *looking* at a point on a graph and *saying* "Show disaggregated data." The available equipment (hardware and software) may require the user to position a cursor at the point on the graph by using function keys, key in the desired data name using a typewriter keyboard, push the enter key, place the cursor on a menu command labeled TABLE, and push the enter key again. Even though thought, action planning, and translation for the system are inextricably mixed together inside the user, for the purpose of illustration we show them schematically separate to emphasize where the designer can accommodate the discretionary user. The computer "processor" completes the loop by interpreting the user actions, accessing stored data where necessary, calculating needed values, and translating the data into a form understandable to the user. If the user does not need to know the internal structure in order to use the system,

FIGURE 3.1   *Schematic Representation of a User Interface*

User/Terminal Interface

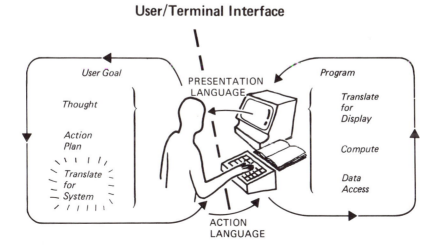

then the system implementation (aside from its impact on response time) is not of concern to the user.

The challenge to the designer is to provide a *presentation language* which the user finds appropriate to the task being carried out and which the user can interpret with a minimum of extraneous thought. The designer must also provide an *action language* through which the user conveys instructions to the system as naturally (minimal steps, minimal "translate for system," easily remembered, and not leading to user error) as the available equipment permits. Presentation and action are closely linked, for example, when action language commands are presented as menu items on the screen. This design approach is consistent with a fact about human performance. It is easier for the user to *recognize* information presented in a familiar format and then to select it than for the user to *recall* the same information accurately from the user's memory. This menu approach can be supplemented by allowing the user who does recall a needed command (which is not displayed at the moment) to key its name directly without waiting for the system to display it. We can also observe that the sequence of menu items needed for carrying out a task must be displayed rapidly, in harmony with the rhythm of user action, if the system is to support the user's train of thought.

WHAT THE USER SEES, HAS TO KNOW, AND CAN DO

A person can use intelligence and memory in sensing a context for interaction, can adapt to the context, can respond to the requirements of the environment, and thereby (within limits) can change the environment—if the person knows how to interpret what is seen. This observation is often taken for granted as a familiar aspect of our everyday experience. We may find it useful to analyze human-computer interactions by asking the following questions:

1. What does the user *see* (or sense) at the terminal as a context for interaction? The terminal establishes a visual (or sensory) context. How well does this context match past user experiences so that the person will recognize information displayed (through hardware and software) and know what action to take?

2. What must the user *know* about what is seen (or sensed) in order to interpret its meaning?
    The user must know both the task to be done (i.e., the problem to be solved) and operation of the system.
    (a) The user can describe the workstation content as a series of white lines on the screen, an illuminated function key, and strings of green text on the screen. Or if the user relates the content to a task, the display can be interpreted as a map outlined in white lines showing a geographical distribution of service calls listed in green, and the user can recognize that the system is signaling via the lighted function key its readiness to accept data for a possible territory reallocation decision.

(b) In addition, if the user takes an action and an error message results, is understanding of computer program logic required in order to interpret the error message and take corrective action?

3. What can (or must) the user *do* with the system in order to accomplish the purpose of using the system?

What functions are available at the terminal, and what interaction sequence is needed to achieve the task results (e.g., the functions needed to center the map on a point, enlarge it, and show the workload for last month)? How easy is it to get help when it is not clear what action to take?

Designer answers to these questions provide an initial point of view for examining the quality of a user interface. This analysis is not limited to single interactions. We also need to determine how the *see*, *know*, and *do* requirements fit within the overall sequence of interactions needed to complete a task [1].

A person learns many languages—oral, written, action, even the sounds of nature—while adapting to the world. Here we are asking "What are the languages a DM needs to know to use a display-based DSS?" We are using the term "languages" in a broad sense not limited to programming languages such as FORTRAN or APL. We mean the patterns of signs and symbols which are used by the display system to present information to a person and the patterns (typically different) of signs and symbols used by a person to give commands to the computer. The signs and symbols may be shown dynamically (a trace on a display screen) or statically (an array of keys on a keyboard). The person gives commands by selecting displayed entities or by moving hardware elements (e.g., keys). Thus the languages include the rules for formation of admissible output and input expressions both on the screen and on supporting equipment at a display terminal. One might say that the terminal characteristics provide the syntax for the interaction languages.

We can contrast the nonsymmetric graphical display and action languages with person-to-person spoken communication. During oral conversation the speaker and listener are in some sense interchangeable because of symmetry in capability. That is, a listener can often "look within" to deduce the meaning of symbols used by another person. This is possible because the listener perceives a mutually shared basis for understanding, a comparable language-processing capacity. Because of technological limitations (physical terminal characteristics and computer information processing capabilities), today's system is in effect a tool which the problem solver uses to achieve a desired result rather than a conversational partner. This contrasts strikingly with an interaction between equals. The system, through graphic presentations, can only suggest possible courses of user action. The user, unable to rely on the system to "do what I mean," must give commands to be interpreted literally. The designer of this environment for interaction (see Fig. 3.1) must compensate for technological limitations through the design of the output and input languages which are provided to foster communication. Thus in designing the system the designer must consider both the human factors of the user's relation to the physical equipment and the more challenging "psychology of information processing." The user must process the information intellectually as well as physically while interacting with the displayed data during the task.

We can look upon interaction as a communication process. The language design provides for successful communication if the user can learn the rules for interaction, can accept the conventions and limitations of the language, and then can interpret and compose the messages required for interaction almost automatically while concentrating energy on the problem to be solved. Failure to achieve this "level of communication" [2] means that interaction is limited to literal interpretations of the displays and the mechanical actions at the terminal needed to operate the system. If the user is presented with too much or too little information or must know a great deal about the internal details of the system in order to interpret what is seen and to take appropriate action, then the user is going to have trouble using the system effectively in the conduct of work.

THE DSS DESIGNER CANNOT IMPOSE PROCESS
WHEN A PROBLEM IS UNSTRUCTURED

In many applications where graphic facilities have been used to good advantage, the structured nature of the process being supported has guided the design of the system. That is, the sequence of functions needed has been somewhat predictable, so that the designer could prescribe, at least in part, the order in which a user would carry out operations. Perhaps the best examples occur in those applications in which the system asks the user explicit questions; the answers determine the next presentation. Many computer-assisted instruction courses follow this pattern.

We seek to aid DMs working on complex, unstructured tasks. By "unstructured tasks" [3] we mean problems in which:

1. The solution objectives are ambiguous, numerous, and not operational;

2. The process required to achieve an acceptable solution cannot be specified in advance; and

3. It is difficult to say either in advance or after the fact which user steps are directly relevant to the quality of a decision.

Thus, there may be a number of acceptable decision outcomes. In unstructured tasks, control over selection of actions to be performed on data and over the sequence in which actions are taken (the decision support process) must lie with the user. Typically, there are far too many possible combinations of user actions to make a question-asking approach feasible. Further, if the system is used to present a result to others who have not participated in development of that result, the user must be able to control the system while responding to particular questions which must be answered to justify decision acceptance.

The display of data in various graphic representations seems clearly relevant in applications such as portfolio management, budget preparation, and personnel allocation, but the problems to be solved have very little inherent structure to guide designers in telling users what representations they should use (and in what order) to arrive at an effective decision.

A DEFINITION AND MEASURES OF USABILITY

It is clear that a usable interface depends on successful solution of design problems. While the dictionary definition—"the quality or state of being convenient to use"—is not much help to the designer who is trying to achieve usability, the definition does allow for inclusion of the dynamics of a task. Usability must be examined within the personal *relationship* which holds between *user* and *terminal* as the user carries out a *task* (see Fig. 3.2). Usability refers to the quality of the interaction which takes place. It can only be meaningfully measured during task performance. The information processing required of the user must be studied in addition to the mechanical actions necessary to operate the terminal.

FIGURE 3.2   *The Usability Relationship of User and Terminal While Carrying Out a Task*

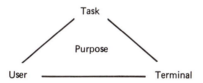

We can think of usability as relating to cognitive support for a user, involving those computer system features which in practice promote effective user thinking and learning during tasks. This is in addition to the mechanical processes needed for operating a keyboard. For example, a usability issue would be how easily a user can find a workable series of commands to design a district map which represents a service allocation decision. This contrasts with determining the speed of using a single command during a clerical task or with determining how rapidly a user can issue a series of commands once it is clear what commands to issue.

It is hard to define the intrinsic user interface attributes which make one interface more usable or less usable than another. Clearly usability is influenced by those characteristics of the user and of the computer terminal which affect performance. But it should also be clear that usability cannot be defined solely in terms of a list of attributes for the user (e.g., 6 feet tall, age 33, IQ 120) and a list of attributes for the terminal (e.g., 14-inch screen, color, transmission speed 9600 baud). That is, there are many attributes of the user and of the terminal which influence effective interaction and many others which are irrelevant for a particular action sequence.

Usability measures are closely related to "ease of use" measures cited by Miller [4]. Sample ease of use measures are

1. Training time for the population of intended users.

    If an interface is "obvious" and fits smoothly into the user's preset or preconceived way of doing things, then the actions taken by the user will be "correct" and the training time will be short. For example, a manager may be very proficient with the tools currently used in the particular work. How long does it take the manager to learn to operate the DSS? In addition, a powerful tool will provide new ways of achieving practical results. How long does it take the manager to discover how to make what is perceived to be a qualitative (as well as quantitative) improvement in the decision-making process?

2. Elapsed time until a user can enter actions "automatically."

    When tasks involve creative thinking, a person's limited cognitive capacity makes it desirable that mechanical actions not require conscious thought. The manager, having learned how to operate the DSS terminal, will then require additional time to become facile so as to be able to concentrate full attention on the decision-making task.

3. Kind and rate of errors.

    Errors can be a revealing indicator of where the "correct" action of a user in terms of a personal model of task and terminal does not agree with the action expected by the computer (its model as represented in the design of its hardware and software). The manager in our example may frequently make an error in selecting a component presented on the screen. The DSS designer responsible for the computer application can use this as a diagnostic cue. The designer can make a trade-off decision on whether to try to change the user model (through training) or to change the interface (redesign).

4. Time to recover from (user or equipment) errors.

    Whatever the task, users can be counted on to make mistakes. This is especially true for people who are infrequent users. A very important inhibitor to increased use of computer power is a fear, real or imagined, that work will have to be repeated. A user who is hurt for this reason is not likely to forget or forgive. Data resulting from creative thinking and laboriously entered must not be lost. Sure and rapid recovery from an error is extremely important to discretionary users.

5. Warm-up time after time away from the equipment.

    The wide variety of functions available through a computer terminal makes it unlikely that a user will be able to sit down and begin immediately to get useful results without some review. The amount of review needed is an especially important consideration for discretionary users who are irregular in their time spent at the terminal. Even for as fundamental a task as altering text with an editor, the same (to a user) actions are accomplished in different ways with different editors. This inhibits the user's ability to switch smoothly between editors. The result is that a user can remember the functions available in a DSS but is frustrated with the mechanics of invoking a function.

6. Attitude toward wanting to use.

    If users feel the equipment puts a physical or mental strain on them, they are not likely to be favorably disposed toward using it. In fact they may find active ways to prove that their use of the terminal is not in the organization's best interest. On the other hand, users who feel that the interface is well matched to the way they do things and aids them in doing the kind of job they want to do are more likely to expand usage by finding new ways to use the terminal in their work.

It should be clear that making trade-offs against these measures (and others listed by Miller) depends on the purpose of the system. The DSS designer must consider the subrelationships between task and user, task and terminal, and user and terminal. A shift in any one of the elements can alter the relative importance of the measures within the usability relationship. Another fact makes evaluating the impact of usability trade-offs particularly tricky. If the equipment gives the highly motivated user a function that is unobtainable in any other way and is perceived to be important, the user may cope with a poorly designed computer interface. Nonetheless, the impact of defects in the design will appear in an analysis of usability as low efficiency, fatigue, and dislike of using the terminal.

There is a temptation to strive for a single number to compare the usability of two interfaces. This is not likely to be very meaningful. Too much information is discarded when the measures are given arbitrary weights and combined into a single number. Thus the DSS builder must consider the purpose of the design work and the DSS environment and must be creative in gleaning as much insight as possible from each individual measure in order to evaluate against a profile of measures.

All these measures are *performance measures*—they can be measured only during use of the system. They are not at all like the *analytic engineering measures* which can be used to predict equipment performance. The DSS developer who wishes to implement a computer terminal workstation protocol which is "easy to use" does not have analytic engineering models of the kind that can be relied on for making design decisions relating to computer data flow.

Usability is associated with both the "physical" aspects of the terminal equipment and cognitive processes within the user. Typical human factors literature addresses questions of visual contrast on the screen, phosphor color, and dot resolution. On the input side, studies of such issues as keyboard layout, direction and amount of key motion, and use of audio feedback to the operator to increase throughput within keying tasks have all been important contributions [5]. Satisfying these physical human factors is necessary but not sufficient for successful applications. For example, Carlson (see Chapter 4) links terminal capabilities to application requirements (e.g., the system must be interruptible at any time because the user may not know a map is "the wrong one" until it starts appearing, or the user may realize a mistake was made only after the program starts a lengthy computation).

TRANSLATING USABILITY CONSIDERATIONS INTO DESIGN IMPACT

Much of the power of a display lies in the capability to present information in a variety of forms. The same numerical data placed on a map, shown in a graph, or shown in a tabular format can lead to different user insights [6]. Given that a user may want different formats at different times during a series of interactions (depending on user judgment of current information needs), the user requires control over the sequence of presentations. This control must be "high level" to be attractive to a discretionary user. The person does not wish to interrupt problem-relevant thinking processes to cope with computer-oriented details.

Where can we look for further guidance both in identifying those attributes relevant to successful interaction and in choosing values for the attributes which define trade-off design decisions? Foley [7] has given an excellent outline of the design problem including a detailed set of typical questions to which the designer must respond. We can also look for answers in the human factors literature. Representative work which can be applied to specific problems is reviewed by Kriloff [8], McCormick [9], and Meister [10]. However, it is important to note the gap between the typical systems (cognitive) questions posed by Foley and the (physical) information found in these sources.

In a series of observations Brooks [11] points out that the work of building tools for others to use is much more like engineering than science. The engineer studies in order to build; the scientist builds (laboratory equipment) in order to study, to discover facts and laws. The engineer tests a design by its usefulness and its cost; engineering progress is evaluated on the basis of user successes. There is no direct way, Brooks continues, to derive form from a list of requirements; satisfactory person-machine systems will always be the product of iterative design.

Meister [10] makes particularly helpful distinctions between system studies of user interaction with machines and the studies typically carried out in an experimental psychology laboratory setting. In a system:

1. Output from the machine influences the input from the person and vice versa;

2. Both person and machine contain logic and function enabling them, once activated, to carry out operations independently;

3. Both person and machine are observed in an environment where the activities of each are directed to a common purpose.

To identify those attributes of the person and the machine which are relevant to a particular design situation, we should look at precisely those outputs which could be provided by the machine and those corresponding inputs from the person which will advance accomplishment of the task being supported [1]. That is, we want to present only what the user understands and needs for the job, and we want to support all (and only) job-relevant user actions on the presentations. For example, a user can bring experience with maps to bear on a graphics representation, and the designer should support the user in such operations as moving and "zooming" on the map. As Meister [10] observes, this makes our arena of study at the same time broader than experimental psychology (where the focus tends to be on how the individual subject is influenced by a stimulus in a controlled laboratory setting) and narrower than experimental psychology (we are here interested only in those aspects of the person which have an effect on the tool design needed to support the task at hand).

Second, the requirement that both person and machine be able to carry out operations independently is met in interactions with computers. At one extreme (i.e., in a batch mode), the user specifies input parameters in advance (e.g., to run a resource allocation model). At the other extreme, a computer can support an interactive display workstation where an individual step itself is not a useful result but where a sequence of such steps under direction of the user (each one building on output from a previous step) can lead to a valuable result when interpreted by the user. Control must be passed between user and computer in such a way that the user will know how to intervene successfully when a computer process does not produce desired results. For example, interaction with a resource allocation model can be more effective when starting conditions are displayed graphically, parameters are set by the user through interactive input, and the user can interrupt at any time to receive a status report and possibly to reset parameters.

Third, the inclusion of purpose separates usability design work from "pure" scientific (i.e., stimulus/response) studies. In science the focus is on the capability of the human subject (facts and laws) rather than on motivation and intent. Giving consideration to the purpose of a DSS during its building can provide a focus for achieving an engineering solution. Looking at what the person is trying to *do* through use of the machine makes it possible to eliminate many scientifically interesting but irrelevant-to-engineering factors. This does mean that we may accidentally overlook some subtle (though important) effects, but it allows us to proceed with what otherwise would be a scientifically unmanageable problem. It also suggests that we consider in our design analysis some factors which might be ignored in a laboratory setting. For example, it is entirely relevant to consider in a usability analysis the effect on results (value to the user) when a manager feels a threat to job security from a computer-aided allocation program accessed through a display terminal.

The studies needed to influence design of systems are likely to be intensely pragmatic. The designer who is seeking system usability must move through a thicket of poorly understood physiological, cognitive, and motivational issues. The designer is searching for a system design which supports the work rhythms of the intended users, which is matched to their particular skills, and which uses hardware and software based on the available computer technology.

An example of a usability factor with deep-seated implications for system design is the control structure required for a user to issue commands through a keyboard or alternatively to select commands presented on a menu. Typically a user finds menu-driven access to function easier when learning the system or when returning after some time away from a once-familiar system. A menu-driven approach can remind the user quickly of the route through a procedure. On the other hand, a user quite familiar with a procedure may know exactly what is to be done and may grow quite impatient with (as well as be needlessly delayed by) a menu-driven approach, even if successive menus appear within one second or less. One way to satisfy this demand for rapid computer response may be to allow the user who knows the appropriate command or command sequence (and is willing to key it) to achieve the result directly. Thus the fundamental system design can support the user who is expert in exercising control over the desired function. At the same time the system can provide a step-by-step approach (upon request) for the user who welcomes guidance. The design objectives must spell out and cost-justify this requirement in a way meaningful to (and measurable by) the development team. Otherwise the capability designed to support "soft" usability objectives may disappear during the trade-offs made against "hard" technical, economic, and schedule constraints that are a part of development. It would be difficult to retrofit a menu-driven system to be command-driven and still maintain a usable interface. However, it should be feasible to operate a command-driven system in a menu-driven mode if the design team knows early in the development cycle that this is a requirement for marketplace acceptance.

Such far-reaching and fundamental design implications are in striking contrast with some strongly held beliefs of system developers that usability issues typically involve localized isolated "cosmetics" such as the placement of a caption on a screen.

These observations about usability apply to all interactive systems, not just those which use a display terminal. In addition, they are especially important for systems using graphics terminals. As Foley [7] states, "The payoff [from graphics applications] is high because of the bandwidth [capability for rapid interaction with high-resolution, directly relevant pictures] of the communications channel. . . . The risk is [also] high because the cost of implementing . . . is typically greater than for non-graphics applications." Graphics offer potential for decision makers who can benefit from interaction with computer-generated representations but who are repelled by computer-oriented detail.

THE USER NEEDS MORE THAN A GRAPHICS PROGRAMMING LANGUAGE

Flexibility of use is clearly needed because we cannot predict the decision process. One approach might be to give a user a graphics package embedded in a programming language. Unfortunately, many managers who could make productive use of the graphics function do not have the capability or motivation to cope with the level of detail typically required. With respect to the three guiding questions listed earlier in this chapter, a manager must know how to visualize mentally a computer-oriented data structure, must know how to build the computer-oriented information structure, and must be fluent in the syntax and semantics of the programming language. Given current graphics packages, the limited creative power of the person will be focused on building a tool to support the information-access process rather than on applying the tool for decision support.

DESIGNING A CONTEXT FOR INTERACTION—THE USER INTERFACE

We cannot build in process (a prescribed sequence of function use) because process is unknown in advance, changes over time for a manager, and often is different for different managers [6]. We cannot ask a manager to build a personally tailored system from a programming package because that requires a specialized skill the manager does not have, and personal construction is therefore too expensive in time, money, and personal energy. There are, however, ways for us as designers to build graphics systems which contain function at a level of detail compatible with the goal of effective manager exercise of control.

With this as background, we present three principles for design of a graphics system user interface to support managerial decision making. These represent one approach to design and are a partial synopsis of what we have learned. They are based on past project work in information retrieval, Negotiated Search Facility [12], and the design of graphic operations on map data, Geo-data Analysis and Display System (GADS) [6, 13]. They have also been influenced by observations of other systems [14] and by analysis of the difficulties people have in learning to use interactive facilities [15]. The principles are in the nature of policy statements or broad objectives rather than fundamental laws. They follow in the spirit of other sets of principles and guidelines, such as those offered by Foley and Wallace [16], J. Martin [17], T. Martin [18], Hansen [19], and Engel and Granda [20]. Each of these sets represents a slightly different point of view, is stated in different terminology, but is directed to an objective of increased usability. While all state desirable goals (e.g., "avoid psychological blocks," "facilitate the carryover of problem solving styles," "know the user"), none is easily made operational in the sense of specifying exactly how to achieve the goal. All are subject to evolution as designers gain increased practical experience.

The principles which follow contain many statements with which there will be disagreement. We hope to encourage others to join with us in verifying or disproving them. We need to establish the conditions under which they are applicable. This kind of exploration advances our understanding of what is or is not user-oriented design.

Principle I. Presentation Guides User Action

Arrange text and graphic symbols on each presentation to establish an explicit context for user action.

Consider the user-computer interaction cycle. User action leads to system response, which in turn leads to user action, and so on. Technically, it does not matter where we start. Behaviorally speaking, it does matter. Principle I is followed when a menu of action words is shown along with a graphic representation upon which the actions operate. Another example is the showing of appropriate subcommands after an editing mode is selected by the user. Additional examples will be mentioned as the principles are explained.

Carlson (Chapter 2) contrasts in his Figs. 2.12 and 2.13 a question-and-answer approach and a representation-oriented approach for guiding the display of a scatterplot. The first approach in effect forces users to visualize mentally how the answers to program questions are shaping the scatterplot being constructed (invisibly) by the program. The second approach displays the object so that the users may make use of defaults which are already set, may focus on adjustments in whatever order they come to mind, and can see the object change as actions take effect. For example, the user who edits the minimum or maximum values for an axis will thereby cause the object (the graph) to be rescaled when it is next drawn.

Design in accord with Principle I contrasts strikingly with the "command first, followed by system response" approach taken by some systems (particularly command languages found in an operating system). In these cases the user must create the context for action while inferring the current state of the computer. We suggest that a user will always be influenced by context when taking action. The system will be judged easier to use if it makes the context explicit rather than relying on the user to infer what action is needed from a (possibly incorrect) understanding of an implicit context. Thus an effective design will both allow actions which a user wants to take on a given representation and offer indicators showing how to invoke these actions. As Mann [21] has observed, command languages "are a narrow, limiting subset of people's familiar range of expression." Through consideration of the surrounding context in which we expect a user to take action, we hope to reduce the strain which command languages place on users. This is one approach to "seek[ing] ways to include commands as part of much more comprehensive schemes," as Mann recommends.

Principle II. Representations Provide a Focus for Design

When user process is not known in advance, concentrate on displayable data representations; then design operations to act upon these representations.

By displayable data representations we mean such schematic shapes and structures as tables, maps, and graphs. These formats for showing data can be understood on sight by users. That is, a user can take for granted the conventional relationships between format cues such as axes, scale indicators, and labels.

The application of Principle II may be made clearer by considering a process-oriented alternative. In an early GADS design [13], a map representation appeared

in two separate contexts. In the first context the data values resulting from a forecast model could be shown on a map and the detail for a zone could be retrieved.
In the second context the zones on a displayed map could be aggregated to form
new areas such as census tracts. This design was acceptable to a class of urban
planners. In later applications users wanted to aggregate zones on the basis of
data values and found that the needed operations were not all available in the
same context. A subsequent design for the map representation included all the
data display and editing operations in the same context. This was a harder context to design because the operations had to be subsetted to avoid presentation
clutter and yet be available whenever, and in whatever order, needed by the user.
Thus, anticipating a series of steps which will occur as part of a problem solution
and limiting actions to separate contexts can be successful, but the designer must
be able to predict accurately which actions a user will want to perform in each
context.

In a particular application a natural unity of design may be made possible by
the content and relationships allowed in the data base. For example, in GADS
[13], values for an attribute such as total calls for police service for zones in a city
can be shown in a tabular list by zone number, can be represented as a histogram
to show the relative distribution of number of calls by zone, or can be presented
on a map to show spatial location. Each different representation of the same
underlying data conveys different information to the user. Most important for
decision support, a user can interpret a particular representation regardless of the
decision-making process that user is carrying out at a particular time.

Principle III. The System Provides an Explicit Framework for Representations to Promote User Control

> The framework gives a uniformity of structure within which the user can synthesize
> problem solutions. This framework can be developed even though the problems them-
> selves are unstructured.

Throughout this chapter, context refers to what the user sees while interacting
with displayed data. Framework refers to what the user must know about the
system in order to control the course of interaction with it. A framework can be
defined at several levels of detail, as shown schematically in Fig. 3.3.

1. In the discussion of Principle II we drew on the fact that users recognize commonly accepted representations (e.g., a scatterplot). Thus a scatterplot is a
   context for showing data derived from a source file. A user who changes data
   attribute names and scale values will know how to interpret the resulting
   changed relationships between points on the scatterplot.

2. The user can think of the data in a representation (e.g., a scatterplot graph) as
   being contained in a "workspace." The workspace content (the data attri-

FIGURE 3.3   Several Levels of Detail
Defining a Framework

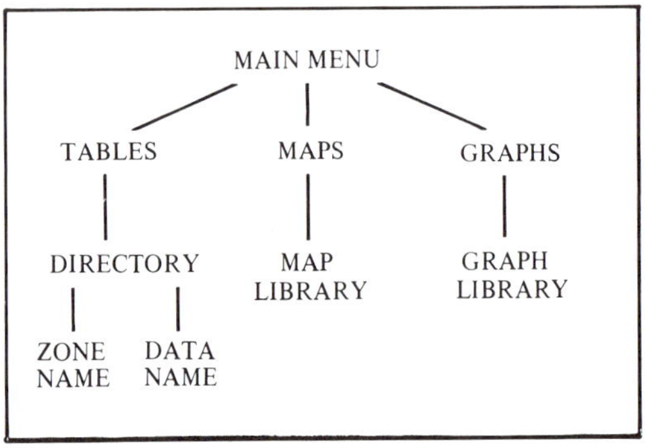

butes being graphed, extreme axes values, a trendline) is constructed with respect to a format for display. The user edits parameters and manipulates the content (see Carlson, Chapter 2, Fig. 2.13) in the workspace in ways that are relevant to current problem-solving needs. The user may then want to save the content while working with a different graph. The concept of a "library" of explicitly saved workspaces becomes useful. A family of operations for saving, retrieving, and preventing accidental destruction of workspaces forms a framework for control of this memory aid.

3. We have suggested organizing DSS system design around different representations (e.g., graphs, tables). The structure found in one representation context will generally apply in other representation contexts. For example, the library for tables will be similar in operation to that for graphs. Because a user will need to move between representations (literally, bring different representations to the screen), commands to support this aspect of the framework are necessary. The framework, defined at these several levels of detail, provides a structure into which the user can place content. The basic outline remains stable regardless of the specific data being viewed.

The ultimate test of a framework is the transfer of its concept to the mind of the user as evidenced by the ability to understand what is seen and to take action to transform what is seen into the decision support information needed. That is, the framework serves to orient user action. As such, the construction of a specific framework is a creative, empirical process often requiring iteration directed by feedback from initial users (see Hurst et al., Chapter 6; Keen and Gambino, Chapter 7). The effect of a framework can be conveyed to the user through the symbols the designer chooses and their placement at the display interface as the designer defines the output and input languages used during interaction.

Relationship Between Principles

As you may have observed, the principles in this set are interdependent. Principle I is quite general and applies to all interactive display systems. Given that a process is unstructured, Principle II applies. A different principle—perhaps "focus on process"—could be developed if the activity to be carried out by the user were highly structured. Given, however, that the user is responsible for choosing the sequence of actions and that the designer is guided by Principle II, then Principle III becomes important. Thus the order in which the principles are presented here is not arbitrary.

Principles Are Implemented Through Design Conventions

Abstract principles, to be useful, must influence the reality of design. Practical design trade-off decisions are based on a number of factors. Hardware characteristics (e.g., line speed, storage tube versus refresh display) constrain in part what the user can see during interaction. The designer initially estimates the skill level and knowledge which will be available as a result of the user's professional background. User action is anticipated as the designer plans for frequency and sequence of operations on a representation (e.g., how often will parameter editing be followed by an explicit screen clear and a redisplay of workspace content?).

The design conventions which are established by the design team codify the design decisions and help implementers and users perceive a uniformity of structure. Conventions are typically concerned with parameter editing, scrolling data, and saving intermediate results. Conventions may be utilized to signal action-options made available to a user by standard placement (location on a screen) of standard operations and by explicit coding (e.g., color, an underscore to indicate an editable field) of selectable commands. The totality of the conventions for moving between contexts conveys an impression of a framework within which the user can exercise effective control over operation of the DSS.

The *designer* who establishes a set of "standard details" to draw upon when developing a presentation can focus creative energies on anticipating and meeting user needs in the application (i.e., providing a complete set of actions). Ideally, the completeness and quality of the conventions are such that it becomes easier for the DSS developer to use existing conventions than to invent new ways of doing standard operations.

The *user* who can sense the framework resulting from utilization of the conventions can concentrate on interpreting what is seen with respect to its relevance to the given task, confident that standard operations (e.g., scrolling) can be accomplished in a standard way whatever the representation currently being used. The conventions (as embodied in the framework) can be explicitly taught, or the user can deduce them from observed uniformity of presentation during interaction. The resulting uniformity of structure is an aid for transfer of learning from one presentation to another. We want the user to be able to say, in effect, "I've seen something like that before, and I know how to work with it."

FIGURE 3.4 Example of a Design Framework Illustrating the Three Principles

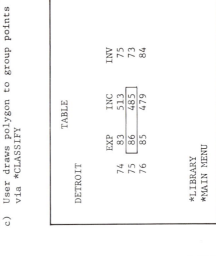

c) User draws polygon to group points via *CLASSIFY

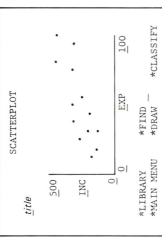

b) Points plotted and more commands shown.

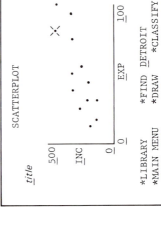

e) Find the source of a point.

a) Initially suppressed detail.

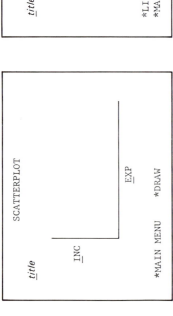

d) Library of saved scatterplots.

f) See tabular data for the point identified at GRAPHS.

60

Applying Principles and Conventions to Design

We are now ready to suggest how conventions based on these principles can be applied to a hypothetical design. The example (Fig. 3.4) is diagrammatic and abbreviated because of space limitations. In particular, we do not describe conventions for moving from one representation to another. The example illustrates the concept of a framework and makes explicit some assumptions underlying the principles.

For a given representation (e.g., a scatterplot) it may be desirable to suppress details upon initial display (Fig. 3.4a) to avoid visual overload. For example, the screen indicates the type of representation (e.g., scatterplot) along with default parameters and an initial subset of action commands. After verifying the parameters visually (i.e., determining that the attribute names are the ones desired), the user can request that the system draw the graph (Fig. 3.4b). The underscores indicate fields containing parameters whose value can be changed by editing. The leading * on words indicates command buttons [16] which will be executed when picked by the user. These conventions are used in every frame and suggest the kind of action the user can take.

The problem being solved by the use may involve grouping data points with similar properties into classes. The user may be able to identify these classes visually by the position (the clustering) of points on the scatterplot. The user can then use the *CLASSIFY command to draw a polygon around those points that are to become members of a class (Fig. 3.4c).

If seeing displayed information on one scatterplot leads a user to seek information displayed on another scatterplot, the user can synthesize a new graph or retrieve a previously saved scatterplot from the library associated with the representation (Fig. 3.4d). The workspace-library framework enables the user to explore several alternatives with confidence, knowing that the current workspace content can be recovered as needed.

The displayed information on a particular scatterplot may cause a user to seek information located in some other representation. For example, the user may want to identify the source of a point on the scatterplot (e.g., "What factory does that represent?" on Fig. 3.4e) and then see data about that source in a table. The framework should allow the user to bring the new presentation (the table) to the screen, be reminded of the link (i.e., DETROIT) established on the other representation (scatterplot), and review the tabular data (Fig. 3.4f). When the user's need for information processing has been satisfied, the user should be able to return to the original representation (scatterplot) and have the computer reconstruct the picture exactly as last seen (Fig. 3.4e). The system should support this kind of user sequence by saving all parameters necessary to reconstruct the workspace for any representation.

An underlying assumption relating to Principles I and II is that the user will recall a mental image of the representation in which the data were seen. Given a list of titles (including perhaps a time and date of entry for each title) in a library of saved workspaces, the user will recognize the key to the workspace content whose retrieval is desired (Fig. 3.4d). The framework, organized around representations, is intended to aid the user in making effective use of personal memory.

Principle III is addressed to the challenge of supporting a user in the undertaking of unstructured tasks. Without explicit task cues a high degree of user creativity is required to synthesize the sequence of operations necessary to achieve a problem solution. This is hard work for a problem solver under any circumstances, and a system perceived as difficult to operate may go unused even though results produced using it would be of potential value. Though we cannot provide problem structure to guide the user where that structure is inherently lacking, we can look for micro-processes based on representations in accord with Principle II in the belief that these micro-processes will generalize over classes of users and over task models. The goal of the framework is to make it easy for a user to cope with the structure of the DSS. The user's creative powers may then be focused on generating the macro-processes necessary to discover a structure in the problem, thereby leading to a decision outcome.

Practical DSS Will Require Combined Representations

The application of these principles (and others like them) is intended to guide designers to a basically sound set of presentations. However, task structure and patterns of anticipated use found in specific applications will make it desirable to combine representations (e.g., a graph and a table on the same presentation). We assume that attention to fundamentals in accord with these principles will enable the designer to arrange the presentation in such a way that user skills developed through interaction with basic representations (i.e., graphs and tables) will transfer to successful interaction with more complex presentations.

SUMMARY

We have given an exposition of three principles which have helped to guide our project work. The principles are stated and discussed in a necessarily abbreviated form. We can summarize as follows:

I. Design the context presented to the user at each interaction point so as to suggest the actions which a user can take upon that context.

II. When user processes are not determined in advance, focus design on displayable data representations.

III. Provide an explicit framework (uniformity of structure) to promote effective user control over the graphics system.

These principles, if they are to become generally useful, must be tested by observing:

1. Beneficial effects which appear to result from applying them, and

2. Failures which appear to result from not applying them.

We have suggested throughout the chapter ways in which the principles apply to considerations of what the user sees, what the user must know in order to interpret what is seen, and what the user can accomplish through use of the system.

ACKNOWLEDGMENTS

These ideas were developed in collaboration with colleagues at the IBM Research Laboratory in San Jose. I particularly acknowledge the clarifying contributions of E. Carlson, P. Mantey, P. Reisner, J. Sutton, and S. Zilles.

REFERENCES

1. Miller, R. B. The human task as reference for system interface design. In *User-Oriented Design of Interactive Graphics Systems*, S. Treu, ed., Association for Computing Machinery, 1977, pp. 97–100.

2. Adams, E. N. The computer in academic instruction. Research Report RC3063. Yorktown Heights, N.Y.: Watson Research Center (IBM), 1970, p. 18.

3. Stabell, C. B. Decision research: description and diagnosis of decision making in organizations. Working Paper A 79.006. Bergen, Norway: Norwegian School of Economics and Business Administration, June 1979.

4. Miller, R. B. Human ease of use criteria and their tradeoffs. TR 00.2185. Poughkeepsie, N.Y.: IBM Corporation, April 12, 1971.

5. Rupp, B. A., and R. S. Hirsch. Human factors of work stations with display terminals. San Jose, Calif.: IBM Human Factors Center, HFC-22, 1977 (also appears as IBM Publication G320-6102).

6. Carlson, E. D., J. A. Sutton, and B. F. Grace. Case studies of end user requirements for interactive problem solving systems, *Management Information Systems Quarterly*, Vol. 1, No. 1, March 1977, pp. 51–63.

7. Foley, J. D. The human factors—computer graphics interface. In *Symposium Proceedings, Human Factors and Computer Science*. Washington, D.C.: Potomac Chapter of the Human Factors Society, June 1, 1978, pp. 103–114.

8. Kriloff, H. Z. Human factors considerations for interactive display systems. In *User-Oriented Design of Interactive Graphics Systems*, S. Treu, ed., Association for Computing Machinery, 1977, pp. 45–52.

9. McCormick, E. J. *Human Factors Engineering*. 3rd ed. New York: McGraw-Hill, 1970.

10. Meister, D. *Behavioral Foundations of System Development*. New York: John Wiley & Sons, 1976.

11. Brooks, F. P., Jr. The computer "scientist" as a toolsmith—studies in interactive computer graphics. In *Proceedings of IFIP '77*. Amsterdam: North-Holland, 1977, pp. 625–634.

12. Bennett, J. L. Spatial concepts as an organizing principle for interactive bibliographic search. In *Interactive Bibliographic Search: The User/ Computer Interface*, D. E. Walker, ed. Montvale, N.J.: AFIPS Press, 1971, pp. 67–82.

13. Carlson, E. D., J. Bennett, G. Giddings, and P. Mantey. The design and evaluation of an interactive geo-data analysis and display system. In *Proceedings of IFIP '74*. Amsterdam: North-Holland, 1974, pp. 1057–1061.

14. Bennett, J. L. The user interface in interactive systems. In *Annual Review of Information Science and Technology*, Vol. 7, C. Cuadra, ed. Washington, D.C.: American Society for Information Science, 1972, pp. 159–196.

15. Bennett, J. L. Integrating users and decision support systems. In *Proceedings, Sixth and Seventh Annual Conferences*, J. D. White, ed. Chicago, Ill.: Society for Management Information Systems, 1976, pp. 77–86.

16. Foley, J. D., and V. L. Wallace. The art of natural graphic man-machine conversation, *Proceedings of the IEEE, 62*: 4 (April 1974), pp. 462–471.

17. Martin, J. *Design of Man-Computer Dialogues.* Englewood Cliffs, N.J.: Prentice-Hall, 1973.

18. Martin, T. H. Feature analysis of interactive retrieval systems. NTIS PB 235 952/AS (Report to the National Science Foundaion). Stanford, Calif.: Institute for Communication Research, 1974, 81–82.

19. Hansen, W. J. User engineering principles for interactive systems. AFIPS Fall Joint Computer Conference, Las Vegas, Nevada, 1971. In *Proceedings, Vol. 39*. Montvale, N.J.: AFIPS Press, 1971, pp. 523–532.

20. Engel, S. E., and R. E. Granda. Guidelines for man/display interfaces. TR. 00.2720. Poughkeepsie, N.Y.: IBM Corporation, December 19, 1975.

21. Mann, W. C. Why things are so bad for the computer-naive user. In *National Computer Conference.* Montvale, N.J.: AFIPS Press, 1975, pp. 785–787.

DEVELOPING THE USER INTERFACE FOR DECISION SUPPORT SYSTEMS

Eric D. Carlson

CHAPTER 4

DSS users are discretionary users. Their use may be frequent or infrequent, routine or *ad hoc*, interactive or batch mode, "hands-on" or via an assistant. Whatever the form of use, there is an interface between the user and the DSS. Even if a DSS provides extremely powerful functions, it may not be used if the interface is unacceptable. Even when a decision maker uses a DSS via an assistant, the interface must provide a meaningful framework within which information is presented and inputs are given.[2,9]

This chapter is intended to provide a guide for developing the user interface for a DSS. It presents a description and examples of design techniques, hardware devices, software packages, and programming techniques. Design techniques are the methods used to specify the user interface. Hardware devices and software packages are the technologies available for constructing the user interface. Programming techniques are the means for using the technologies to implement a design specification. Since there are no absolute rules for developing a user interface, examples and comparisons illustrate the economic, technological, and usability trade-offs that will be required. It is the examples and trade-offs that make this chapter specific to DSS. The topics covered are relevant to the design of any user-computer interface.[16] The chapter is not intended to provide a complete coverage of all the technical details necessary to develop an effective user interface for a DSS. These technical details will change over time and among DSS. The chapter is intended to identify the issues and alternatives that will need to be considered.

It will become obvious in reading this chapter that there are very few studies comparing alternative designs or clarifying basic issues (e.g., are color graphics really useful?). Even for such fundamental questions as "What query language should I use?", there is very little information on which to base a choice.[17] Therefore this chapter should provide researchers with a large set of unanswered questions. Until these questions have answers, developing the user interface for a DSS will remain engineering rather than science.

EXAMPLES

The examples given in this section certainly do not cover all possible designs, nor do they necessarily represent the best designs. The examples, taken from DSS which have been used, are classified according to the "style" of the dialog which takes place between the user and the DSS. All of the DSS cited in the examples are interactive, but the designs also can be used in batch DSS.

Question-Answer (Q/A) Interface

A user interface design that is very common in DSS employing line-at-a-time terminals is the *question-answer design*. Figure 4.1 shows a Q/A dialog from the MYCIN system. With Q/A design, the DSS asks the user a question (possibly multiple choice), the user answers the question, and so on, until the DSS produces the answers needed to support the decision. As shown in the MYCIN example, the Q/A interface may use "natural" language and may determine the next question based on the answer(s) to the previous question(s). If the DSS can-

FIGURE 4.1   Q/A Interface in MYCIN [7]

```
--------PATIENT - 248--------
1)   Patient's name: (first-last)
**   C.R.
2)   Sex:                          Questions from MYCIN preceded by: 1), 2),...
**   MALE                          User answers are typed in following: **
3)   Age:
**   52
4)   Have you been able to obtain positive microbiological information about
     a possible infection of C.R.?
**   YES

        --------INFECTION - 1--------
        5)   What is the infection?
        **   ENDARTERITIS (.6)
        6)   Please give the date and approximate time when signs or symptoms of
             the endarteritis (INFECTION-1) first appeared.  (mo/da/yr time)
        **   21 JULY 1975
        The most recent culture yielding positive microbiological information
        about the endarteritis (INFECTION -1) will be referred to as:

            -------CULTURE - 1--------
            7)   From what site was the specimen for CULTURE -1 taken?
            **   BLOOD
```

not "understand" an answer, or needs additional information, clarification questions may be asked. In some DSS the user can redirect the questioning by giving answers such as "SKIP QUESTION" or "BEGIN WITH QUESTION 25."

Q/A interface design tends to be most successful with inexperienced or infrequent users who are unfamiliar with the problem to be solved. Q/A design tends to be least successful with sophisticated or frequent users who get tired of proceeding through the questions. To accommodate both frequent and infrequent users, a Q/A design may provide more than one mode of use (e.g., full sentence mode and abbreviation mode) or may have default answers. The Q/A design leads to awkward usage patterns if, during a dialog, users need to modify answers to previous questions.

Command Language Interface

A second technique for designing the user interface is to develop a *command language* for invoking DSS functions. The usual format of this interface design involves commands of verb-noun pairs (e.g., PLOT SALES) with short spellings (i.e., 6–8 characters) for the nouns and verbs. Figure 4.2. gives an example of a

FIGURE 4.2   Command Language Interface in PLANCODE [12]

COMMANDS:

```
'INPUT VALUES'
CASH_INFLOW
CASH_OUTFLOW
AMOUNT,   CHAR = '-'

'NET PRESENT VALUE', NET_PRES_VAL,LEVEL=2,TOTAL=NO
'CUMULATIVE PRES.VAL.',CUMPV,LEVEL=2,TOTAL=NO
```

RESULTING OUTPUT:

INPUT VALUES				
CASH_INFLOW	18.00	31.00	43.00	92.00
CASH_OUTFLOW	3.00	6.00	8.00	17.00
AMOUNT	15.00	25.00	35.00	75.00
NET PRESENT VALUE	13.64	20.66	26.29	
CUMULATIVE PRES.VAL.	13.64	34.30	60.59	

Implied verb in commands is "PRINT"

command language interface. The implied verb is PRINT, and the output commands are a set of nouns. Several existing DSS use this style of interface.[4] For simple applications, a command language is easily learned, but it will probably need to be relearned by infrequent users. For complicated applications, a command language can easily become a programming language, thereby requiring more skill to use. It is, however, possible to develop a "layered" command language. In a layered language there are simple commands for simple or frequently used functions, and these commands can be combined with other, more complicated commands for complex or infrequently used functions.

Menu Interface

An interface design that is popular for DSS which utilize display (CRT) terminals is the *menu interface*. Unlike the command language interface which requires the user to type commands, the menu interface design lets the user select from a menu of alternatives such as report names or computation commands. Selection is accomplished with a keyboard or a "picking" device such as a light-pen. Figure 4.3 illustrates a menu interface from IBM's Trend Analysis.

FIGURE 4.3 Menu Interface in Trend Analysis 370 [13]

```
                       REPORT TYPE SELECTION
                                                          EXAMPLES
        10 SINGLE PERIOD COMPARISON REPORT                D/E #1   D/E #2
             ROWS ARE ORGANIZATIONS               ORG #1    X        X
             COLUMNS ARE DATA ELEMENTS            ORG #2    X        X

        20 HISTORICAL COMPARISON REPORT                   TIME 1   TIME 2
             ROWS ARE ORGANIZATIONS               ORG #1    X        X
             COLUMNS ARE PERIODS OF TIME          ORG #2    X        X

Menu—   30 HISTORICAL ANALYSIS REPORT                     TIME 1   TIME 2
             ROWS ARE DATA ELEMENTS               D/E #1    X        X
             COLUMNS ARE PERIODS OF TIME          D/E #2    X        X

        40 ROTATE AXES FOR SELECTION 10 ABOVE

        50 ROTATE AXES FOR SELECTION 20 ABOVE

        60 ROTATE AXES FOR SELECTION 30 ABOVE

        ENTER YOUR TWO DIGIT SELECTION(S)
        20
Selection
```

The menu interface seems to be quite effective for inexperienced or infrequent users who are familiar with the problem to be solved. For DSS which provide a large number of functions, menu interfaces often require many menu items, and

FIGURE 4.4   Input Form/Output Form Interface in Query by Example [22]

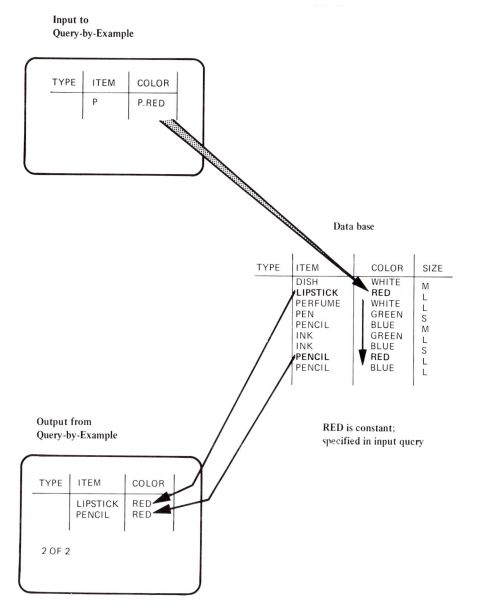

**Input to
Query-by-Example**

TYPE	ITEM	COLOR
	P	P.RED

Data base

TYPE	ITEM	COLOR	SIZE
	DISH	WHITE	M
	LIPSTICK	RED	L
	PERFUME	WHITE	L
	PEN	GREEN	S
	PENCIL	BLUE	M
	INK	GREEN	L
	INK	BLUE	S
	PENCIL	RED	L
	PENCIL	BLUE	L

**Output from
Query-by-Example**

RED is constant;
specified in input query

TYPE	ITEM	COLOR
	LIPSTICK	RED
	PENCIL	RED

2 OF 2

in such cases the menus should be structured. Restaurant menus are examples of structuring by grouping (entrees, desserts, wines, etc.). Another structuring technique is to use hierarchies of menus. In Fig. 4.3, the menu lets the user select the types of reports to be displayed by the DSS.

Input Form/Output Form Interface

Input form/output form designs provide input forms in which the user enters commands and data and output forms on which the DSS produces responses. After viewing an output form, the user can fill in another input form to continue the dialog. If the system determines which input form is next, this design parallels the Q/A design, with input forms corresponding to a set of questions and output forms corresponding to a set of answers. Figure 4.4 shows an input form and an output form from IBM's Query by Example.

This design can be very successful if there is a correspondence between the input/output forms in the DSS and paper forms or thought patterns familiar to the users. For example, an input form can correspond to an existing check list, or it can be arranged to group items that a decision maker is likely to think about together.

Input-in-Context-of-Output Interface

An extension of the input form/output form design is to combine input and output forms so that *user inputs are always given in the context of the previous output* from the DSS. In this style, the DSS presents an output (e.g., a table or a graph or a list) within which the user may fill in or select inputs that will either modify the current output or result in a different output. For example, a skeletal report giving sample or standard data can be used as an input form if the user can write new data names or selection criteria on the report for subsequent use as inputs to the DSS. More sophisticated versions of this type of design combine menus of commands which can be used to create and modify an output form. Figure 4.5 gives an example from a DSS where inputs are given in the context of previous DSS outputs. The output is a scatterplot, and the inputs for any scatterplot are given beneath the output. The inputs are the variable names (TBASE, CEIDENT) and the x and y axis scales (0–200, 100–610). The output/input context design can provide a "high-function" user interface which supports complex decisions.[1,2] To use a system based on this design, however, one is likely to need a few hours of training.[10]

Combinations

It is likely that the user interface for a specific DSS will combine more than one style. For example, a Q/A interface could be used in a "help" or "tutorial" feature of a DSS along with a command or menu interface used for routine interactions.

FIGURE 4.5   *Input-in-Context Interface in GADS [5]*

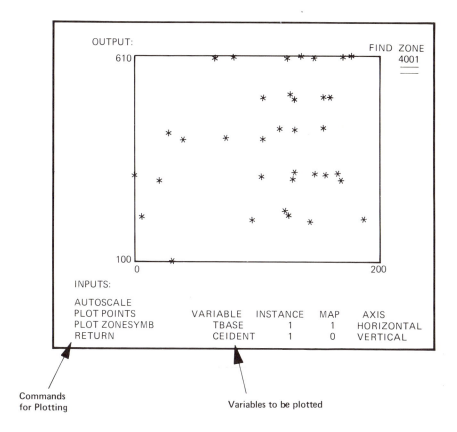

In such a DSS, the HELP command would invoke a Q/A dialog to assist the user in accomplishing a task. The multiple-choice answers could cause invocation of commands which the user could have selected from the menus to accomplish the same task. Thus the Q/A dialog can help train the user. Another possible combination is to use menus for command selection in a command language interface or to use menus for inputs in an input-in-context interface.

TRADE-OFFS

If alternative designs for the user interface are considered, trade-offs are involved in selecting among the alternatives. Whether or not the designers recognize or enumerate design trade-offs, they are made in any event. These trade-offs affect the usability of the DSS as well as its cost. Reducing hardware or development costs is often the predominant consideration in making trade-offs. Better measures of the costs of poor user interface design are needed to help compare reduced development or hardware costs with the increased costs of poor usability. Training time, number of errors, number of potential users, and time to do a given task are examples of such measures.

A list of trade-offs is a useful guide for evaluating alternatives. For each DSS the list will involve trade-offs unique to the users, application, and organizational environment of the DSS. For example, Donovan and Madnick illustrate the differences that "type of decision" makes in the design of DSS.[8] Table 4.1 gives a list of some of the trade-offs that need to be considered in designing the user interface, and Table 4.2 compares Q/A designs with input-in-context designs using the list in Table 4.1. Note that the list is not necessarily complete and that the comparison is qualitative.

DESIGN TECHNIQUES

Carlson (Chapter 2 of this book) describes an approach for designing DSS which involves an analysis of the representations, operations, memory aids, and control aids used by the decision maker(s) in the decision(s) to be supported. This approach to DSS design is particularly appropriate when one is developing the user interface for a DSS. For example, the representations can be used to specify the output formats for the user interface, and the operations indicate the commands

TABLE 4.1   Trade-Off Variables in User Interface Design

Variables	Examples of Alternatives
Hardware	
1. output media	line-at-a-time, full-screen graphics
2. input media	keyboards, pointing device, voice recognition
Software	
3. available programs	graphics subroutines, natural language parsers
4. amount of code to write	device drivers, control logic, simple subroutine calls
User	
5. interaction style	batch, slow speed, high speed
6. training constraints	will accept, must minimize
7. control style	"hands-on," tell someone else
8. familiarity with problem	low, high
9. familiarity with computer	low, high
Decision-making	
10. type of decision	ad hoc, institutional [8]
11. number of participants	few, many

Explain this

TABLE 4.2   *Sample Comparison of User Interface Alternatives*

Trade-Off Variables	Alternatives	
	Q/A	**Input-in-Context**
Hardware		
1. output media	line-at-a-time terminal	full-screen CRT
2. input media	keyboard	keyboard and/or pointing device
Software		
3. available programs	computer-assisted instruction packages	graphics subroutine packages
4. amount of code to write	large	large
User		
5. interaction style	slow speed	high speed
6. training constraints	low training time	high training time
7. control style	"help-me"	"do-it-myself"
8. familiarity with problem	low	high
9. familiarity with computer	low	some
Decision-making		
10. type of decision	institutional, infrequent	ad hoc, frequent
11. number of participants	one	several

which the DSS will need to provide. The control aids which are identified can help the designer choose from among the alternative dialog styles (e.g., Q/A or input form/output form) for the user interface.

Regardless of the techniques used for systems analysis, the design of the user interface requires a selection of representations and operations. That is, the design team must specify the output and input formats that will be used in the interface. Simultaneously, it is useful to establish user interface conventions (see Bennett, Chapter 3 of this book) which can be used to guide the user interface design. For example, a convention could be that only one style of user interface will be used for the DSS. Other conventions might cover error message formats, restriction of error messages to certain locations in the output formats, restriction of input formats (e.g., all commands will be alphabetic, eight characters, and mnemonic), and requiring of feedback (e.g., each user input in an interactive system will be acknowledged by the system). These conventions can serve as standards to which the design should conform. A useful technique is to allow exceptions to the conventions only if the design has first been completed using the conventions and a good reason can be given as to why this design is not satisfactory. For example, a convention may not be followed because it is too expensive to implement, or it conflicts with another convention, or it will severely degrade performance.

Once a set of output and input formats has been developed, the next step in the design of the user interface should be a "usability walk-through." For a usability walk-through, a sample set of output and input formats is developed on paper or as part of a prototype system. A design review group, containing some potential users, then "walks-through" (simulates the steps needed for) sample decision-making tasks using the sample formats. Every system output and every user input should be recorded as part of the walk-through. Planned responses to possible user errors also should be checked. The walk-through gives the designer (and potential users) a chance to get a feel for what it will be like to use the DSS *before* any implementation. A walk-through is even more effective if real data are prepared for use in the sample outputs, if actual inputs are required to get the output, and if a real decision-making situation (even a past decision) is used. The walk-through should generate numerous suggestions. These are checked against the conventions, trade-offs are assessed, and the user interface design is revised. Additional walk-throughs may be necessary.

Where the necessary tools exist (e.g., interpreted languages like APL or BASIC and interactive computer systems), a prototype of the user interface (and possibly of the entire DSS) can be very useful both in the design of the user interface and in usability walk-throughs. Prototypes are especially important for DSS which are expected to be large (i.e., over 10,000 lines of code). A danger with prototypes is that the users may think the prototype is the final DSS. If the prototype is not satisfactory, then the users may lose interest. If the prototype works well, the users may not want to wait for a second implementation. Thus before users are shown a prototype they should be aware that it is not intended to be the final DSS, and the designers should have good estimates of the implementation time required for the next version of the DSS.

A final step in designing the user interface is to establish measures which can be used to evaluate the design. The choice of measures should be based on the types of users and tasks which the DSS is to support. For example, for infrequent users, time needed to "sign-on" may be an important measure. These measures are valuable in making design trade-offs, and they can help the design team to decide if modifications to the user interface are necessary. The measures should be checked with the users because the users will often have suggestions concerning what usability criteria are important to them. Examples of measures which could be used are training time, number of input errors per session, time to relearn after a week (month, etc.) away from the system, time to select the correct inputs, time to enter the correct inputs, and number of alternative choices at each user decision point.[1] After the interface is implemented, of course, there will be one obvious measure: is the DSS used or not? For more detailed evaluations, experiments can be designed.[17]

HARDWARE SELECTION

Hardware affects the functionality and the usability of any design. Therefore the user interface cannot be designed without concern for the hardware. The choice of hardware may be made before, during, or after the design of the user interface for a DSS. In many cases the hardware choice is specified by what is already

TABLE 4.3   *Parameters for Choosing Hardware for the*
DSS User Interface

	Sample Values	
Parameter	**Batch DSS**	**Interactive DSS**
Group 1 (output)		
composed of	text, lines	text, lines, audio
size/page	8½" × 11"	19" diagonal
resolution	100–200 points/inch	50–100 points/inch
volume/page	over 1000 characters or 1000 vectors	over 500 characters and 100 vectors
refreshed	daily	many times/second
must last	several months	several seconds
Group 2 (input)		
devices	forms	pick (e.g., light-pen) keyboard, switches, audio
text	several hundred characters, at least 2 fonts, at least 2 sizes	same
graphics	none	2-D drawings
colors (shades)	2	2–8
Group 3 (programming)		
interface to computer	standard communication codes	same
interface to program	high-level language	same
Group 4 (product quality)		
performance	600 lines/minute output, 400 characters/minute input	9600 bits/second communications, refresh 60 times/second
price	$600,000 shared	$10,000/terminal
package	remotable, low noise, fit in small room, standard power and operating environment	remotable, portable, low noise, no glare, fit on desk top, standard power and operating environment

available within the organization. In such cases the hardware becomes a constraint in the design. For batch-mode DSS the relevant hardware includes the output device (usually a printer) and the input media (e.g., cards, forms, etc.). For interactive DSS, the relevant hardware is the terminal and its associated input and output devices (e.g., keyboards, light-pens, audio units, and tablets).

⌐ The variety and price/performance ratio of the relevant hardware for the user interface in a DSS are changing rapidly. For example, the price of an eight-color, medium-resolution (512×512 picture elements) graphics terminal decreased by a factor of three (to about \$15,000) between 1974 and 1978. The number of vendors of these terminals increased by at least the same factor (to at least nine). In choosing among hardware alternatives there are a number of parameters to consider. Table 4.3 lists some of these parameters and gives sample values for the parameters which would be "typical" of those required by batch and interactive DSS. The values for batch DSS assume a printer for output and keypunched input; the values for interactive DSS assume a CRT (cathode ray tube) terminal. If the CRT has an associated printer, its characteristics should approximate those of the output parameters for batch DSS. (A more detailed discussion of these parameters, as applied to graphics terminals, is given by Carlson [3].) The parameters in Table 4.3 are divided into four groups. The parameters in Group 1 characterize output capabilities, and those in Group 2 refer to input capabilities. Group 3 is a set of parameters relating to how the hardware is programmed. Group 4 includes performance, price, and packaging parameters.

The sample values given in Table 4.3 are not nearly as important as the parameters they exemplify. In choosing the hardware for a specific DSS, the designers should develop "required" values for each parameter based on the design and "provided" values for each parameter for each hardware alternative. The parameters thus serve as a framework for comparing hardware alternatives based on design requirements. For example, a DSS that displays computer-stored photographs (e.g., satellite pictures) would require an output resolution of about 100 points per inch. Such a requirement would greatly reduce the number of hardware alternatives that could be considered.

SOFTWARE PACKAGES

The largest costs in developing the software for a DSS probably will be the development and maintenance of the software which implements the user interface. As an example, about 60 percent of the code written for the DSS GADS [5] is code for the user interface, and about 75 percent of the changes made to GADS over a four-year period were changes to the user interface code.

Software packages are collections of programs which can be used as part of, or to implement, other programs. For the user interface the most useful software packages are those which support output from and input to user interface devices. This section focuses on such packages, and the terms "output" (or "write") and "input" (or "read") refer to communication to and from the user. The reason for using these packages is to reduce the implementation costs. Software packages are available from a variety of computer vendors, software vendors, and government agencies. Most of the packages can only be used with a small set of hardware, so the hardware choices for the user interface usually reduce the choice of software packages (or vice versa). A few software packages are free; some can be leased for from about $100 to over $1000 per month; some can be purchased for from about $1000 to about $20,000. Because of high development costs and small markets, the prices of the software packages for DSS are unlikely to decrease as rapidly as hardware costs. The number of available software packages, however, should increase.

Types of Software Packages

The types of software packages are characterized more by the languages programmers use to invoke the packages than by any significant differences in function. The predominant type of software which could be acquired to help implement the user interface for a DSS is a subroutine package. Subroutine packages are sets of programs which are accessed via CALL statements from a high-level programming language, such as FORTRAN or COBOL. CALL statements usually require the programmer to know a second, small language (that of the CALL statements) in addition to the language used to implement the other parts of the DSS. For parameters to the calls the programmer gives the data to be written or read and a series of attributes telling how the data are to be written or read (i.e., format or position). The subroutine name and parameters are the only details the programmer needs to know. The details of how the subroutine works internally should not be of concern. Subroutine packages can be quite flexible, so that almost any user interface (which can be designed for the hardware which the package supports) can be implemented using the packages. A report from an ACM SIGGRAPH committee compares ten packages designed to support graphics terminals and/or plotters.[21]

A second type of software package is a programming language with high-level constructs (i.e., more than WRITE and READ commands) for data output and input. The high-level constructs simplify programming of the output and input formats and the interpretation of the inputs. Such languages are not common today, but are likely to become more common as programming languages reflect the advances in hardware. Programming language constructs for supporting dialogs allow the code for the user interface to be written in the same language used for the code which implements the DSS. There are no CALL statements required as in subroutine packages. Because high-level constructs in a programming language are consistent with the language, they are often easier to understand than subroutine calls. Because high-level constructs are integrated into the language and can be compiled directly into the program, they tend to produce a more efficient implementation than that produced by subroutine calls. LaFuente designed a set of such constructs as an extension of the programming language PASCAL.[14]

Although the extensions were not implemented, they are indicative of what can be done to improve the support which the commonly used high-level languages (COBOL, FORTRAN, etc.) provide for programming the user interface.

Data definition languages describe the outputs and inputs for the user interface. The data definitions are invoked by a subroutine call, similar to that for subroutine packages. However, there is only one call to the data definition interface per output or input "page" in the user interface, whereas a subroutine package requires several calls. In addition, calls to the data definition package give the device and format names plus parameters for the formats, whereas the calls to a subroutine package specify the entire formats. Data definition languages help specify the attributes to be used in writing or reading the data passed as part of the call. Historically, data definition packages have supported fewer devices than subroutine packages, and they have required more skill to use than high-level constructs in a programming language. However, there are no technical reasons why these differences need exist. Since the data definitions are stored separately from the program, they are easy to modify and reuse. In addition, data definition packages may be more efficient than either subroutine packages or high-level constructs because they are tailored for specific devices and because they tend to be "lower-level" languages. IBM's Message Formatting Services (MFS) is an example of a data definition package.[11]

A final type of software package is the "skeletal" or "base" DSS out of which others can be built. In most cases the main extensions which can be made to the skeleton (base) involve the user interface. A skeletal DSS may provide functions to define new reports, to modify the formats of reports provided by the DSS, or to create new input formats (e.g., inputs to a new forecasting routine which has been added to the DSS). This type of package usually provides fewer functions and control structures than the other three types of software packages do (because it is developed for specific DSS applications). This restriction, however, often makes it easier to program using this type of package. In fact, the only examples of "users" developing a DSS involve use of a skeletal DSS. IBM's PLAN-CODE is an example of one of several skeletal DSS from which specific DSS can be built.[12]

Figure 4.6 gives examples of program segments in a hypothetical language for each of the four types of software packages. The examples show code segments used to produce a table comparing up to five balance sheet items for up to three different companies. The inputs are the names of the balance sheet items and the names of the companies. The exact meaning of each program segment is not given here; the figure is intended to illustrate the syntactic differences among the types of software packages. Figure 4.6a shows subroutine calls to read data from a display terminal (INTEXT), to clear the display screen on the terminal (ERASE), and to draw the tabular output (DRAWTABLE). In Fig. 4.6b the table is described (DECLARE TABLE), the input fields are described (DECLARE INPUT-AREA), the input is read, and the table is displayed. Figure 4.6c shows an output data definition (TABLE FORMAT) and an input data definition (INPUT FORMAT).

FIGURE 4.6   *Examples of Languages for Programming the
User Interface*

a) Subroutine package

```
CALL INTEXT (DATANAMES(5), Length(10), CHARACTER,
              ROW(10), COL(30));
CALL INTEXT (COMPANYNAMES(3), LENGTH(25), CHARACTER,
              ROW(12), COL(30));
CALL ERASE;
CALL DRAWTABLE (DATANAMES, COMPANYNAMES,
              HEADINGS = YES, LOWER LEFT = (24,1),
              UPPER RIGHT = (1,70);
```

b) Constructs in a programming language

```
DECLARE TABLE
              COLUMNS = DATANAMES(1-5),
              ROWS = COMPANYNAMES(1-3),
              LOWER = 24, 1,
              UPPER = 1, 70,
              HEADINGS = YES;
DECLARE INPUT-AREA
              DATANAMES(5) CHAR(10) ROW(10) COL(30),
              COMPANYNAMES(3) CHAR(25) ROW(12) COL(30));
          .
          .
          .
READ INPUT
DISPLAY TABLE;
```

c) Data definition package

TABLE	FORMAT
FIELD 1	LTH10, POS(1,1)
.	
.	
FIELD 24	LTH5, POS(24,66)
TABLE	END
INPUT	FORMAT
FIELD 1	LTH10, POS(10,30)
.	
.	
FIELD 8	
INPUT	LND

d) Skeletal DSS

```
DATA = SALES77, S
COMPANIES = IBM,
TABLE DATA FOR C
```

These descriptions would be stored in a file and could be requested by name in a program which wanted to write or read that particular format. The identicalness of names in the output and input formats is intentional and is required if the input fields are to be associated with specific output fields. In Fig. 4.6d the inputs are specified (DATA =, COMPANIES =), and the output is requested (TABLE DATA) using a command language interface to a skeletal DSS. Note that the formats of the input and output data are not specified. If the user is not willing to take the default formats for inputs and outputs in a skeletal DSS, the user can specify new formats, if allowed, usually in a language similar to that of one of the other three types of software packages. The main advantage of the skeletal DSS approach to programming the user interface is the availability of these default formats.

Criteria for Choosing Among Software Packages

Table 4.4 lists some criteria that could be used in selecting a software package. In addition, the table indicates the author's ranking of the four types of software packages with respect to each criterion. A ranking of 1 indicates that existing software packages of this type currently are the best of the four types (in the author's

TABLE 4.4   *Criteria for Choosing Among Software Packages for the User Interface in a DSS*

Criteria	Software Packages	Language Constructs	Formatting Languages	Skeletal DSS
Hardware				
1. devices supported	1	3	2	4
2. hardware independence	1	3	2	4
Software				
3. interface to existing programming language	2	1	3	4
4. interface to data base	4	1	2	3
Functionality				
5. number of output representations possible	1	2	3	4
6. transformation (e.g., scaling) of output representation	1	2	3	4
7. number of input formats supported	2	1 (all are weak here)	3	4
8. support for specifying responses to inputs	4	3	2	1
Costs				
9. acquisition costs	1	4	3	2
10. installation costs	2	3	4	1
11. execution costs	3	2	1	4
12. ease of programming	3	2	4	1

opinion) with respect to the criterion; a ranking of 2 is next best, and so on. In the criteria related to costs, a 1 indicates lowest cost. A DSS design team should do its own ranking of the software packages being considered.

The first two criteria relate to hardware/software interaction. If the software package is limited to a small set of hardware, then the set of user interfaces that can be described will be limited accordingly. Criteria 3 and 4 are important if the software package will be used in connection with other software packages in order to implement the DSS. Criteria 5 through 8 indicate what user interface designs it will be possible to implement with the software package. For example, if the package only supports display of a single line of text at a time, then a contextual design for the user interface cannot be implemented. Similarly, a package that does not provide support for "parsing" of text input will be of limited value for a question/answer design. The last four criteria in Table 4.4 deal with the costs of acquisition and of the use of the package.

PROGRAMMING TECHNIQUES

Programming techniques are methods for using programming languages and/or software packages to implement the user interface. Good programming techniques can reduce the implementation costs of the user interface as well as improve its quality. Cost reductions are achieved in two ways. First, good programming techniques reduce the programming effort because they simplify program structure or because they specify the alternatives available to the programmer. Second, good programming techniques reduce maintenance costs because they make it easier to understand the programs. Good programming techniques help improve the quality of the user interface because they encourage (or enforce) use of design conventions (see the section titled "Design Techniques" in this chapter) and because they make it easier to change the interface when improvements are needed. In fact, programming techniques are often developed in connection with the conventions for the user interface, which are established during the design phase. The conventions are the guidelines for programming, and the programming techniques are methods which make it easier for the programmer to follow the guidelines.

As an example of the relationship between design conventions and programming techniques, suppose that the following design convention is adopted: all error messages will be preceded by ****, will not contain any numbers, and will appear at the lower left of all output reports (or display screens). A programming technique corresponding to this convention would be to provide a subroutine (ERROR-MESSAGE) which would insert the ****, check that the message was only alphabetic, and display it on the lower left of the appropriate report (or display screen). The programmer would use the subroutine by a CALL statement such as:

CALL ERROR-MESSAGE (REPORT3, 'REQUESTED DATA NOT AVAILABLE');

The subroutine would take care of the details. Programmers are likely to follow the guideline because using the subroutine is less work than programming all the details for printing error messages.

A variety of programming techniques can be developed for use in implementing the user interface. Some of these rely on subroutines, as in the preceding example. Others involve constraining the use of constructs in the programming language. For example, if the DSS users are not familiar with scientific notation, floating point formats should not be displayed on outputs. Some programming techniques involve adding constructs to the programming language (via macro statements or external data structures). For example, a REPORT construct could be added to enforce standard formats for reports.

The value of programming techniques which simplify implementation of the user interface is largely independent of the design chosen for the interface. For example, the use of an error-message subroutine would benefit a Q/A design as much as it would benefit an input-in-context design for the user interface. However, the content of the routine would be different for each design, since in the Q/A design the error message would be displayed immediately following the answer to a question, and in the contextual design the error message would be displayed with a context that would be used to correct the error. Thus programming techniques are intended to affect the cost of building the user interface rather than its design.

The remainder of this section gives three examples of programming techniques likely to be useful for implementing DSS. Additional techniques should be developed for a specific DSS project. To develop the techniques, two questions are useful:

1. What program segments or data are likely to be reusable or frequently modified?

2. What program segments or data can be provided to programmers to support use of the design conventions?

Use of Data Types and Structures

Data types in a programming language are the constructs available for describing variables used in the program. In general, a data type defines a set of values which can be assigned to a variable in a program and defines the set of operations that can be performed on that variable.[15] Character, decimal, and floating point are examples of simple data types found in most programming languages. Compound data types, such as "record," can be formed from simple ones. Data structures are essentially compound data types. They are formed from groups of variables where each component has a (possibly different) type.

Data types and data structures usually are thought of with respect to storing, retrieving, and operating on variables in a program or a data base.[15] The data types and structures provided by existing languages tend to have operations associated with modifying or storing values of variables of that type (e.g., arithmetic and data base operations). However, data types and data structures can also be very useful in programming the user interface. As an example, the data type ERRORMSG could be used to implement the error message convention discussed previously. Because most languages do not provide this data type, it would have to be defined in terms of those data types that are provided. In a programming language like PL/1, the structure construct could be used to define the error message data type. Note that a language like PL/1 does not permit the definition of "new" operations which can be performed on the type, nor will it provide any "type checking" for any operations (such as assignment) performed on the type to guarantee that the results do not violate the definition of the type.

```
DCL  1  ERRORMSG,
     2  TEXT,
        3 HDR CHAR(4) INIT('****'),
        3 MSG CHAR(50) VARYING INIT(' '),
     2  POSITION,
        3 ROW FIXED BIN(15) INIT(24),
        3 COL FIXED BIN(15) INIT(1);
```

To use this data type the programmer would write code such as:

```
ERRORMSG.TEXT.MSG = 'ILLEGAL ACTION';
DISPLAY (ERRORMSG.TEXT, ERRORMSG.ROW, ERRORMSG.COL)
```

If the ERRORMSG structure is also an array, then it can contain all the error messages, and the programmer need only write:

```
DISPLAY (ERRORMSG(7).TEXT, ERRORMSG(7).ROW,
ERRORMSG(7).COL)
```

To determine where error messages will be displayed in the output formats, a programmer need look only at the definition of ERRORMSG, not at all the lines of code that display an error message. In fact, only the programmer who creates the ERRORMSG type needs to understand the details concerning the location of error messages. If the convention for the location of error messages changes, only the data type (i.e., the PL/1 structure) need be changed (new ROW and COL values). All the lines of code that refer to the data type (e.g., the DISPLAY statement) remain unchanged. If the programming technique of defining an ERRORMSG type had not been used, then all the lines of code that displayed error messages would need to be modified to reflect the new convention.

Display of an error message can be tied to the data type to make coding easier. If DISPERR is defined as a procedure which can access the ROW and COL items of ERRORMSG, then the programmer need only write:

```
CALL DISPERR (ERRORMSG(7)),
```

and the DISPERR procedure will use the ERRORMSG type and the DISPERR procedure to display the error message in the output format at the row and column defined as part of the type. This concept of associating data types and operations together and requiring that all operations on a particular data type be restricted to those associated with it is called "abstract data types."[15] For the data type ERRORMSG we could define operations such as:

> ADDMSG to define an error message,
> DELMSG to eliminate a message,
> DISPMSG to display a message,
> ERASEMSG to erase a message.

There are many uses for data types and structures in programming the user interface for a DSS. Two obvious uses are to define each report as a data structure and to store each set of related user inputs in the same data structure. The data structure for inputs can also contain default input values. If the conventions for the user interface design include conventions for report formats, input values, or input checking, then the data structures can often facilitate implementing these conventions.

Skeletal DSS software packages may be thought of as collections of the skeletal data structures and the operations on those data structures (i.e., a skeletal DSS is a set of abstract data types). Thus a specific DSS built from the skeletal DSS is actually a program in the language of the skeleton. The programs are sequences of operations on instances of the data types provided by the skeletal DSS.

Modularization of the User Interface Code

Modular means "standard design," so modularization means to make standard. Modularization is a common programming technique, and it usually involves dividing the program into well-defined, self-contained, small units with one entry and one exit. Determining module boundaries requires an analysis of how the programs are likely to be used and how they are likely to be changed over time.

Because of the high probability that the user interface will need to be modified during the life cycle of the DSS, the code for the user interface should be in program units (modules) which are separate from the remaining code. The code that reads and writes data to the hardware devices (e.g., terminals) should also be in modules separate from the code that defines the output and input formats for a specific interface. This separation of device-specific code will facilitate locating errors in that code, and it will isolate the impact of adding or changing hardware. The code that produces the output formats and the code that interprets the inputs should also be in separate modules. This separation will permit reuse of the separate parts, and it will simplify changes to outputs or inputs.

The definition of the modules depends on the design of the user interface. For batch DSS the output formatting and the input handling should be in separate modules because output and input are separate phases of the operation of the DSS. If the formats are complex, each output report should be in a separate module. For interactive DSS groups of related outputs and inputs can be coded in a single module. For example, each question/answer pair in a Q/A interface can be in a single module. In a command language design, the interpreter of each command and its associated output can be in separate modules.

A high-level modularization scheme for a program structure for a DSS is shown in Fig. 4.7. The structure contains five sets of modules: access modules for the display and data base devices, user interface modules, data transformation modules, and data base management modules. This division separates the device-specific code (the access modules) and the code for three general functions of any DSS (user interface, data transformation, and data base management). The separation is intended to group logically related components of a DSS.

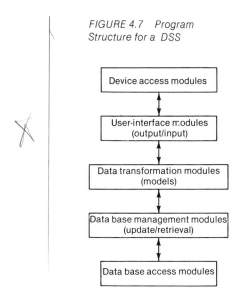

FIGURE 4.7   Program Structure for a DSS

Readers with programming experience will note that a program with a large number of modules often executes more slowly than a program which is one large module. Thus modularization involves a trade-off between development and maintenance costs on the one hand and execution costs on the other. New programming languages and programming techniques, such as modularization by use of internal subroutines, can help reduce the magnitude of the trade-off.

Use of External Data Structures for Memory

DSS, particularly interactive DSS, usually provide a variety of memory aids for the user. Examples of functions of these aids include saving the previous inputs, providing default inputs, and providing a workspace for storing temporary inputs or outputs. Rather than coding such memory aids as part of modules for the user interface, the designer should use data structures which are external to all the modules. External data structures facilitate sharing of the data among modules, which is the purpose of the memory aids. Using external data structures facilitates changing the memory (without recompiling the program), but it may be less efficient than using program parameters to pass memory information among modules. Note that this is another example of a trade-off between development/maintenance costs and execution costs.

External data structures can also be used for memory aids, such as parameters for report formats, which are not shared among parts of the user interface. The reason for so using external data structures is that they are easily modified and preserved over time. Use of a programming technique (external data structure) helps the programmer support a DSS requirement (memory aids).

SUMMARY

An effective user interface does not guarantee the success of a DSS, but it is a necessary ingredient. There is little research which indicates the relative importance of the user interface with respect to the many other factors which influence the success of the DSS. Two facts, however, do indicate its importance. The first is that the code for the user interface often represents the largest percentage of the total code in a DSS and is the most often modified code.[20] The second is that communication is known to be an important ingredient in effective decision making, and the user interface in a DSS is the means through which the users communicate with the DSS. In one of the first published works on DSS, Scott Morton emphasized the importance of the user interface,[18] and research on DSS has indicated that attention to the user interface can enable a variety of decision makers to use a single DSS.[5,6]

To develop a user interface which supports effective communication between the decision maker and the DSS, the designer must begin with an analysis of the decision makers and of the decision-making processes which the DSS is to support. This analysis should focus on the representations (outputs) which are, or are intended to be, used and on the operations (inputs) which are used to create and manipulate those representations. Following the analysis a first version of the user interface can be designed. During the design hardware and software constraints should be identified, but the focus of the effort should be on effective representations and understandable operations. Once there is a design proposal, a usability walk-through can help designers evaluate effectiveness and understandability. At this stage in the development process, the design can be used to establish the criteria for selecting among hardware devices and software packages. Often, however, external constraints such as availability and costs will limit the alternatives or will require revisions in the design. These revisions should be checked by another usability walk-through.

If acceptable trade-offs can be made among the technology (hardware and software), the economics (cost and availability), and the usability of the design (training times, error rates, and user acceptance), then implementation can begin. Implementation costs will be reduced and the implementation will be more likely to conform to the design if conventions are established and if programming techniques are developed to assist in implementation. The choice of programming techniques should be based on supporting the conventions, and the choice should make it easier for the developer to follow than to not follow the conventions.

To evaluate the user interface during walk-through, prototyping, implementation, testing, and installation, ease-of-use measures are needed. These measures should focus on performance (time or number of errors), process (how decisions are made), and perceptions (what users say).[19] Evaluation is needed throughout development of the user interface, because the earlier that errors in the interface are detected, the cheaper they are to fix.

In the future, better hardware and different (although often not better) software can be expected to be available for use in developing the user interface in DSS. Color display terminals and printers, capable of producing extremely high-quality outputs, and new, easier-to-use input devices (e.g., voice input) will be the most noticeable hardware improvements. Software will become available for these devices, but programming the user interface is likely to remain difficult unless high-level constructs are provided in software packages to reduce the complexity and detail of programming the devices. The power of skeletal DSS should increase, and the use of these will remain the cheapest way to implement a DSS.

As the number of DSS increases, there will be more information available on successes and failures in design of the user interface. Because the design of the user interface is likely to remain more an engineering discipline than a science, experimental data will be extremely valuable in reducing costs and increasing the effectiveness of the user interface for a DSS.

REFERENCES

1. Bennett, J. L., Chapter 3, this book.

2. Carlson, E. D., "Decision Support Systems: Personal Computing for Managers," *Management Review*, 66:1 (January 1977), 4–11.

3. Carlson, E. D., "Graphics Terminal Requirements for the 1970's," *Computer*, 9:8 (August 1976), 37–45.

4. Carlson, E. D. (ed.), "Proceedings of a Conference on Decision Support Systems," *Data Base*, 8:3 (Winter 1977).

5. Carlson, E. D., Bennett, J. L., Giddings, G. M., and Mantey, P. E., "The Design and Evaluation of an Interactive Geo-data Analysis and Display System," *Proceedings of the IFIP Congress 74*, Amsterdam: North Holland, 1974, 1057–1061.

6. Carlson, E. D., Grace, B. F., and Sutton, J. A., "Case Studies of End User Requirements for Interactive Problem Solving," *Management Information System Quarterly*, 1:1 (March 1977), 51–63.

7. Davis, R., "A DSS for Diagnosis and Therapy," *Data Base*, 8:3 (Winter 1977), 58–72.

8. Donovan, J. J., and Madnick, S. E., "Institutional and Ad Hoc DSS and Their Effective Use," *Data Base*, 8:3 (Winter 1977), 79–88.

9. Eason, K. D., "Understanding the Naive Computer User," *The Computer Journal*, 19:1 (February 1976), 3–7.

10. Grace, B. F., "Training Users of a Decision Support System," *Data Base*, 8:3 (Winter 1977), 30–36.

11. IBM Corporation, *IMS/VS Message Formatting Services User's Guide*, SH20-9053. White Plains, N.Y.: IBM Corporation.

12. IBM Corporation, *PLANCODE General Information Manual*, GH19-1103. White Plains, N.Y.: IBM Corporation.

13. IBM Corporation, *Trend Analysis/370 General Information Manual*, GH20-1961. White Plains, N.Y.: IBM Corporation.

14. Lafuente, J., and Gries, D., "Language Facilities for Programming User-Computer Dialogues," *IBM Journal of Research and Development*, 22:2 (March 1978), 145–158.

15. Liskov, B., Snyder, A., Atkinson, R., and Schaffert, C., "Abstraction Mechanisms in CLU," *Communications of the ACM*, 20:8 (August 1977), 564–76.

16. Martin, J., *Design of Man-Computer Dialogues*. Englewood Cliffs, N.J.: Prentice-Hall, 1973.

17. Reisner, P., "Human Factors Studies of Data Base Query Languages: A Survey and Assessment," *Computing Surveys*, 13:1 (1981), 13–32.

18. Scott Morton, M. S., *Management Decision Systems*. Boston, Mass.: Graduate School of Business Administration, Harvard University, 1971.

19. Sutton, J. A., "Evaluation of a Decision Support System: A Case Study with the Office Products Division of IBM," IBM Research Report RJ2214. San Jose, Calif.: IBM Research Laboratory, March, 1978.

20. Sutton, J. A., and Sprague, Jr., R. H., "A Study of Display Generation and Management in Interactive Business Applications," IBM Research Report RJ2392. San Jose, Calif.: IBM Research Laboratory, November, 1978.

21. "Status Report of the Graphics Standards Planning Committee," *Computer Graphics*, 13:3 (August 1979).

22. Zloof, M. M., "Query by Example," *Proceedings of the National Computer Conference 1975*. Montvale, N.J.: AFIPS Press, 1975, 431–37.

INTEGRATING OPTIMIZATION MODELS WITH INFORMATION SYSTEMS FOR DECISION SUPPORT

James S. Dyer • John M. Mulvey

The purpose of OR/MS optimization models is insight, not numbers (Geoffrion [1976c]).

INTRODUCTION

Many authors carefully distinguish between an optimization model and a Decision Support System (DSS). The former is presented as being appropriate for the solution of well-structured problems, while the latter is characterized as being appropriate for the analysis of more loosely structured problems. Here we emphasize the similarity, rather than the difference, between the effective use of an optimization model and a DSS and offer suggestions for the design of DSS that incorporate optimization models.

The key to recognizing that optimization models *must* be viewed within the context of DSS is the observation that a mathematical model only approximates the real world. While this statement has been repeated so frequently that it has become almost trite, its implications for the design of effective optimization models are often overlooked.

An optimization model provides a set of decision variables that optimize a well-defined goal—called an objective function. For example, maximizing profit could be an objective function subject to the real-world constraints of production equipment and labor skills available to a company. All other solutions that satisfy this set of constraints will result in an inferior value of the objective function. Thus the model provides the "best" vector of decisions, provided that it is a perfect representation of its corresponding real-world system. The class of real-world systems that can be represented perfectly by an optimization model is extremely limited and would seem to be confined almost exclusively to physical systems that are subject to well-known physical laws. Thus the results from optimization models that are used to solve some engineering design problems may actually provide answers that can be implemented directly in the corresponding real-world systems.

In contrast, the role of the optimization model in managerial decision making is to *support* the discovery of an *adaptable* plan of action, rather than to dictate what the decisions should be. Since managers are ultimately responsible for their decisions, the recommendations generated by the model must be treated as such—only as recommendations. Very often these recommendations will only be relevant to a limited part of a much larger problem, and they may be subject to numerous modifications that are required by the consideration of other factors that were not explicitly incorporated into the optimization model. Since DSS are designed for flexible problem solving, the integration of an optimization model within a DSS is crucial for a successful implementation.

The optimization model used by a manager is generally an incomplete model of the corresponding real-world system. The model is often simplified because of a desire (or need) to reduce complexity, or perhaps to reduce its information requirements or computational costs. In addition, many of the constraints in the model may be very "soft," in the sense that they can be modified by managerial actions if the optimal solutions are not considered to be satisfactory.

In the context of managerial problem solving, the key to the successful implementation of an optimization model is to imbed it within the concept of a DSS. The essential features of a DSS are flexibility and usability. The DSS must be flexible enough so that the model parameters and model structure can be tuned in an interactive fashion and easy enough to use so that nontechnical decision makers can operate the system without being overburdened by a need for assistance. If an optimization model meets these criteria, it can provide valuable insights even though the model is only a crude approximation to the corresponding real-world system.

In this chapter we introduce two examples of applications of optimization models that are imbedded within DSS. Next we consider five criteria for the choice of an appropriate optimization model within a DSS. We stress the increasing importance of system flexibility and ease of use as the approximation of the real-world system by the model becomes more crude. Our guidelines for DSS designers are then illustrated in the context of the two applications.

A PREVIEW OF TWO PROBLEMS

We are now ready to discuss the nature of the two problems to be addressed.

Faculty/Course Scheduling in an Academic Department

The first problem involves the determination of the annual assignments of faculty members to courses within the Graduate School of Management (GSM) at UCLA. In 1973 GSM revamped its Master of Business Administration (MBA) curriculum. This necessitated an increased centralization of the annual scheduling of faculty to courses and time periods (quarters). Scheduling had previously been conducted by each curriculum area in relative isolation since faculty and courses were uniquely assigned to these areas. The integration of these subschedules was carried out primarily by a departmental administrator in conjunction with the curriculum area coordinators. However, the new MBA program increased the number of overlapping responsibilities among these areas, and the need for coordinated scheduling was more evident. The large size of the problem (100 faculty numbers assigned to teach 500 courses over 3 time periods) suggested that a computerized system might be useful to support the departmental administrator in developing the schedule.

The relatively high degree of structure associated with this problem indicated that an optimization model might be used to match faculty members with course offerings during the three quarters of the academic year. Yet the problem is difficult to represent completely in a mathematical model because of the ill-defined preferences of the faculty members, the lack of information regarding the desires and needs of the students, and, occasionally, the uncertain budget of the administration.

During the analysis of this problem, three alternative optimization models were proposed as the heart of a DSS.

A Network Formulation

The structure of the network optimization model that was proposed for this problem is illustrated in Fig. 5.1. Each faculty member is provided with a faculty node and three related faculty/quarter nodes on the left-hand side of Fig. 5.1. Each course is provided with a course node and up to three related course/quarter nodes on the right-hand side of Fig. 5.1. The model determines the optimal matching of the left- and right-hand sides. Variables are defined as flow across the arcs; the flow on the arcs of the network is in course-section equivalents. The flow on these arcs is restricted by lower and upper bounds indicated by the values of the numbers in parentheses. (1,2) indicates a lower bound equal to 1 and an upper bound equal to 2. Thus Buffa is assigned a total of five courses for the three quarters since the arc connecting the source node to Buffa's node has the restriction (5,5). Courses are similarly constrained.

The objective function for solving this model is the maximization of the sum of the preferences of the faculty for teaching their assigned courses while satisfying the arc restrictions. Faculty desires are also considered when the lower and

FIGURE 5.1   Network Representation

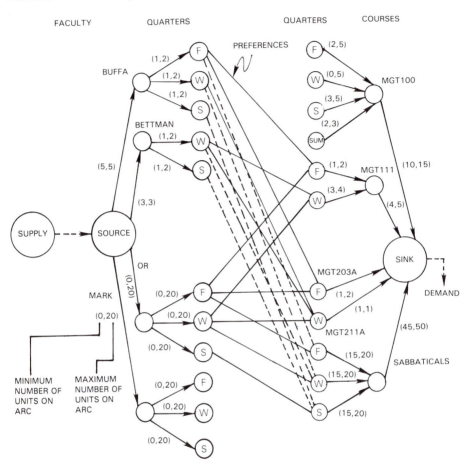

upper bounds are established on the faculty/quarter arcs. Subject to administrative policies, faculty members may determine the number of courses they will teach each quarter. For example, a faculty member may request a heavy teaching load in the fall and winter in order to have uninterrupted time for research during the spring.

Information concerning the needs and desires of the students can be used to determine the upper and lower bounds on the number of sections of each course offered per academic year and by quarter. At UCLA we utilized a statistical forecasting model, which predicted the number and types of courses required for the following academic year.

It should be noted that the network model is an important special case of the general linear programming model. Highly efficient strategies are available for solving this type of problem. See Glover *et al.* [1974], Glover *et al.* [1978], and Mulvey [1978] for details.

An Integer Program

The second alternative model formulation that we considered took the form of an integer linear program (see Mulvey [1972]). The network constraints and the objective function of the network model shown in Fig. 5.1 were an essential part of this formulation. In addition to these network conditions, an expanded set of restrictions was incorporated into this model. Restrictions such as the following were allowed:

1. If course A is taught by Professor X, then course B must be taught by Professor X.

2. Professor X could teach two sections of course A in the fall quarter *or* one section in the winter quarter.

3. Professor X wants to teach one course from the set A,B,C,D,E .

4. Professor X will teach one section of course B if and only if Professor Y does not teach course B.

Faculty members were asked questions via a detailed questionnaire to obtain information on these issues, and their responses formed the basis for modeling the extra constraints. The addition of these extra constraints meant that the problem could no longer be modeled as a network.

Although the resulting model was large for general integer programming, a specialized enumeration procedure was developed to capitalize on the structure of the problem. Tables 5.1 and 5.2 illustrate the approach. Courses are shown as columns in the assignment matrix, whereas faculty members are shown as rows. The matrix simply indicates who can teach what course. A clustering of faculty and courses was performed on the matrix of Table 5.1, resulting in the three compact subgroups presented in Table 5.2. The integer linear programming algorithm takes advantage of these relatively distinct subgroups.

An Auxiliary Model

The third formulation (Fig. 5.2) incorporates considerably less detail than the previous two models. This model is an aggregation of the pure network model. To derive this model we first observed that the faculty members can be clustered into areas of common interest, with some overlap, as was done in the previous model. Instead of four unique nodes for each faculty member, there are faculty group or cluster nodes. For instance, one group is the "finance" faculty. Faculty members who are able to teach finance courses are assigned to that group node. In an entirely analogous manner, the individual courses are assigned to course group nodes. All of the arcs in the network model of Fig. 5.1 linking faculty/quarters

TABLE 5.1 Faculty/Course Assignment Matrix

Courses

Faculty	101	102	106	108	201	210A	210B	210C	215	411
Andrews	1	1								
Bettman							1	1	1	1
Buffa			1	1	1			1		
Dyer						1	1	1	1	
Geoffrion	1	1		1		1				
Graves				1						
Lippman					1		1			
MacQueen			1					1		1

TABLE 5.2 Clustered Faculty/Course Assignment Matrix

Courses

Faculty	108	106	201	215	101	102	210A	210B	210C	411
Buffa	1	1	1						1	
Lippman			1					1		
Graves	1									
Andrews					1	1				
Geoffrion	1				1	1	1			
Dyer				1			1	1	1	
MacQueen		1							1	1
Bettman				1				1	1	1

94

FIGURE 5.2   An Auxiliary Model for the Personnel Scheduling Example

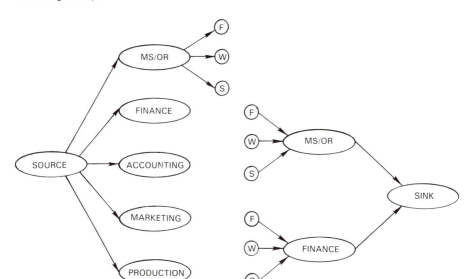

with course/quarters are preserved in the aggregate model. For instance, an arc from Professor Smith (Group A) to course MGT 101 (Group I) in the fall quarter would be assumed by the arc (A,I). An arc in the aggregate network will typically replace many arcs in the original network. The preference weight for the new arc is a simple weighted average of the arcs it replaced.

Following Geoffrion [1976c] this formulation is called an auxiliary model. It possesses the structural characteristics of the original network model shown in Fig. 5.1, but the number of arcs and nodes is greatly reduced.

Computer-Based Corporate Planning

The second problem involves the determination of a strategic plan for a large corporation. The planning process begins with the definition of corporate-level objectives, many of which can be associated with quantifiable measures for evaluating alternatives. Examples of these measures include market share, net wealth of the stockholder at a future horizon date, return on equity, and a stable growth in earnings per share.

A large number of computer-based corporate models have been implemented in recent years, as is reported by Gershefski [1970]. The majority of these models may be described as descriptive simulation models that are composed of standard accounting relationships in which the onus for generating new alternatives lies with the strategic planner. The role of the model is confined to the production of the results that would occur *if* a particular alternative were selected.

In large, decentralized organizations, however, the number of alternative strategic plans that could be generated from the suggestions of their subsidiaries may be enormous. Hamilton and Moses [1973, 1974] noted that an optimization model could be used as an efficient means to sort through the alternative combinations of actions that would be aggregated into a strategic plan. The accounting relationships that exist in a more traditional corporate planning model provide the natural basis for an optimization model. However, there were several candidates for the formulation of the optimization model.

A Mixed Integer Programming Model

The optimization model for corporate planning is complicated by two issues: 0/1 (all or none) decision variables and an arbitrary distinction between goals and constraints. The strategic decisions involve acquisitions, divestments, and market and product line expansions. These go/no-go or yes/no decisions are generally modeled with 0/1 integer decision variables. Unfortunately, integer programs are much less efficient than linear programs for problems of comparable size in terms of the numbers of decision variables and constraints.

The often arbitrary distinction between objectives, goals, and constraints ensures that a single "solution" from the computer model will not be sufficient to select the final strategy. Mathematical expressions that could be considered as either goals or constraints can be developed in the following areas:

1. Guarantee a stable pattern of growth in earnings per share.

2. Maximize the return on assets.

3. Maximize the return on stockholders' equity.

Other constraints can be used to ensure that certain financial ratios remain in a range that indicates good operating performance and financial stability. However, the range of the "acceptable" values for these constraints is rather vague, and it seems clear that the planners would wish to test the sensitivity of any solution to small variations in these ranges.

Hamilton and Moses [1973] demonstrate that the corporate planning model can be written as a mixed integer programming model with an objective function that maximizes the total corporate earnings per share of common stock over the planning horizon. Their version of the model contains approximately 1000 decision variables and 750 constraints, including about 200 0/1 variables. This formulation lies within the capabilities of modern mixed integer programming codes, but each solution thus obtained would be relatively expensive.

A Linear Programming Model with 0/1 Round-Off

The second candidate model might be described more appropriately as a solution strategy. The same mixed integer formulation could be solved efficiently with a linear programming routine, with 0 and 1 lower and upper bounds, respectively, on the go/no-go decision variables. In the linear programming solution, we would expect a majority of the 0/1 variables to be at their upper or lower bounds. The remaining fractionally valued 0/1 variables could be set to 0 or 1 by a computerized round-off routine. Alternatively, they could be set judgmentally by the strategic planners. The latter seems particularly attractive since many of the constraints are "soft" and relatively minor violations of them could be tolerated.

A Nonlinear Mixed Integer Programming Model

A more accurate formulation of the corporate planning models would include a nonlinear objective function and nonlinear constraints. The objective of maximizing corporate earnings per share is actually written as a ratio of the total corporate earnings divided by the number of shares of common stock outstanding. Of course the number of shares outstanding is also an important decision variable, so this objective function is nonlinear. As another example, stock prices can be forecast by a nonlinear function involving earnings per share and other variables. Introducing these nonlinearities would make this model much more realistic. In the linear mixed integer model already discussed, Hamilton and Moses used a linearized approximation to this objective function.

THE CHOICE OF AN OPTIMIZATION MODEL

In this section we consider the choice of an optimization model as a problem worthy of systematic study. First, we present five criteria which should be considered when evaluating alternative models. Next, we apply these criteria to the two examples presented above.

Criteria for the Choice of an Optimizing Model

The selection of the appropriate optimizing model is an important decision in itself. Although no algorithms exist to simplify this choice, we can offer some

FIGURE 5.3 *Five Dimensions for Evaluating Mathematical Models*

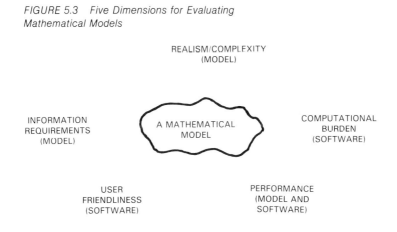

rules of thumb and five criteria that might be considered (Mulvey [1979]). These five criteria are illustrated in Fig. 5.3. Two of these criteria (computational burden and ease of use) deal with the computer software for solving the optimization problem; two criteria (realism/complexity and information requirements) involve the underlying mathematical model; and one criterion (performance) involves both the computer software and the mathematical model.

It should be obvious that the objectives implied by these criteria are often conflicting. Formulating a totally realistic model, one which duplicates the original system to arbitrary precision, usually conflicts with the objective of building an affordable system. Implicit or explicit trade-offs in these objectives are inevitable. The goal of this section is to illustrate how these trade-offs might best be made in an effort to select the appropriate models for faculty/course scheduling and for corporate planning.

Performance

By performance we mean the ultimate usefulness of the information that is generated by the solution provided by the model. Since the purpose of modeling is gaining insight, the amount of understanding that results from interacting with the modeling system measures its performance.

The primary user of the faculty/course scheduling system was an administrator who had previously determined the schedule by hand. From her perspective the abilities of a modeling system to generate a complete schedule and to provide a method for altering that schedule were critical measures of performance. Since both the network model and the integer programming formulation can determine complete schedules, they are equal on this criterion. Both dominate the auxiliary model, however, which only provides aggregate information in each curriculum area.

The strategic planning staff using a corporate model is also seeking a complete comparison and evaluation of the alternatives. Both the mixed integer formulation and the nonlinear formulation can provide a complete solution, with each 0/1 variable indicating whether an alternative should be accepted or rejected. However, the 0/1 round-off solution strategy is inferior on the performance criterion, since heuristic round-off strategies might violate some constraints, or the planning staff might be required to determine some values manually.

On the basis of performance, we might be tempted to eliminate the auxiliary model from consideration for faculty/course scheduling and the 0/1 round-off strategy from the corporate model alternatives. Yet the model performance ranking does not tell the entire story.

Realism/Complexity

We define the realism of a model as the relative closeness of the mathematical form to the situation which is being modeled. How well does the model mirror reality? Generally, realism and complexity are synonymous—more realism requires more complexity in the model.

The relative realism of the alternative faculty/course scheduling models is obvious. The integer linear programming formulation has the most general structure; it can accommodate any situation that can be handled by either of the other models. The integer linear program requires about 5000–6000 variables and 1500 constraints. Approximately 150 of these constraints are non-network constraints. Next in realism is the network formulation; it has more capabilities than the auxiliary model, which is an aggregate subset of it, but less realism than the integer program. The network consists of 5000–6000 arcs and approximately 1200 nodes. Remarkably, because the auxiliary model is a well-defined aggregation of the network model, the amount of detail which is lost by using the auxiliary model instead of the unabridged network can be precisely measured. For further details about the theory of aggregation, see the work of Geoffrion [1976b] and Zipkin [1977].

The nonlinear mixed integer formulation of the corporate planning model is more realistic than the linearized approximation. Since the 0/1 round-off model is actually an alternative solution strategy for the linear mixed integer programming model, these two alternatives provide identical realism.

Unfortunately, in some instances when diverse modeling techniques are compared (such as simulation versus optimization or heuristics), a simple ranking of model realism is not obvious. Elements of one model may be more realistic than elements of a competing model, and vice versa. This adds a serious complication to the decision of selecting alternatives. A mechanism for describing the extent of these differences is sorely needed and should be an important topic for future research.

Computational Costs

An important consideration which is often overlooked relates to the available software and the resulting computational costs. By adding a criterion which involves the computer software for solving each model, we are incorporating what Simon [1978] calls procedural rationality into the decision problem. In this manner, the decision comes to depend on the techniques that are available at a given point in time. Thus the "best" decision today may not be the "best" decision tomorrow.

The cost of solving the network model of the faculty/course scheduling problem with the out-of-kilter code (Barr *et al.* [1974]) was only about $5.00, even though this formulation included 1200 nodes (constraints) and 6000 arcs (variables). This included the costs of preprocessing and postprocessing the data. The auxiliary model could be solved for $.50 per run. By contrast, we determined that it would cost at least $250.00 to find a *feasible* solution for the integer programming formulation, and it would be too costly to guarantee optimality.

Hamilton and Moses [1973] do not report computational costs for the nonlinear formulation of the corporate planning model, but we can assume that they would be extremely high. By contrast, the optimal integer solution to the linear mixed integer formulation was typically found in 15–30 minutes of CPU time additional to that required to determine the optimal continuous solution with a standard linear programming code. If CPU time costs approximately $.04 per second, this integer solution costs between $36 and $72 more per run than the linear programming solution that could be used as the basis for the 0/1 round-off strategy.

Information Requirements

The amount of information which is collected and processed can impose a considerable burden on the user. In many applications, the sheer weight of these data may lead to the ultimate demise of an implementation. Thus information requirements should be considered when one is performing an evaluation of competing models. Generally, more realistic models will require more information, as indicated in Fig. 5.3.

The integer formulation of the faculty/course scheduling problem would require more information than either the network or the auxiliary model. The auxiliary model does extremely well on this criterion, since the bulk of the data can be gathered by interacting with curriculum area representatives rather than individual faculty members. Both the integer and network formulations require all faculty members to assign a preference weight (from -2 to $+2$) to all courses that they are eligible to teach. The integer model would also need data concerning "if-then" and other non-network restrictions.

The information requirements of the three corporate model alternatives would be essentially the same. The nonlinear relationships in the more complex mixed integer formulation would not require any additional data.

Ease of Use

Ease of use describes the relative flexibility (or inflexibility) which is encountered when running a computer system. Many programs are awkward to use on a regular basis, and the criterion of usability must be taken into account in the selection process. Otherwise a perfect model may be developed, but the unavailability of correspondingly perfect software may prevent efficient usage.

Again, the introduction of software into the decision of selecting the best model complicates the decision problem. The development of a model is no longer time-invariant; the "best" model today may come to be considered inferior when additional software becomes available. Although a systematic way of measuring the usability of a system is difficult to achieve, this criterion is essential and cannot be avoided. (See Bennett in Chapter 3 of this book for details concerning measurement for this criterion.)

The faculty/course scheduling system was designed in 1973, when the available optimization software was limited to RIP3OC, which is a general integer programming package (see Geoffrion and Marsten [1972]), and an advanced out-of-kilter algorithm developed by Barr, Glover, and Klingman [1974]. Since the network system possessed a data base management facility, it was rated better than the integer programming system with regard to ease of use. Thus the two network models were superior to the integer programming formulation on this dimension.

The nonlinear mixed integer programming formulation of the corporate planning model was at a disadvantage because optimization codes were unavailable for solving this problem when the system was designed in the early 1970s. The size and structure of the linearized mixed integer model meant that it could be solved by most mixed integer programming algorithms available at that time (from CDC, IBM, and Univac). A linear programming solution to this formulation could be found easily, but the 0/1 round-off strategy would require the development of new software if a computerized round-off scheme was required. Thus the round-off alternative would be most usable if the fractional variables in the optimal solution were set to 0 or 1 manually, but its usability would probably fall between the linear and nonlinear mixed integer formulations if new software was needed.

Selecting the Model

Once the alternative formulations have been ranked on these five criteria, the analyst must weigh the relative merits of each criterion to make a final selection. In some cases it may be possible to construct and empirically test two or more competitive models with real data, especially if their basic structure and data requirements are not too dissimilar.

Sample rankings of the three formulations suggested for the faculty/course scheduling model in the previous section are summarized in Table 5.3. A rank of 1 indicates that a model is superior in terms of a criterion, while a 3 indicates that it is inferior to the other two alternatives.

TABLE 5.3   *Summary Rankings of Alternatives for Faculty/Course Scheduling Problem (1 = best, 2 = moderate, 3 = worst)*

Criteria	Network Model	Integer Program	Auxiliary Model
Performance	1	1	2
Realism/complexity	2	1	3
Information requirements	2	3	1
Ease of use	1	2	1
Computational costs	2	3	1

The simple rank scores are generally not a sufficient basis for a decision. For example, one model may be clearly superior to another on a criterion, but the difference may not be considered significant because of the relative unimportance of the criterion. Another alternative may be considered so poor on a criterion that this essentially disqualifies it from further consideration.

From Table 5.3 we can see that the auxiliary model is the easiest and cheapest to use for faculty/course scheduling, but it suffers on the realism and performance dimensions. The reverse pattern of rankings appears for the integer programming formulation. In fact, the network model would seem to be a good compromise. It offers considerably better performance and realism than the auxiliary model, and the computational costs are still quite modest. The only potentially serious problem concerns the information requirements. However, similar data were collected when the scheduling problem was solved by hand. The only additional cost incurred is in typing these data into the computer system.

Table 5.4 summarizes the scores of the formulations of the corporate planning problem. The nonlinear mixed integer model is disqualified because of the

TABLE 5.4   Summary Rankings of Alternatives
for Corporate Planning Problem
(1 = best, 2 = moderate, 3 = worst)

Criteria	Mixed Integer Model	Round-Off Model	Nonlinear Mixed Integer Model
Performance	1	2	1
Realism/complexity	2	2	1
Information requirements	1	1	1
Ease of use	2	1*	3
Computational costs	2	1	3

*Assumes fractional 0/1 variables are set manually.

excessive computational costs and the lack of a usable software package. The mixed integer programming formulation solved with a mixed integer software code offers better performance than the round-off solution strategy, but at higher computational costs. If the task of setting any fractional values from the linear programming solution were not too burdensome, this round-off approach might be preferable.

Hamilton and Moses [1973] explored this issue in some depth. They found that the corporate strategies selected by the mixed integer formulation were often quite different from those suggested by the fractionally valued variables in the continuous solution. For example, they reported that two 0/1 variables with values of 0.89 and 0.03 in the optimal continuous linear programming solution were given values of 0.0 and 1.0, respectively, in the optimal mixed integer solution. They also found that the objective-function values that were determined by simply rounding off the continuous solution were significantly inferior to the objective-function values of the corresponding optimal mixed integer solutions. Hence the performance of the mixed integer model was superior to the performance of the round-off model.

INTERACTIVE DECISION MAKING WITHIN A DSS

On the basis of this discussion, it would seem advisable to select the network formulation of the faculty/course scheduling problem and the mixed integer formulation of the corporate planning model. As Tables 5.3 and 5.4 emphasize, however, *neither* model was rated highest on the realism/complexity dimension. Thus we must compensate for this deficiency in some way in the design of the decision-making *process* that involves these models.

As a model becomes more approximate and sacrifices reality in order to gain information and computational advantages, generally the model must be run more times in order to gain insights equivalent to those that would be obtained from a single solution of the more realistic alternative model. Therefore the successful use of an "approximate" model will depend on imbedding it within a flexible, interactive DSS.

The term "interactive" does not necessarily imply the use of on-line, real-time terminals at the decision maker's desk. However, a fully automated interactive system may be an attractive option if the approximate model is to be used periodically to address a recurring problem. For a one-time major decision, the cost of the interactive software may not justify its development, but maintaining the spirit of an interactive DSS is crucial. For an excellent discussion of the concepts of a DSS that does not involve the use of on-line terminals, see Geoffrion [1976a].

An Interactive Decision-Making Strategy
for Faculty/Course Scheduling

The network model of the faculty/course scheduling problem was imbedded within an integrated optimization/information system (for details, see Dyer and Mulvey [1975]). An on-line terminal is used to enter and modify the data in the system in a convenient manner. The actual run of the optimization model is carried out in batch mode, with the lengthy output being routed to a high-speed printer.

The report writer (or query facility) portion of the optimization/information system allows the user to print the schedule for any selected subset of faculty members or courses. This feature is especially important, since the pattern of course offerings within each area of specialization, such as accounting, is always of concern. The report writer can also provide the intersection of a subset of faculty members and a subset of courses for any particular quarter for the academic year. For example, the user might wish to see a listing of the full professors who are teaching undergraduate courses in the fall quarter. The query facility was set up so that this information could be provided in a convenient fashion.

A second feature of the report writer originally introduced as a computational convenience has proved to be of extreme importance in enhancing the value of the system to the user. We were concerned that, in some instance, the network model would have no feasible solution. That is, some instructors would not have sufficient courses to teach, while other courses could not be staffed. This situation can easily arise, given a relative undersupply of instructors in one area (such as accounting) and an oversupply in another. Therefore we added a "super-prof" to our list of faculty members, a person with the ability to teach any course offered within the department but with a low interest in doing so (preference weight of -9). Similarly, we added a "supercourse" that every instructor could teach, although we assigned the low weight of -9 to the course for each instructor. We elected to print the schedule for superprof and the instructors assigned to supercourse along with the normal assignments. It quickly became evident that these two features were extremely important in helping the user isolate the problems that had to be resolved before a schedule could be final. Superprof and supercourse highlight the planning needs of the department and provide a reference point for possible actions. By studying the courses assigned to superprof, the decision maker can determine immediately what teaching abilities additional lecturers, new faculty members, and visiting faculty members should have during the forthcoming academic year. And the list of faculty members assigned to supercourse indicates the areas that have excess teaching capacity.

Since the network formulation cannot include all the considerations relevant to the determination of a faculty/course schedule, the solution strategy must involve the user in an interactive scheme. The general strategy we have used in implementing this system is summarized in Fig. 5.4 and can be described step by step as follows:

Step 1: Generate the data required for the approximate model. These data include faculty information and course information, both modified to reflect the administrative policies.

Step 2: (Approximation) Formulate the network model, and solve.

Step 3: (Evaluation) Determine whether or not the candidate schedule is a feasible alternative. If not, return to Step 1.

Step 4: (Evaluation) Determine whether or not the candidate schedule is acceptable. If not, go to Step 6.

Step 5: Print the schedule.

Step 6: Decide whether or not to persist in attempting to improve the candidate schedule by hand. If not, go to Step 8.

FIGURE 5.4 The Solution Strategy for the Faculty/Course Scheduling Model

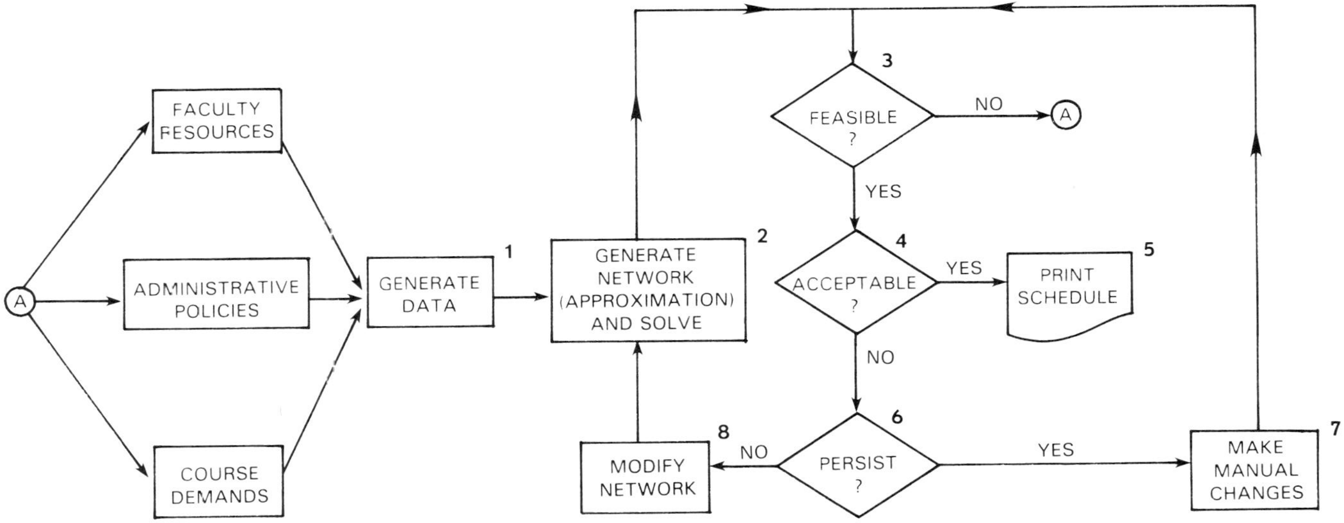

Step 7: (Modification) Make manual changes in the candidate schedule. Go to Step 3.

Step 8: (Modification) Make changes in the network formulation. Go to Step 3.

Remarks

If the candidate schedule is considered infeasible (*Step 1*), the user may attempt to resolve the imbalances in the schedule by (a) hiring new faculty, visiting faculty, lecturers, or apprentice personnel; (b) canceling sections of some courses, or shifting them to other quarters; or (c) adding additional sections of courses in areas where the available resources permit.

The determination that a schedule is either feasible or infeasible (*Step 3*) can generally be accomplished quickly by studying the superprof and supercourse.

The primary consideration in determining whether or not a schedule is acceptable (*Step 4*) is whether any faculty members have been assigned a high proportion of courses they do not wish to teach. The final schedule should be consistent with the expectations of the faculty members.

An Interactive Decision-Making Strategy for Corporate Planning

Hamilton and Moses [1973, 1974] also adopted the philosophy that their "approximate" model of corporate financial planning would be useful only if it were imbedded within an interactive environment. Since the planning decisions are made annually and occasionally on an *ad hoc* basis during the year, Hamilton and Moses considered it worthwhile to design their system for on-line operation. They also provided an input/output system with the explicit capability of performing a parametric analysis of many of the "soft" constraints in the model, such as those involving financial ratios.

They finally imbedded this optimization subsystem within a larger strategic planning system. The strategic planning system includes an econometric subsystem that provides projects for the economies and industries in which the company operates or may operate. These forecasts are often converted into model parameters in the optimization subsystem. Also included is a risk analysis subsystem that evaluates the alternatives generated by the optimization model in an uncertain environment. This analysis provides insights into the possible effects of errors in the econometric forecasts and other planning data. For additional details, see Hamilton and Moses [1974].

IMPLICATIONS FOR BUILDERS OF DSS

An optimizing model imbedded within the context of, and in harmony with, a DSS can have a number of important advantages. Often a computerized system cannot be guaranteed to determine the best alternative for a given scenario—either because the system has no mechanism for generating alternative plans or because it uses a heuristic search procedure that is incomplete. In most serious analytical studies, a number of individual runs of the computerized system are desirable in order to study the impacts of changes in the future scenario and other discretionary constraints on the solution. With an optimization capability, the users can be assured that the *differences* between these runs are a result of the changes in the scenario and the constraints, rather than a result of the accidental behavior of a heuristic computer program. Of course, the problem must be well enough structured that it can be approximated by a mathematical objective function and mathematical constraints.

A DSS which is easy to use and which supports an adaptable plan of action requires integration of the optimization model and the data base (information system) design. Too often the design of these elements is left to different groups in the organization (e.g., the operations research department and MIS division), with disastrous results.

Figure 5.5 depicts the usual view of an optimization model within an information system; for instance, see Madnick [1977]. The applications-dependent software for solving the optimization problem is separated from the data base management system (DBMS). Unfortunately, this separation makes it difficult to achieve a system that is easy to use. A key element under the criterion "easy to use" for optimization modeling is the user's ability to adjust model parameters and even model structure in a simple, direct fashion. Parametric and sensitivity

FIGURE 5.5   *Relationship of the Optimization Model Within an Information System*

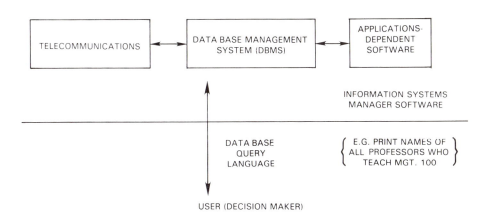

analyses must be carried out before users gain confidence that the results are consistent with their beliefs and are the best attainable.

What are the alternatives? Figure 5.6 depicts the three main approaches. In the first instance, the data base management system is kept separate from the optimization software—a disjoint state of affairs. In the second instance, the optimization program is constructed from macro-instructions in the data base management query language. Bonczek, Holsapple, and Whinston [1976] have shown

FIGURE 5.6   *Alternatives for Coordinating Data Base Design and Model Optimization*

What Alternatives ?

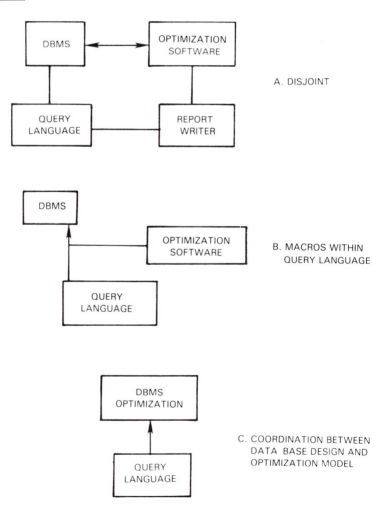

the feasibility of this approach for linear programming. Finally, the third possibility is to coordinate the design of the data base management system and the optimization routine. We suggest that this last approach will lend itself to successful implementations.

SUMMARY AND CONCLUSIONS

The primary conclusion of this chapter is that the successful use of an optimization model is dependent on its being imbedded within the context of a DSS. This may require the development of an elaborate on-line software system complete with a sophisticated data base, as illustrated by the corporate planning model, or of a more modest system that provides sufficient user convenience to encourage interaction, as illustrated by the faculty/course scheduling system.

The notion that an optimization model must be a precise mirror of reality in order to be of value is incorrect. In the context of managerial decision making, a relatively crude approximate model may still be an efficient way to provide useful insights to the decision maker. In such a case, however, the manner of placing the optimization model into the DSS will be crucial.

In conclusion, we offer the following suggestions to designers who are incorporating optimization models into DSS:

1. Involve the ultimate decision maker in initial phases of system design.

2. Encourage interaction between OR modeling group and data base group (i.e., coordination of these functions).

3. Provide the decision maker with an *active* role in determining a final solution.

4. Develop a DSS which is easy to use in the sense that parametric and sensitivity analyses can be readily performed.

REFERENCES

1. Barr, R. W., F. Glover, and D. Klingman (1974). "An Improved Version of the Out-of-Kilter Method and a Comparative Study of Computer Codes," *Mathematical Programming, 1,* 60–86.

2. Bennett, J. L., Chapter 3, this book.

3. Bonczek, R. H., C. W. Holsapple, and A. B. Whinston (1976). "Mathematical Programming within the Context of a Generalized Data Base Management System," Paper No. 578, Krannert Graduate School of Management, Purdue University.

4. Dyer, J. S., and J. M. Mulvey (1976). "An Integrated Information/Optimization System for Academic Planning," *Management Science, 22,* 12.

5. Geoffrion, A. M. (1976a). "Better Distribution Planning with Computer Models," *Harvard Business Review, 54,* 4, 92–99.

6. Geoffrion, A. M. (1976b). "Customer Aggregation in Distribution Modeling," Working Paper No. 259, Western Management Science Institute, UCLA.

7. Geoffrion, A. M. (1976c). "The Purpose of Mathematical Programming Is Insight, Not Numbers," *Interfaces, 1,* 81–92.

8. Geoffrion, A. M., and R. F. Marsten (1972). "Integer Programming Algorithms: A Framework and State-of-the-Art Survey," *Management Science, 18,* 465–491.

9. Gershefski, G. W. (1970). "Corporate Models—The State of the Art," *Management Science, 16,* 6, 8303–8312.

10. Glover, F., J. Hultz, D. Klingman, and J. Strutz (1978). "Generalized Networks: A Fundamental Computer-Based Planning Tool," *Management Science, 24,* 1209–1220.

11. Glover, F., D. Karney, D. Klingman, and A. Napier (1974). "A Computational Study on Start Procedures, Basis Change Criteria, and Solution Algorithms for Transportation Problems," *Management Science, 20,* 5, 793–819.

12. Hamilton, W. F., and M. A. Moses (1973). "An Optimization Model for Corporate Financial Planning," *Operations Research, 22,* 2, 677–692.

13. Hamilton, W. F., and M. A. Moses (1974). "A Computer-Based Corporate Planning System," *Management Science, 21,* 2, 148–159.

14. Madnick, S. E. (1977). "Trends in Computers and Computing: The Information Utility," *Science, 195,* 1191–1199.

15. Mulvey, J. M. (1972). "Preliminary Application of a Resource Allocation Procedure for the Educational Sector," Discussion Paper No. 22, O.R. Study Center, Graduate School of Management, UCLA.

16. Mulvey, J. M. (1978). "Testing of a Large-Scale Network Optimization Program," *Mathematical Programming, 15,* 291–314.

17. Mulvey, J. M. (1979). "Strategies in Modeling: A Personnel Scheduling Example," *Interfaces, 9,* 1, 66–77.

18. Simon, H. A. (1978). "On How to Decide What to Do," *Bell Journal of Economics, 9,* 2, 494–507.

19. Zipkin, F. H. (1977). "A Priori Bounds for Aggregated Linear Programs with Fixed-Weight Disaggregation," Technical Report No. 86, School of Organization and Management, Yale University.

GROWING DSS: A FLEXIBLE, EVOLUTIONARY APPROACH

E. Gerald Hurst, Jr. • David N. Ness
Thomas J. Gambino • Thomas H. Johnson

CHAPTER 6

NURTURING A DSS

The experience reported in this chapter is garnered from the seventy-five collective years its four authors have spent working with computers, mostly on managerial problems. In that time, they have managed operations using DSS, operated DSS built by others, built special-purpose and general-purpose DSS, supervised construction of DSS, studied users, and written on the conception, design, and other aspects of DSS development. This composite experience of four people working for the most part on different problems has produced remarkable unanimity about how to "grow" a successful DSS.

An agricultural analogy has been chosen as the theme of this chapter, since this is very close to the authors' view of the way DSS are cultivated. DSS are nurtured in the same sense that planting, cultivating, and harvesting take place continually in a garden, with no well-defined time at which one activity ceases and the next begins. The danger with organizing the discussion around the life cycle of a DSS is that the reader will get the mistaken impression that a DSS is grown in fixed steps separated by well-defined boundaries.

The headings in this section provide a useful outline of the growth stages of a DSS. They are presented as a convenient way of organizing the gardener's manual, not as a mandatory step-by-step procedure to follow in growing all DSS. After this life cycle of DSS growth is presented, three case studies are used to illustrate additional issues on appropriate organizational environments, desirable technical support, and other points about DSS cultivation.

Preparing the Ground

Most gardeners soon realize that not all soil is tillable. Even if it is tillable for some kinds of crops, it may not be suitable for others. DSS cannot be successfully "planted" where growing conditions are not favorable. People with problems amenable to DSS must recognize that they indeed have a problem, although it is not necessary at first that they know very much about DSS or even that DSS might be applicable in their situation. After the need is recognized, it is necessary that they realize that the use of a DSS is promising. This is not always easily brought about. The successful DSS almost certainly involves the users in the process of its development. Getting the users involved can be difficult because it is often hard to estimate the benefits which will come from the use of the DSS. Since such users are computer novices, they are not committed to the use of this technology on their problems. Potential users must be helped to understand both the possibilities of the DSS and the investment required. If the users simply cannot fathom where a DSS might be helpful, move on—like Johnny Appleseed—to more fertile ground.

Choosing the Crops

Successful DSS growers are more like truck farmers than cotton farmers. Prudent truck farmers have several crops planted, so that even if some fail, those remaining provide a successful harvest. In developing DSS, choosing the appropriate number and kind of problems requires judgmental skill. More than one problem should be picked in order to hedge the bets, but not so many should be picked that the developer is spread too thin. Problems, especially early ones, should be important enough to attract the users' attention, but not so important that a failure is seen by them as a disaster.

Cultivating

Truck gardens need continuous cultivation. Soon after they are planted, the farmer must check that all the seeds have sprouted. Those that haven't should be resown, or the crop should be changed. Those seeds that sprout must be watched carefully throughout their growth. DSS are much the same. They must be continuously monitored. Early DSS attempts usually must be modified several times. A DSS which does not work the first time must be redone or abandoned. An established DSS must be maintained so that it remains current and relevant to the problem of interest. The vigilance of the DSS grower must match that of the truck gardener.

Transplanting

It is often possible to take a cutting from an existing plant and root it in new ground. This can both reduce the time it takes to get a full-blooming plant and simplify its early care and feeding. DSS are similar. While it is generally not simple to take a system from one environment and plant it in another, such transplanting, if done carefully, is often much easier and more effective than growing a new system from the ground up.

Harvesting

Like cultivation, harvesting in the truck garden is a continuous process. Different crops mature at different times, have a period in which harvesting is possible, and then have no further yield. Through timing of the various harvests, something valuable can be produced nearly continuously. This is especially important if there are several sharecroppers who depend on the garden for support. DSS cultivated continuously produce results in this fashion. Each version of a system should provide not only useful results, but also feedback leading to its further development. Successful DSS also tend to produce early results and continue to be valuable until the problem is solved or the situation is no longer a problem. If more than one DSS is in process for several users, the aggregate result can be almost continuously useful to the sponsoring organization.

Dealing with Crop Failure

No matter how hard the farmer tries, some crops are going to fail. The plant and the soil are not right for each other, the cultivation is improper, or the harvest is poor. So it is with DSS. The wrong problem is being addressed, the wrong DSS is being proposed to help with it, the development is not proceeding as planned, or the results are not as expected. Given all the things which can go wrong, it would be startling if no DSS ever failed.

Considerable system design literature is devoted to the problem of avoiding failures. For systems of the scale and magnitude of the typical data processing system, this is not surprising. It is like suffering the complete failure of a single cash crop. In the truck garden of DSS, however, it is a different picture. The failure of one crop, especially a favorite, can be undesirable, but it is not disastrous. A mixed-crop strategy minimizes the risk from failure of any one of them.

Further, with DSS—especially experimental ones—the developer should feel rewarded if more than 20% of the systems turn out to be useful. Nearly 80% are destined for only very limited usage and eventual scrapping. While this success ratio might terrify some, notice that the figures concern the *numbers* of systems, not the amount of energy invested in them. If 80% of DSS are failures, the skills to recognize this fact early should become honed so that such DSS can be abandoned quickly before they absorb significant resources. This leaves the bulk of effort to be invested in the successful systems, perhaps in the reverse ratio of 80% on successful DSS, 20% on failures. Even the 20% of effort is not wasted, since the experience helps develop the ability to spot a bad DSS early.

CASE EXAMPLES

Three cases drawn from the authors' experiences are used as background for presenting the collective insights the authors have garnered about the process of growing a successful DSS. The cases illustrate user types, organizational and technical environments, and the educational value of DSS. They differ markedly in type, level, and application area of the DSS, type of company, degree of success with the system, and even country of origin.

Alpha Services

Alpha Services was formed in the late 1960s to provide on-line access to data bases using the then-new technology of time sharing [1]. The first data base consisted of the responses of a large consumer panel to a questionnaire. Tabulations of these data were available in a number of volumes, and special tabulations not in the books were available at extra cost from daily sequential computer runs through the magnetic tape files of the responses, which were organized by respondent.

The founders of Alpha proposed to invert this data base so that it was organized by question rather than respondent. They further proposed to make this data base accessible through an interactive terminal via a specially designed inquiry language, which could process complicated queries and produce the tables required within a few minutes. The decisions supported by the system concerned mix and placement of advertising, and the prospective users were buyers of advertising, sellers of advertising (the media), and advertising agencies.

The developers of the system were three college professors with a good deal of consulting experience but no track record in developing money-making systems. The financial backing was to be provided by the owners of the data base, who had limited knowledge and experience in computers, and none in interactive systems. The backers were understandably skeptical that such a system could work, and they insisted on an early demonstration of a limited prototype. The parties involved finally came to terms only six weeks before the demonstration was due.

The odds of success under these circumstances appeared to be slight, but what seemed to be stringent constraints of time and promised delivery date turned out to be blessings in disguise. The design team was forced to construct modules which were quite separate and separable, since only a few pieces could be implemented in time. They were forced to make many early engineering compromises to get a system operating. Most importantly, because the financial backers wanted to try before buying, the developers were forced to present quickly a working system, albeit a limited one, rather than simply to present a design on paper.

After the demonstration of the prototype, substantial backing was given to finance the next stage of development. The backers also had useful suggestions for improvements. The system was finally developed and introduced to the market. It proved to be successful, and it was then embellished as user needs and desires became clearer. Ten years later, the gross income from this single DSS product was approximately $3 million per year.

Beta Industries

Beta Industries is a large, multinational conglomerate which started to develop a DSS for planning at about the time it began to diversify. Diversification was forced by the threat that the government would nationalize the industry from which Beta's major revenue was derived. The rapid expansion into a variety of businesses convinced management of the need for a staff to develop a plan.

To start this effort, they hired an aggressive young manager with significant DSS training and experience. He in turn staffed the department with still younger computer science and information system specialists, and he hired outside consultants to aid in the development process and in selling the system to management. Corporate planning systems and utilities with the latest audio-visual and computer technology were installed. An extensive DSS for planning was outlined. Many managers were interviewed and sold on the project. Public presentations explained the concept to the world at large.

After the early promises were kept, the going became tougher. The overall system did not take shape on schedule. Data were impossible to obtain as the jealousy of the data processing organization toward the DSS team surfaced. Based on his early successes, the DSS manager was promoted to head of special projects, and his team was split into planning departments for different autonomous divisions of the company. The DSS developers became programmers for the finance operations, doing more and more transaction process programming and less and less DSS development. The large, integrated, company-wide planning DSS that was originally proposed was never realized.*

Gamma Products

Gamma Products is a largely decentralized company which manufactures and sells a range of health and beauty products. At one of their manufacturing divisions, two DSS developers [2] worked closely over a period of months with the finance and production managers to develop a series of DSS to solve the various planning and operating problems each of them identified. Three different complete DSS were developed, with the efforts of users and designers averaging 130 hours per system and elapsed time averaging twelve weeks. For each DSS developed there were several "minicycles"—complete design, building, and evaluation cycles—included as part of the overall process. These were completed in two to three weeks and averaged 50 hours of effort.

---

*This is an instance where valuable experience has not previously been published in the literature.

Both of the involved managers expressed satisfaction with the process and with the results. The DSS developed were used in a variety of ways. Parts of some were used once and discarded, their one-time purpose served. Other parts were never used, or they were extensively modified when it became clear, once the prototype was developed, that they addressed the wrong questions. Parts of others are still used, either on a sporadic basis when the need arises or as a regular part of the operational decision-making process.

INSIGHTS INTO DSS CULTIVATION

The following sections discuss the experiences illustrated in each of the cases just presented. Table 6.1 summarizes this discussion.

Users

Users don't know what they want or need, but they do know what they like.

During its lifetime a single DSS may have a number of different people as users. For the purpose of this discussion, four different types of users are identified, ranging from the person with perfect problem knowledge and no systems knowledge to the opposite extreme. Of course, these paradigms seldom fit perfectly in a real situation, but they furnish a useful categorization of the types of users with which a DSS must interact.

The *manager* (the owner of the garden) for whom the DSS is built is the person with the most authority over what the DSS does. This person has the best problem knowledge but often knows very little about the workings of the DSS. The *staff assistant* (overseer) knows the problem well, but has only enough knowledge of the DSS to interpret the information requests made by the manager to the system and to interpret for the manager the responses received from the system. The *operator* of the system (tenant farmer) knows the system well and understands enough of the manager's problem to make a straightforward interpretation of the information requests. This user knows much less about the real problem than the assistant and is therefore less able to pose reasonable questions about the real world for the system to answer. The *mechanic* (farmhand) who has built the system maintains and updates its technical aspects but knows little about its use.

Several observations about this user population are in order. In the first place, the usual data processing system (DPS) does not have to deal with the first two classes of users to any great extent. The involvement of the manager and the staff assistant, after they have identified the need for the DPS and authorized its development, is indirect and infrequent, usually limited to periodic reviews of progress summarized (by the management of the DPS) in the broadest terms. With a DSS, their involvement is much more direct and frequent. Further, this greater direct involvement of the high-level people means that they must continue to be satisfied with the result, or they will find some reason to eliminate the activity. Bennett [3] has highlighted this difference by distinguishing the *committed* from the *discretionary* user; managers and staff assistants are in the latter category. In Beta Industries, the highest-level managers were involved early; indeed, they may have been oversold. They spent less time later; this may have caused some of the problems the DSS encountered. In contrast, at Gamma there was a hands-on involvement of the two managers throughout the entire process.

Of course, as emphasized above, the user roles are not likely to be played by a single person. The typical situation, especially for a small DSS in a well-defined area like planning, is to have two actors, the manager with the problem and an assistant (for example, a member of the planning department) who serves in the other three roles. This was the case, for example, in Gamma Products. In Alpha, the role of the user was assumed at first by the data base owners; only later were real users involved. When they arrived on the scene, they did provide feedback which led to changes in the system. Occasionally the person with the problem will construct and maintain the DSS, thus playing all four roles. This will become even more common as personal computers with manager-oriented software become widely used.

Whatever the split of responsibilities, the relative need for different skills seems to evolve. There is generally a heavy need for both managerial definition and technical competence in the early stages of implementation. Later, use of an already built and slowly changing system involves principally the staff assistant and operator, with only the sporadic involvement of the manager and mechanic. This pattern was closely followed in Alpha Services, for example.

It is important in implementing a DSS to recognize that all the user types described above are required at various points in its life. The mix may change, but both managerial and technical people will continue to play roles because of the changing nature of both problems and technical support tools. A DSS which is ignored by the technical people because the technical problems are apparently all solved will sooner or later fall into disuse.

Technical Tools

The new technology makes decision support possible, but it still doesn't make it easy.

Technical tools are needed to support the people developing and using DSS. The most obvious of these tools is the hardware. Since many DSS are computer based, the hardware needs center on the computer and the peripheral equipment the DSS require.

The evolutionary approach advocated in this chapter suggests user interaction through a readily available terminal, whatever the size or location of the computer system. Interactive response is necessary for both the development and the use of the system. Because the development is evolutionary, fast turnaround between the developer and the DSS is essential; this can only be obtained through

Crock summary

TABLE 6.1   Summary of the Case Examples

	Alpha Services	Beta Industries	Gamma Products
Type of business	Supplier of consumer panel data	Multinational conglomerate	Health and beauty products
DSS purpose	Summarize and present data	Long-range corporate planning	Support various production and finance decisions
Initial approach	Assemble prototype from a few new (plus many off-the-shelf) modules	Completely develop several working modules (e.g., graphics)	Continual iteration with managers
Follow-up approach	Used feedback from prototype demonstration to guide development	Attempted to finish according to original plan	Same as initial approach
Outcome	Enhanced system still used by many customers	Effort finally abandoned when company decentralized; group disbanded	Developed several versions of DSS for three different problem areas
Reasons for success or failure	Quick, early demonstration gave clients confidence and gave developers insights	Large system oversold; could not easily respond to organizational change	Iterative, evolutionary approach kept clients involved

118

User roles			
Manager	Data base owners; later, customers	Top management of company	Production and finance managers
Assistant	Developers; later, customers	DSS group manager	Developers
Operator	Developers; later, customers	DSS staff	Developers
Mechanic	Alpha company staff	DSS staff and DP staff	Developers
Hardware	Commercial time-sharing service	Large, in-house computer	Micro-computer
Software	FORTRAN; assembler	APL	TROLL
Other technical tools	System software utilities	Tektronix graphics terminals	—
Organizational support	Development funds; data	DSS group formed; DP computer support	Managerial (client) time
Evaluation	Several phases, each ending with demonstration, to get funding for next phase	No formal criteria established	Managerial satisfaction with results
Communication	Sporadic, mostly at demonstrations	Largely through formal meetings and presentations	Continuous, informal
Education and training	User's manual prepared for ultimate customers; on-line help available	Not done after DSS was abandoned	Nothing formal; provided as byproduct of continuous communication

human-paced, conversational responses. During the use of the DSS, interaction is even more important. A user poses questions and wishes to receive answers at human thinking speed, not days, hours, or even minutes later.

Computer services are available in two modes—time-shared and dedicated. Time-shared computation in turn can be obtained from two different sources. The first of these, an in-house computer, is generally the preferred source of time-sharing service. It is usually less expensive than buying time-sharing service outside. System expertise is available on the premises. If it is necessary to access the operational data of the firm, the data are more easily available and controlled if they stay within the organization. The disadvantages of using an in-house time-sharing service are related both to the control that the data processing organization has over the machine and to the availability of languages suitable for DSS development. If the transaction processing activities of the system make its services available only at hours inconvenient for DSS users, or if all uses of the system are controlled by the data processing organization, then it is better to obtain the time-shared computer support from the second type of source—purchased service. Also, some of the languages which are most suitable for the development of DSS might not be available on the in-house machine. Some of those which are obtainable may not easily fit the in-house computer. In summary, the principal advantages of in-house time-sharing are cost and convenience, and the principal disadvantages are constraints imposed by the mainstay data processing use of the machine.

Beta Industries used a company computer for development of their large-scale planning system and realized both the advantages and the disadvantages described above. Because the data of the firm were accessible, the DSS could easily make use of them. However, when the development group began to be absorbed into data processing, it was harder to resist the absorption because of the dependence on the equipment of the data processing group.

The advantages and disadvantages of a purchased time-sharing service are essentially the reverse of those of the in-house computer. Commercial time-sharing services offer a variety of software, probably more extensive than is usually found on the company computer, and these programs may be more suitable for DSS development. Commercial time-sharing services are accustomed to helping beginning users, an aid not normally provided by the in-house data processing center. The lead time to get started can be extremely short. On the negative side, outside facilities generally cost more, although in the current market the cost to the DSS development unit for an outside competitively obtained service may be less than the charges assessed by a monopolistic in-house service. If the operational data of an organization are necessary in the DSS, they will be harder to transfer to the external service, particularly if they must be kept up to date. Occasionally a myopic organizational policy forbids the use of outside services, even when the advantages are shown to outweigh the disadvantages.

Alpha Services developed their system on a commercial time-sharing service. In their case the question was not whether or not to do this, but rather which service to use. The developers did not own a computer; the suppliers of the data base had only a batch computer. It was clear that large data files would be required, so a small computer was not feasible. And because the system was highly speculative, investment in hardware at the prototype stage would have been extremely risky.

An alternative source of interactive systems, one that is becoming increasingly attractive with the wider availability of personal computers, is the dedicated mini- or micro-computer system. Prices are falling, and the support available is improving, most notably in the area of high-level and special-purpose languages. The main advantage of the small stand-alone computer is that interference with the principal computer and its data processing applications is totally avoided. Because the system is dedicated, it can be used at any time for DSS applications. The principal disadvantages of such a system are the limited size of the DSS and data base which can be accommodated and the lack of direct access to the data base of the organization. This second disadvantage is lessening; many micro-computers can now be used either as stand-alone units or as devices which can communicate with larger computers when the occasion demands it. A third disadvantage is the fixed cost of acquiring the system, although these costs are falling rapidly. For example, the various DSS developed for Gamma Products made use of two micro-computers and were written in a high-level programming language. This approach required minimal investment and caused no interference with the major computers in the operation.

The second major component of the technical tools for building DSS is software. Because of variation in the sophistication of the users as well as variation in the problems to be solved, it should be no surprise that a variety of languages are used in DSS construction [4]. For a standard application and/or a novice user, a special problem-oriented language is appropriate. Good examples are found in the various planning systems available for exploring the implications of a strategic plan. These are available on time-sharing services, both in-house and commercial, and on micro-computers. For a new application developed by a problem-oriented set of users, a high-level general-purpose language is most appropriate. Both Beta Industries and Gamma Products did their development work using languages of this sort. Beta Industries used APL on their in-house large computers, and Gamma Products used TROLL and a dedicated micro-computer. Finally, for coding a generic or general-purpose DSS, especially when it is developed by computer professionals, efficient programming languages, even assembly language, can be used to good advantage. As an example, the Alpha Services media selection package was coded in a mix of FORTRAN and assembly language. Of course, this system was built from the start as one in which heavy use was anticipated, and therefore efficiency was important.

A typical pattern of development might at first involve the use of a high-level language requiring little time to program. If and when the evolution of the DSS stops or slows, and if the DSS will continue to be used, it should be reprogrammed in a more efficient language. As desirable as this step appears, it is seldom taken, even when abandoning the old system and totally reprogramming it has been shown to be advantageous.* People have an aversion to scrapping working programs. Similarly, for hardware, the development might be started on a time-sharing computer with high variable cost and low fixed cost; when usage justifies, the DSS might be switched to a dedicated mini- or micro-computer.

Along with languages at a variety of levels, some utilities are also desirable. In particular, some sort of editing or string processing capability is essential, since this makes it convenient to build the system and to operate it easily. Another essential utility is a powerful debugging capability, either built directly into the language or available as a part of the overall operating system. This is obviously useful when iterative changes are being made during the building of a system. In general, the more modules there are available from the "public library" of software, the more effort can be concentrated on developing the modules which are unique to the problem as well as the interfaces which tie them together.

One additional set of technical tools that is highly desirable in developing DSS is graphics capability. Graphics capability is important for the presentation of complicated information in large "chunks" to managers. For example, Beta Industries made extensive use of graphics in the development of their corporate planning DSS, well before the availability of the business-oriented color graphics systems currently on the market. Graphic input via light-pen, track-ball, or other similar device is also becoming important as a means of eliciting components of the problem and their relationships from decision makers, as contrasted with supplying parameters once a problem model is specified. Software support for graphic interaction is not well developed currently, but improvements are being made as interest and demand increase.

Organization Support

> DSS don't need many organizational resources; that's fortunate, because sometimes resources are hard to justify.

Perhaps even more than for standard data processing systems, the support of the organization is critical to the success of DSS. The organization must recognize that the problem is important and must provide the resources necessary for its solution. On the one hand, this is harder than it is for standard data processing systems (DPS), since the benefits are more difficult to quantify. On the other hand, it is easier because fewer resources are required. Further, if the support of the decision maker to whose problem the DSS addresses itself is obtained, the rest of the necessary support usually becomes available. The decision maker can free appropriate people from standard "fire fighting" duties so that they can work on developing the DSS.

---

*McLean and Riesing argue in Carlson [5] that reprogramming would have been effective.

Surprisingly, the support of the data processing (DP) department is required in only a few cases, and then aid is needed only on technical aspects of the problem. Cooperation from the DP department may be necessary to obtain data or access to data maintained by that department. Cooperation may also be necessary to get computer systems support, in the form of people and special programs, when the machine being used for DSS development is operated by that department.

Placing the DSS effort under the organizational control of corporate data processing can lead to failure. The major cause of failure in these cases is a basic incompatibility between the automation philosophy of data processing and the decision support philosophy of the DSS effort. A successful data processing application is typically characterized by the high-volume repetition of an unvarying process. This is appropriate behavior when one is dealing with the highly structured problems of accounts receivable, accounts payable, payroll, and the like, but is of questionable value when dealing with the unstructured problems typical of DSS. The adoption of an automation philosophy by corporate data processing results in a production-line orientation in which the objective is to process as many different transactions as possible in a single standardized manner. In fact, DSS builders must sometimes guard against the scuttling of their whole effort by a jealous DP department whose members feel that they have a monopoly on any such effort and retaliate when responsibility is not given to them. This occurred in Beta Industries after the early successes of the prototype, and this may have been responsible in part for the fact that the DSS was not completed.

Continual Change

The only constant is change, and you can't even count on that.

In all aspects of a DSS—users, technical tools, organizational needs—the one unchanging fact is that change will occur throughout its life. The humans who interact with the system change. A novice user of the system becomes expert in its use and learns to take shortcuts, emphasizing the useful features and discarding the rest. There is evidence that a smaller number of options are used more extensively in a shorter elapsed time as a novice user becomes expert. In addition to this change which occurs as the user learns about the operation of the system, there may be a change which takes place as the user learns how to "program" previously unprogrammed decisions. Beyond that, the role of the decision maker in the context of the organization may change, expanding as more responsibility is assumed. This change may happen in any case; it can be accelerated or aided by the DSS. Also, there may be one-of-a-kind special tasks, such as mergers, on which decisions must be made. Finally, the original DSS user often departs, if lucky, for greener pastures. The whole cycle begins again as a novice decision maker arrives with different biases and expertise. As it did in Beta Industries, the DSS development experience may actually accelerate the promotion and therefore the departure of the decision makers involved.

Not only do users change, but the problems on which they work also change. A "problem" is, after all, a perceived discrepancy between the behavior of the real world and someone's model of the ideal behavior of that world. Thus the problem will change if: (1) the world changes, (2) the perceptions of the individual involved change, or (3) the person who is perceiving changes (a new individual in the job). Given the likelihood of change occurring in at least one of these three dimensions, it is a wonder that problems are ever stable. The answer utilized in Gamma seems the best one: many problems were confronted during the project as the decision maker and analyst learned together which were most important.

The tools available are also changing, as discussed in the section on technical tools. Powerful computers are becoming cheaper, and their capabilities—notably reduced size, increased language power, and display graphics—enhance their value for DSS. More important, the software options are becoming more extensive. Planning languages and other special-purpose systems are widely available on large computers. The primitive languages available on small personal computers a few years ago have even given way to high-level and special-purpose systems. All this makes building DSS easier than it was a few years ago. For example, the mini-computer and general-purpose language on which Gamma Products developed its DSS were not even available when Alpha and Beta began their DSS developments.

Organizational structures and the people who staff them change. A highly centralized organization can become decentralized, changing the scope of the decisions made by its managers and, with that, the need to be served by a DSS. The developers of the planning system in Beta Industries encountered just such a change; their system, designed for centralized planning, could not easily respond to the changed needs brought by decentralization. Managers and other personnel in organizations are being replaced by those who have received an introduction to the possibilities and limitations of computers in their basic education. As this happens, DSS will be better understood and appreciated, even by those who are discretionary and not committed users.

All these changes should be a positive force in the adoption of DSS in decision-making situations. But a design approach responsive to these changes is necessary in order to take advantage of this force.

Middle-Out Approach

Building tools is wonderful for those in the tool business.

The notion of taking a "middle-out" approach to the development of a system is much less discussed in the literature than are the more conventional "top-down" and "bottom-up" alternatives [6]. The middle-out approach begins close to the level of the problem at hand, and it involves a cyclical process of generalizing (bottom-up) and specifying (top-down) at each stage of the problem-solving process.

Middle-out developments begin with a much less global view of the environment than is conventional with most top-down approaches. In the top-down approach, there is an implicit notion of a wide-range plan, which structures the entire problem area being tackled. In most problem domains, particularly those where the problem structure is not well understood, achievement of such a global view can take a long time. Thus top-down analysis implicitly involves prespecification and prestructuring a problem area. The approach and system plan must be developed completely before being implemented.

Bottom-up efforts, on the other hand, involve developing "tools" which can later be used to construct solutions to problems. In any new problem domain, many useful facilities are always lacking, and this can make the approach of tool construction attractive. However, this tool-building activity can cease to be a means to some end and become an end in itself. A common result of such activities is the "Universal, All-Purpose, Completely General . . . System" which has been abandoned by the organization which paid for its development, but is being advocated in public (without much success) by its originator. To some extent, the planning system in Beta Industries suffered this fate, both because it became too general and because it did not keep in touch with the organizational needs of Beta.

Both the top-down and the bottom-up approaches have proven to have distinct problems. Top-down analysis, if pursued with a vengeance, often means that months or even years will be spent doing global designs without ever getting down to concrete details. Such "blue sky" analysis often proves, in the long run, to have been grounded on dubious assumptions, and the engineering involved in developing the system based on such an analysis then proves to be unusually difficult. The top-down approach assumes that, because there is little to be learned during implementation, prespecification is possible. In decision support situations this is not true, and the feedback obtained in the design and implementation process means that extensive top-down analysis at the beginning has little value.

Bottom-up analysis generally suffers both from lack of any decision-maker perspective and from distraction. Tool building without a problem-focus perspective is likely to produce hopelessly inappropriate tools. Many systems designers and implementers are people who enjoy (and are skilled at) the task of building tools. When given free rein, they not surprisingly develop tools which are aesthetically pleasing to them rather than tools which are well suited to the decision-making task at hand.

In middle-out development, a prototype system that supports an important but separable part of the overall problem is built quickly and used on the relevant part of the problem. It helps solve that part of the problem immediately, but, more importantly, the prototype provides quick feedback on the structuring of the problem and on the use of the technique. The DSS designers can use the information in refining that part or in building other parts. Or the feedback may lead to a decision to abandon the whole prototype. The modules constructed in this fashion are similar to those of a large system, except they are designed to be free standing and to do a job separately rather than as part of an overall system. It may be that later the pieces developed in middle-out mode are connected to solve some larger problem, but this is not a precondition for building the modules. For example, the DSS for Alpha Services was built in this fashion, with part of the system in place, working and generating prototypical results, before the rest was built or even fully planned. Another important purpose of a prototype is to establish the value of the DSS before many resources are spent on it, as also occurred at Alpha Services.

Synthetic Approach

> If you can't have something working within the week, maybe you are working on something too big.

The essential thrust of systems analysis is to study and break down tasks into components. This approach, popular for more than a decade, is very useful in understanding situations that can make effective use of standard data processing. Large-scale problems must be separated into subproblem modules in order for developers to understand and consider the complexities of the tasks. This analytic activity is a key technique for solving such problems. When DSS are designed, however, there is usually not much to analyze. There is only a loose understanding of the problem domain, and profound analysis may become an end in itself rather than simply a means to the accomplishment of the decision maker's objectives. In these circumstances, it is more effective to synthesize than to analyze, and this gives rise to the systems synthesis, as opposed to the systems analysis, approach.

When a system is synthesized, a structure is created by taking a number of components off the shelf and putting them together to form a crude approximation of a system. This activity is well known to electrical engineers, who seldom redesign transistors, capacitors, or resistors when they wish to build something. As engineers begin to structure the solution to a problem, they do not implement the first design on a highly polished chassis in a mahogany cabinet. Instead, a loose connection of existing components is made in an attempt to obtain a quick solution. It is rarely the case that something which fails at this "breadboard" stage would have succeeded if a more refined approach had been tried. If the first attempt fails, not much has been invested, and an alternative approach can be easily tried. If the breadboard design seems promising, then more energy can be invested in refining and packaging it in the sure knowledge that the effort is directed toward an objective worth accomplishing. Making an investment in refinement and packaging before the basic design is proven seems foolish. In order to synthesize systems, it is necessary to have a stock of components and substantial knowledge about how to use them. Even with this knowledge, it is not easy to tie together a system. But then, most engineering tasks are not easy. By building a breadboard DSS, one obtains early and rapid feedback on the critical assumptions implicit in the design.

All three examples of DSS used this approach to some extent. It was especially noticeable in Alpha Services, where some off-the-shelf software for data bases, sorting, and the like were loosely stitched together in a way that gave a quick test of the system concept with minimal investment. After the value of the DSS was proven, specially built efficient routines replaced the less efficient general packages with which the concept had been tested.

Evaluation

> DSS developments should be measured by "yardstones," not milestones.

DSS development projects are undertaken principally because decision makers see value in having some problem solved. The solution is perceived to be valuable because it might enhance the effectiveness of the decision maker, not because it will improve efficiency. This emphasis on perceived effectiveness raises important issues. Measuring effectiveness requires assessment of both benefits and costs, since effectiveness depends on both. Assessing benefits and costs in a DSS is an uncertain proposition at best. Benefits are especially hard to assess, since they depend largely on the decision maker's perception. The decision to develop a DSS should be part of a decision made by the decision maker on how to allocate analytical resources, mainly the decision maker's time [7]. Should time be spent developing a computational tool, or would a consulting study or some telephone calls or a few plant visits be more beneficial? The estimate of benefits should be based on what appears to be the most valuable means for obtaining the knowledge to make the best decision. It is the lack of perceived value of a DSS which generally keeps it from being built, not its cost [8]. Unless the decision maker perceives the need for a DSS as an aid in decision making, the system has no value even if it produces all the "right" answers. (Some other benefits of DSS, communication and education, are discussed in the following sections of this chapter.)

DSS development costs have two principal components. The first is the cost of the hardware or computer service necessary to build and operate the DSS. The second is the cost of the people involved. The major portion of the personnel costs are for the decision maker and the actual builder of the system (assuming they are different people), with additional expenditures required for data gathering and reduction, occasional system and language problems, and the like. The costs of DSS development have two distinctly favorable features. First, they are relatively small compared to the usual costs of data processing system development. For example, as mentioned in the description of Gamma Products, one typical DSS took one week of managers' time and six weeks of analysts' time. All work was done on a micro-computer system costing $15,000. The second advantage is that the costs are applied incrementally. The only real investments are some learning time at first and the cost of the mini-computer if this hardware is chosen. After that, costs are incurred only as long as the (perceived) benefits appear to justify these costs.

Communication

It is a lot easier to answer the question "How *do* you like X?" than to answer the question "How *would* you like X?".

A DSS can serve as an important channel of communication among the people responsible for its development. In this sense, the DSS aids in its own development. By conceiving, designing, developing, using, and evaluating a DSS quickly, and by reconceiving, redesigning, redeveloping, reusing, and reevaluating the modified DSS, the developers establish a routine for rapid communication about the DSS as it is used for the problem's solution. This is like the task an architect would face when designing a custom-built house for someone who had never seen or lived in a house. The communication between client and designer is improved with paper sketches and enhanced with paper models, but it really works best with full-scale operating models. The first-cut DSS is an operating full-scale model of the decision aid needed by a client who does not know what is available or useful and built by a designer who does not know exactly what the client desires or needs. For example, Alpha Services would never have been allowed to build the full DSS without having first developed the prototype for communicating with its backers. On the other hand, the developers would not have known what to build if they had not been able to communicate, via the prototype, with users unfamiliar with computer support and its possibilities.

Beyond the communication required between disparate users to build a DSS to support a given decision, the discipline enforced by the need to encode the DSS in the unambiguous language of the computer can lead to communication which transcends the problem at hand. What is thought originally to be important turns out to be a nonproblem. What is thought to be a trivial issue turns out to be a pivotal one. When used correctly, the communication process required to grow a DSS is integrated into the whole process of problem formulation and solution, rather than treated as just a bothersome add-on to the old way of doing business. This is best illustrated in Gamma Industries, where the two managers communicated with the builders almost exclusively through the iterations of the DSS. Some DSS were scrapped early, and some problems were totally redefined. When all the DSS were finished, both managers had a different view of their environments and the decisions required in them.

Education and Training

If you want to learn something, study it; if you want to learn even more, teach it; but if you really want to understand it, program it for a computer.

Just like communication, the education and training of all of the people involved in developing and using a DSS can be more important than the actual system and its output. During the process of conceiving, designing, developing, using, and evaluating a DSS, these people learn about the decision to be made, problem constraints, and the behavior of the surrounding organization. DSS educational benefits stretch from the initial problem-finding phase to the audit and evaluation of the DSS after its use is completed. In order to structure the problem, decision makers and designers must exchange ideas on difficulties and possible solution methods. In the process, the decision makers can learn more about their jobs, the problem constraints, the limitations of analysis and computer methods, and their organization. Designers learn about the needs of the decision makers, the use and utility of DSS tools in managerial problems, and also about the particular organization. This learning takes place in the task-oriented process of developing a DSS.

Sometimes the educational process is so revealing that it obviates the need for further use of the formal DSS. The process of constructing the DSS can increase understanding of the perceived problem until it becomes a nonproblem, or until its solution is so obvious that no formal use of the DSS is required. Even in cases where the DSS is used to find a first solution, subsequent solutions to similar problems may not require its use because the process of structuring and solving the problem has produced an essential set of calculations simple enough to be done by hand. In these cases, an increased understanding of the problem has been obtained during the process of developing the DSS. Several of the DSS developed for Gamma Products led to this result.

While education occurs during the building of a DSS, training takes place during subsequent uses. For example, a production manager who has developed a method for scheduling machines using a simple DSS can easily pass this managerial insight on to others via the use of the system. Other managers are trained by applying the system to their own tasks—and quite possibly they also learn by refining and changing the DSS so that it better fits their environments and structures their tasks.

Further, applying a DSS can be a better means for teaching management techniques than traditional textbooks or lectures. In particular, the DSS can serve as a prototypical system for demonstrating the value of various methods for attacking a problem. Much more effectively than a discussion about the potential value of a method, a DSS incorporating it can establish the method's value, demonstrate its feasibility, and teach about the possibilities and limitations of its use.

CONCLUSION

In this chapter the case has been made for a flexible, evolutionary, gradual approach to the development of DSS. The examples have highlighted the various characteristics of DSS that the authors find important. As an understanding of the DSS environment changes, as the development of hardware and software makes DSS easier to build, so will the vision of how best to commit resources change. Development will continue apace as new problems, especially in the area of day-to-day operations, are added to DSS experience. Because courses in business schools now include DSS as a natural and integrated part of the educational program, more decision makers will expect to have DSS as a standard weapon in their management arsenal.

REFERENCES

1. Ness, D. N., and C. R. Sprague. "An Interactive Media Decision Support System," *Sloan Management Review*, Vol. 14, No. 1 (Fall 1972).

2. Grajew, J., and J. Tolovi. "Conception et Mise en Oeuvre des Systèmes Interactifs d'Aide à la Decision: L'Approche Evolutive." Third Cycle Doctoral Thesis, Institut d'Administration des Entreprises, Université de Grenoble II, 1978.

3. Bennett, J. L. "Integrating Users and Decision Support Systems," in J. D. White (ed.), *Proceedings of the Sixth and Seventh Annual SMIS Conferences*. Ann Arbor, Mich.: University of Michigan, July 1976, pp. 77–86.

4. Ness, D. N., C. R. Sprague, and A. Moulton. "On the Implementation of Sophisticated Interactive Systems," Working Paper No. 506–71. Cambridge, Mass.: The Sloan School, M.I.T., 1971.

5. Carlson, E. D. (ed.). "Proceedings of a Conference on Decision Support Systems," *Data Base*, Vol. 8, No. 3 (Winter 1977).

6. Ness, D. N., and E. G. Hurst, Jr. "Characterizing Type-P and Type-S Systems," Working Paper No. 78–03–01. Philadelphia: Department of Decision Sciences, The Wharton School, University of Pennsylvania, 1978.

7. Johnson, T. H., J. Grajew, J. Tolovi, J. C. Courbon, and B. Oudet. "Cost/Benefit Analysis of and for the Evolutive Approach," Working Paper No. 78–10–01. Philadelphia: Department of Decision Sciences, The Wharton School, University of Pennsylvania, 1978.

8. Keen, P. G. W. "Value Analysis: Justifying Decision Support Systems," *Management Information Systems Quarterly*, Vol. 5, No. 1 (March 1981), pp. 1–16.

GENERAL BIBLIOGRAPHY

Alter, S. *Decision Support Systems: Current Practice and Continuing Challenges.* Reading, Mass.: Addison-Wesley, 1980.

Alter, S. "Why Is Man-Computer Interaction Important for Decision Support Systems?" *Interfaces*, Vol. 7, No. 2 (February 1977), pp. 109–15.

Bennett, J. L. "The User Interface in Interactive Systems," in C. Cuadra (ed.), *Annual Review of Information Science and Technology*, Vol. 7. White Plains, N.Y.: Knowledge Industry Publications/ASIS, 1972.

Bennett, J. L. "Incorporating Usability into System Design," IBM Design Symposium '79. San Jose, Calif.: IBM Research Laboratory, April 1979.

Carlson, E. D., J. L. Bennett, G. Giddings, and P. Mantey. "The Design and Evaluation of an Interactive Geo-data Analysis and Display System," in *Information Processing 74.* Amsterdam: North Holland, 1974, pp. 1057–61.

Courbon, J. C., B. Oudet, and J. P. Rouet. "Systèmes Interactifs d'Aide à la Decision: Problèmes et Perspectives d'Évolution," Research Paper 76–08. Grenoble: Institut d'Administration des Entreprises, Université de Grenoble II, June 1976.

Courbon, J. C., J. Grajew, and J. Tolovi. "Decision Support Systems: An Evolutionary Approach to Design and Implementation." Grenoble: Institut d'Administration des Entreprises, Université de Grenoble II, 1978.

Ebeling, D. G., and E. G. Hurst, Jr. "PA3: A General-Purpose, Time-Shared Problem Analysis Language," *Proceedings of the Third Conference of Applications of Simulation,* December 1969.

Gerrity, T. P., Jr. "The Design of Man-Machine Decision Systems." Ph.D. dissertation, The Sloan School, M.I.T., 1970.

Gerrity, T. P., Jr. "The Design of Man-Machine Decision Systems: An Application to Portfolio Management," *Sloan Management Review,* Vol. 12, No. 2 (1971), pp. 59–76.

Grajew, J., and J. Tolovi. "Action Research on the Design and Implementation of Decision Support Systems." Grenoble: Institut d'Administration des Entreprises, Université de Grenoble II, 1977.

Keen, P. G. W. "Computer-Based Decision Aids: The Evaluation Problem," *Sloan Management Review,* Vol. 16, No. 3 (Spring 1975), pp. 17–30.

Keen, P. G. W. "Computer Systems for Top Managers: A Modest Proposal," *Sloan Management Review,* Vol. 18, No. 1 (Fall 1976), pp. 1–17.

Keen, P. G. W., and M. S. Scott Morton. *Decision Support Systems: An Organizational Perspective.* Reading, Mass.: Addison-Wesley, 1978.

Krolak, P., W. Felts, and G. Marble. "A Man-Machine Approach Toward Solving the Traveling Salesman Problem," *Communications of the ACM,* Vol. 14, No. 5 (May 1971), pp. 327–34.

Malhotra, A. "Design Criteria for a Knowledge-Based English Language System for Management: An Experimental Analysis," Project MAC Technical Report 146. Cambridge, Mass.: M.I.T., February 1975.

Martin, J. *Design of Man-Computer Dialogues.* Englewood Cliffs, N.J.: Prentice-Hall, 1973.

Meador, C. L., and D. N. Ness. "Decision Support Systems: An Application to Corporate Planning," *Sloan Management Review,* Vol. 16, No. 2 (Winter 1974), pp. 51–68.

Miller, L. W., R. Kaplan, and W. Edwards. "JUDGE: A Value-Judgment-Based Tactical Command System," *Organizational Behavior and Human Performance,* Vol. 2, No. 4 (1967), pp. 329–74.

Scott Morton, M. S. *Management Decision Systems: Computer-Based Support for Decision Making.* Cambridge, Mass.: Harvard University Press, 1971.

Simon, H. A. *The New Science of Management Decision.* New York: Harper & Row, 1960.

Walsh, D. H., and M. D. Schecterman. "Experimental Investigation of the Usefulness of Operator Aided Optimization in a Simulated Tactical Decision Aiding Task," Report No. 215-4. Santa Monica, Calif.: Integrated Sciences Corporation, January 1978.

Young, L. F. "Another Look at Man-Computer Interaction," *Interfaces*, Vol. 8, No. 2 (February 1978), pp. 67–69.

BUILDING A DECISION SUPPORT SYSTEM: THE MYTHICAL MAN-MONTH REVISITED

Peter G. W. Keen • Thomas J. Gambino

CHAPTER 7

1. INTRODUCTION

1.1. Overview

This paper describes the development of a Decision Support System (DSS)—from its beginning as part of a research project through its implementation as a commercial product used by six state agencies and public sector consulting groups. The system was designed by individuals with a long-standing involvement with DSS. As such, it provided an excellent opportunity to test the conventional wisdom on principles and techniques for DSS design.

We had clear expectations concerning what would be easy and what would be hard to implement. We wanted to see if the DSS field is at a stage where one can give builders reliable rules of thumb—not a cookbook, but the sort of pragmatic advice that would be welcomed by a capable systems analyst, consultant, or programmer setting out for the first time to deliver an interactive computer system to support decision makers in a complex task.

Interactive Support System for Policy Analysts (ISSPA) is a DSS written in APL that supports administrators, analysts, and researchers concerned with public policy issues at the state and local level. The initial application this paper discusses is in the area of school finance—the funding of public education in individual states. However, ISSPA is of general relevance to planning and policy making in both the public and private sectors.[1]

The development strategy was based on principles of adaptive design, derived

---

Portions of this material adapted, with permission, from "Selected Papers on Decision Support Systems from the 13th Hawaii International Conference on System Sciences," published in *DATA BASE*, Vol. 12, Nos. 1 and 2, and *SIGOA Newsletter*, Vol. 1, Nos. 4 and 5, Special Interest Groups of the Association for Computing Machinery.

from the recommendations of several researchers and practitioners (see Section 5). These principles assume that the "final" system must evolve through usage and learning. Rather than focus on functional specifications, the designer relies on a prototype system to:

1. Find out quickly what is important to the user as opposed to what the designer thinks ought to be important,

2. Provide something concrete for the user to react to and experiment with, and

3. Define a clear architecture for the DSS, so that it can be easily modified and evolved.

The prototype is a real system, not a mock-up or experiment. It provides the base for learning by using. In addition to the prototype, adaptive design emphasizes:

1. Careful attention to the *user-DSS dialog* and thus to the design of the software interface,

2. The importance of *user learning*, in terms of the *evolution* of the system and the need for *flexibility* in the DSS and *responsive service* by the system builders,

3. *Getting started*, rather than getting finished, and

4. A *command-based structure*. (ISSPA is built up of APL functions that directly correspond to the action words or the "verbs" users employ in their own problem solving. A verb is a statement that says "do this," such as "give me descriptive statistics," which ISSPA performs with a DESCRIBE command.

1.2. The Mythical Man-Month

Both the adaptive design approach used with ISSPA and the choice of APL reflect the hypothesis that is the main topic of this chapter:

Adaptive design resolves the problem of the mythical man-month.

The mythical man-month is F. P. Brooks's (1975) summary of the discrepancy between the expected and actual effort required to develop software products.[2] Designers estimate the time for completion in terms of man-months of effort; their projections almost invariably turn out to be badly underestimated, and the system often does not work.

Brooks identifies a number of explanations for the widespread problems in planning for and delivering software systems. Assessments of man-months are often based on the number of lines of code. However, program coding is only 10% of the total effort. Testing, debugging, interfacing, and generating documentation comprise a far greater percentage of the total effort. Moreover, the effort to develop a system product, as opposed to a single program, is usually under-

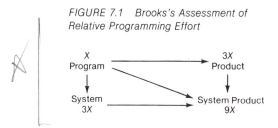

FIGURE 7.1 Brooks's Assessment of
Relative Programming Effort

estimated by a wide margin. Brooks observes that, if X is the effort required to
write and test a single program, $3X$ is needed to integrate it into a *system* and $9X$
is required to make it into a *system product* (Fig. 7.1).

Making a program into a product involves documentation, additional testing
to ensure "robustness" (i.e., the program should be able to handle inputs and uses
outside the range of the initial special-purpose program), error-handling routines,
etc. Integrating a program into a system requires substantial testing of linkages,
and often additional code must be written to ensure consistency.

Brooks recommends several techniques to solve the problem of the mythical
man-month. He emphasizes the importance of a clear design architecture, the use
of "sharp tools," and systematic testing procedures.

We were particularly concerned about the mythical man-month, since we
wished to make ISSPA into a system product and had an extremely limited
budget. In essence, we started with a set of hypotheses about DSS development—
about adaptive design, system architecture, APL, and the mythical man-month.
The rest of this chapter describes our experiences, focusing on the surprises. We
found that:

1. The principles of adaptive design, which are unique to the DSS faith and
    stand in sharp contrast to the methods of the systems development life cycle,
    hold up well. Given APL as a tool, we have been able to evolve a complex
    system out of simple components and to respond quickly to our users' chang-
    ing needs.

2. We underestimated the importance of having skilled users; much of the test-
    ing process relies on them.

3. Although APL immensely speeds up the development process, it has some
    hidden costs. It is extremely difficult, even for expert programmers, to esti-
    mate the relative efficiency of the source code. We suspect that many of the
    highest-level languages share with APL a characteristic we term opaque-
    ness—the surface (the source code) gives no clear indication of the depths (the
    machine level).

4. Brooks's estimate of $9X$ seems to hold. Even with APL, adaptive design, and
    a highly skilled programmer, the initial development effort has to be supple-
    mented by continuous attention to improving the usability of the DSS. Of
    course, since APL reduces X, it also makes the total effort, $9X$, acceptable.

2. SCHOOL FINANCE POLICY ISSUES

Since the early 1970s, the funding of public schools has been a major legislative and judicial issue in at least half of the states in the country (Garms, Guthrie, and Pierce, 1978). The Serrano case in California in 1973 established that children's opportunities for education—expressed in terms of expenditures per pupil in each school district in the state—should not be determined by their parents' and neighbors' wealth. Towns with high wealth and property values can raise large revenues with less effort than must be expended by poor ones. Since local property taxes are the major component of school revenues, this has resulted in huge disparities between neighboring districts. To resolve this inequity, the state must both limit rich districts' expenditures and provide substantial aid to poor ones. States must now consider the notion of equity when formulating school finance legislation.

The main result of school finance reform has been to place responsibility on state legislative and executive branches to determine the "formula," the set of equations on which each district's state aid is based. In states where school finance is not a major issue, the legislature can incrementally adjust last year's funding formula through an increase in state basic aid of, say, 5%. This incremental process, which has worked reasonably well for a century, breaks down when a judge declares the state's existing system unconstitutional, or when school finance becomes a "hot" issue because of taxpayer revolts, or when inflation affects the ability of local districts to raise adequate revenues. Such circumstances have forced certain states to undertake fundamental rather than incremental analyses. Unfortunately, the professional staff responsible for performing the fundamental analysis in these states can rarely provide it.

The whole aim of ISSPA is to break through the technical constraints faced by the staff, but many organizational constraints remain. The key problem is that the whole system has *always* relied on incrementalism. There is no policy focus. Even when a court decision forces rethinking, legislators are mainly concerned with the "bottom line," the exact impact of a proposed formula on each of their constituent districts. This "costing out" of the formula leads to a narrow focus; the planning horizon is next year, and longer-term qualitative issues are ignored.

The key issues in school finance concern data. It is a "numbers" game with lengthy arguments about who has the right figures. The state aid formula is generally based on a variety of data: attendance by grade, enrollment (which is not necessarily even close to attendance), local tax rates and revenues, transportation expenditures, special and vocational education information, etc. School finance is a morass of numbers. In New York, for example, every local school superintendent must supply the state with up to 1200 pages of data a year.

Control over these data is the major source of influence for the department of education, which is generally a poor stepchild in state government. A few states have effective collection, control, and reporting procedures, but on the whole the data management process is clumsy and inefficient. There is a shortage of programmers. Low salaries and lack of hardware, management, and training mean the policy analysts' major problem is access to high-quality information.

These analysts are mainly legislative staff or professionals working for executive fiscal and budget agencies. Their responsibilities vary; they are partly watchdogs who monitor the other parts of government (executive or legislative). They may initiate policy alternatives. Above all, they evaluate information on the current state aid system and on competing proposals for change. In general, the only computer-based aids available to them are SPSS (Statistical Package for the Social Sciences) and limited batch "simulations," which do little more than calculate what each school district would have received last year had a proposed formula been used. Only a few states have more advanced tools. These tend to be expensive but highly valued by their users.

While legislative debates on school finance are limited to incremental analysis and the bottom line, the policy issues are complex. There is a rich research literature on measures of equity and alternative structures for a formula (i.e., foundation, guaranteed yield, and pupil weighting). The field has an esoteric jargon—recaptures, hold-harmless, mils, and caps—of its own. The gap between the research concepts and the practices of policy analysts is huge. ISSPA is intended to bridge the gap, to provide analysts with a "portable technology" that can help them add a real policy focus to school finance. Because access to information is the key to effective analysis and to influencing the legislative debate, ISSPA is designed to allow fast and flexible manipulation and display of information. It is a DSS for policy analysts, not for policy analysis.

The state department of education often has a monopoly on data and data processing relevant to school finance. It is difficult for the policy analysts to get appropriations for computer resources; the centralized data processing unit can generally thwart their efforts to use outside services. Thus ISSPA had to be "portable." A portable technology is one that can be easily transferred and maintained. Portability includes:

1. *Low cost.* Even $10,000 may be too much to justify, regardless of potential payoff, if it requires a capital investment proposal and legislative approval.

2. *Installation.* Given the frequent organizational isolation of analysts and the hostility of the department of education data processing unit, it must be easy to build and update the ISSPA data base and to bring up the DSS.

3. *Ease of use.* The need for an intermediary computer person must be removed. The analysts should work directly with their own data to minimize the need for training; it is important to make ISSPA self-explanatory.

Portability is important for political as well as technical reasons.

3. ISSPA DESIGN FEATURES

3.1. Introduction

ISSPA is a command-driven system. There are four categories of commands, as follows:

1. Data management,
2. Data access and display,
3. Data analysis, and
4. User-system linkages (e.g., "help" commands).

Conceptually, the data base is a matrix in this form:[3]

Planning units × Variables
   (Rows)   (Columns)

There is no fixed limit on either the rows or the columns; ISSPA fills up the workspace with variables (via the CHOOSE command) until it is full. In a typical school finance application, the data base contains 500–600 variables for each of 500–750 planning units (school districts).

We deliberately chose a simple data structure and approach to data management for ISSPA. Our assumptions were that policy analysis largely involves exploring and manipulating a small amount of high-quality data and that analysts think of data as a simple table of values. The notion was to match ISSPA's data model with the user's data model.

Commands in ISSPA are simple and kept as close to the users' vocabulary as possible. Almost all DSS claim to be Englishlike, easy to learn and use. The evidence that ISSPA is indeed so is that with use of a manual consisting of examples, users have been able to operate the system, drawing on most of its commands, after an hour of training. The training was simply a one-hour demonstration.

Considerable effort was put into the design of the user-system interface. Most commands involve typing a single word, which is generally self-explanatory, such as LIST, PLOT, REGRESS, DEFINE, or COUNTIF. A structured dialog is used within the more complex commands. For example, ISSPA prompts the user in a fixed sequence such as "DO YOU WANT A OR B?" when an additional choice is required.

The number of artificial, computer-oriented conventions was held to a minimum. The only such conventions that take time to learn and use concern choosing and identifying variables. Since the data base may be of any size, only a part of it can be in the computer's workspace at any time. Users are told to view the DSS as a scratchpad. The commands operate on whatever is in the scratchpad. The user CHOOSEs which variables to bring in from disk (see Fig. 7.2). We assumed that this would not be restrictive since users will rarely want, or be able, to deal with more than 10–20 variables at the same time[4] (see also Carlson, Grace, and Sutton, 1977).

The identification of variables is the second convention. Mnemonics for variables are cumbersome to use and hard to remember, especially since an ISSPA data base often contains over 600 variables. The convention used in ISSPA is that variables are referenced by either a permanent identifier Vxxx, set up when the data base is created, or by a temporary number Axx, showing the variable's location in the workspace ('A'xx = active variable *number* xx). While analysts found

FIGURE 7.2   The ISSPA CHOOSE Command

```
COMMAND: VARS

THE ACTIVE VARIABLES ARE:

A1 V101 TOTENRL79   TOTAL ENROLLMENT 79
A2 V201 TOTREV79    TOTAL REVENUE 79
A3 V505 ASSDVAL79   ASSESSED VALUATION 79
A4      WEALTH79    ASSESSED VALUATION PER PUPIL 1979--WEALTH MEASURE

COMMAND:
```

this convention reasonably easy to accept, they still wished to define their own labels, at least for those variables they used frequently. We added a SYNONYM facility so that now variables can be referred to by V-number, A-number, or a one-word user-supplied label (see Fig. 7.3).

We allowed variable names to be of any length, to ensure that reports would be meaningful and clear. If users—or the legislative or public interest groups for whom they prepare analyses—think of a variable as, for example, "GUARAN-TEED YIELD, GOVERNOR'S PROPOSAL," then that is what must appear on reports, not "GY, GVR." Obviously, providing maximum flexibility on variable labels meant that we had to find a compact and efficient (from the user's perspective) mode of reference (e.g., A-number or V-number).

The current variable identification system was extended to include:

1. A-number and V-number

2. SYNONYM

3. VARNAME (to allow easy and complete identification of a variable)

4. WHAT IS (lists the full label for any A-number, V-number, or synonym)

5. VARS (shows the identifiers for all the variables currently active)

*FIGURE 7.3   An Illustration of ISSPA
Variable-Naming Conventions*

```
COMMAND: CHOOSE
GROUP OR ITEM?   ITEM
ENTER VARIABLE TO BE CHOSEN ('STOP'): TOTENRL79
ENTER VARIABLE TO BE CHOSEN ('STOP'): TOTREV79
ENTER VARIABLE TO BE CHOSEN ('STOP'): ASSDVAL79
ENTER VARIABLE TO BE CHOSEN ('STOP'): STOP

CURRENT NUMBER OF ACTIVE VARIABLES: 3

COMMAND:
```

3.2. System Architecture

The system structure of ISSPA is relatively simple in concept. There are three separate components (see Fig. 7.4):

1. Dialog manager

2. Analytical commands (LIST, REGRESS, etc.)

3. Data management system

Most of the initial effort went into defining the interface that handles the dialog between the users and the system. This interface strongly determines whether or not users will view the DSS as friendly and easy to use. Once the initial system was released for use, significant effort was needed to ensure that the data management routines were robust. Many of the analytical commands use APL functions from public libraries (see Section 6), especially those for statistical analysis.

Brooks draws attention to the "architecture" of a system. The command-based structure we used for ISSPA meets many of his recommendations:

1. It reflects a top-down approach, and the dialog manager is independent of the commands and data management routines.

FIGURE 7.4   ISSPA Architecture

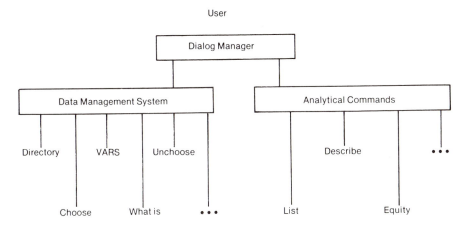

2. Each command is fully independent of other commands; a new one can be added to ISSPA with no change to the logic of the dialog manager or to any other command.

3. Our design methodology is a form of "stepwise refinement." We implemented an initial version of a routine and refined it on the basis of users' experiences and reactions.

Adaptive design assumes that such extensions will be added *as a direct result of system usage*. One cannot predict in advance exactly what will be needed. The early users of ISSPA in effect taught *us*.

4. THE DEVELOPMENT PROCESS

4.1. Introduction

This section briefly summarizes the sequence of the development process. Adaptive design is based on rules of thumb. We will present the rules as we proceed and then list them at the end of the narrative.

The initial system took roughly 70 hours of effort on the part of the programmer (Gambino). The analyst (Keen), in an ongoing research study, had spent six months studying the design and use of the computer models and information systems in state government agencies concerned with school finance policy making. The computer systems available to policy analysts in most states were cumbersome and very limited in scope. The analysts complained of the lack of system flexibility and of the unavailability of data. Generally, they were unable to get programs written to produce special reports; the data processing staff were unresponsive, overworked, or incompetent. A few states had useful interactive systems, but these were expensive ($200,000–$1,000,000).

The initial design aim for ISSPA was to show that a simple, general, flexible, and cheap DSS could be built that would meet the analysts' needs and would also facilitate better and more extensive exploration of policy issues (i.e., permit fundamental analysis of school finance issues). Limited funds were available for the initial system. From the start, however, ISSPA was intended to be a system product in Brooks's sense of the term. It was expected that there would be sufficient demand for such a system and that funds would be available for continued development.

The development fell into three distinct phases:

1. Phase 1: build the initial system, Version 0.

2. Phase 2: extend it, adding new commands and improving existing ones in response to *users' reactions*.

3. Phase 3: create the system product that is portable, stable, and documented.

Each phase posed different challenges and key issues.

4.2. Phase 1: Development of the Prototype

4.2.1. The First Meeting

At their first meeting, the analyst and the programmer began by sketching out the user-system dialog. The analyst had a clear idea of the initial set of user verbs to be supported. For example, it was obvious that analysts relied heavily on rankings. Often they would create a report listing expenditure figures; the district with the largest average revenues per pupil would be shown in the first row. This led to a command: RANK . . . BY.

The analyst presented the verbs, and the programmer suggested the exact dialog. The analyst responded to the recommendation; generally, it would be rejected if it seemed to be cumbersome or clumsy for a nontechnical, inexperienced user.

The meeting lasted three hours. There was a constant give-and-take between analyst and technician. A *general* dialog was agreed on but not made final. This dialog determined the nature of the data management routines. The team had started by focusing on the representation of the data; data had to appear to the user as a simple table of values. Each command had to operate directly on the table; no specific procedures were needed on the part of the user to get, manipulate, or update data.

It is worth noting that this approach was the opposite of standard systems analysis. Analyst and programmer began from the dialog and worked back to the inputs, leaving the procedures to be specified later. This reflects the view that what happens at the terminal determines the "quality" of the DSS; to the user, the interface *is* the system. Most programmers focus on defining the input data and then the procedures, leaving the outputs for later definition.

This strategy also allowed the programmer, who was completely unfamiliar with school finance, to learn a great deal quickly about the intended users. Many programmers have a naïve view of the user. Indeed, the "user" is often only an abstraction. From the start, all our design effort emphasized what the user would say and see. The "quality" of the DSS was defined in terms of ease of use, lucidity, and gracefulness. Far from being an abstraction, the user was included during development. The user became the guiding force within the development process.

This initial phase reflects a key and reliable rule of thumb:

Rule 1. Design the dialog *first*. Forget about input files, functional capabilities, etc.

    a. Define what the user says and sees at the terminal.

    b. Define the *representation* of the data: what the data look like to the user.

    c. Adopt a system model which closely matches the user's conceptual model.

4.2.2. Initial Commands

Keen (1980b) distinguishes between usefulness and usability in a DSS. Usefulness relates to the capabilities of the system: models, retrieval facilities, and report routines. Usability refers to the user-system dialog. Our first rule of thumb stresses usability. Obviously, though, the initial system has to contain something worth using.

The link between users' verbs and DSS commands is a key one for our design strategy (see Section 6). Understanding the users involves identifying their verbs. The verbs provide design criteria for the commands that constitute the useful components of ISSPA. We defined two types of commands:

1. *Generic* verbs

2. *Special-purpose* verbs

Generic verbs, the ones common to most problem-solving and analysis, are required in many DSS. For example, any task involving data analysis requires LIST, RANK, and HISTO(gram) commands. We identified a dozen generic commands, most of which could be provided with minimal programming.

Generic commands have been implemented in other systems. We chose to use APL partly because excellent public libraries are available on several computers. APL is a convenient language for borrowing routines; integrating them into a new program requires very little effort. The majority of statistical routines in ISSPA come from public libraries. We have found that from two to eight hours is required to modify, integrate, and test a routine from a library. Since it has already been at least partially (and in most cases entirely) debugged, we save much of the 9X of effort Brooks identifies. The main modifications needed in adding a function to ISSPA involve the user-system dialog. Many of the designers of APL programs show little sensitivity to the user (see Section 7).

Most special-purpose commands must be programmed. We identified well over 20 special-purpose verbs for policy analysis in general, and we found another 10 were needed for school finance. The generic verbs largely related to statistical techniques and measures; the school finance verbs related to measures of equity and to comparing and ranking school districts.

Examples of the various types of commands we identified for potential inclusion in the initial version are as follows:

1. Generic: LIST, RANK, DESCRIBE (descriptive statistics), HISTO(gram), DEFINE (new variable), FREQUENCIES, ADD (to) DATABASE.

2. Special-purpose:
   a. Policy analysis: SELECT UNITS, COUNTIF, BOTTOM, NTILES, GROUP, REGRESS, ANOVA
   b. School finance: EQUITY, (equity measures), GINI, LORENZ[5]

We put priorities on the commands. This was done informally and based on four criteria:

1. *Priority to the user* (i.e., the extent to which this command reflected a verb the analysts relied on or would immediately find useful)

2. *Ease of implementation* (HISTO and REGRESS could be taken directly from an APL public library)

3. *Clarity of user-DSS dialog* (With REGRESS, we could lay out in advance a simple complete dialog. We found it hard to do so for ANOVA—analysis of variance—and thus left that for a later version.)

4. *Likelihood of acceptance* (We avoided trying to force unfamiliar or contentious routines on the user; we could—and did—add them later.)

The focus on user verbs and the use of a command-based program structure were effective and simple techniques. Our ability to extend Version 0 from 12 to 50 commands directly resulted from these rules of thumb:

Rule 2. Identify the users' special-purpose verbs.

Rule 3. Identify generic verbs relevant to this DSS.

Rule 4. Translate the verbs into commands, and vice versa.

Rule 5. Check public libraries for off-the-shelf routines, especially for generic verbs.

Rule 6. Set priorities for implementing commands for Version 0.

Rule 7. Support first, extend later; aim at giving the users something they will readily accept, and add the less familiar, more complex capability later.

4.2.3. Version 0

A working system was available within 40 hours.[6] It contained the following user commands: LIST, DESCRIBE, RANK, TOP, BOTTOM, HISTO, REGRESSION, CORRELATE, and NTILES (e.g., 10NTILES = deciles, 4NTILES = quartiles). The regression, histogram, and correlation routines were taken from a public library. Version 0 included other commands needed to manage the user-system dialog or to improve the usability of the DSS (e.g., DIRECTORY, CHOOSE, and ENVIRONMENT).

When the preliminary system was ready, we spent substantial time (10 hours) improving what the users saw on the terminal. The major changes that needed to be made concerned the formats of the outputs. Whereas functional specifications involve laying out a report format in some detail, adaptive design is similar to the concept of stepwise refinement. Instead of asking users "What do you want?", we asked "How do you like this?"[7] We entirely redesigned the dialog and style of the outputs by playing with the system prior to showing it to potential users. After an additional 20 hours of programming effort, we had an operational system (70 hours in total) containing more than 30 commands. This was made available to a senior policy analyst and his assistant as part of a research grant. Over the next three months, as they worked with the system, we made many extensions and modifications (see Section 4.3.).

The first phase of development worked out well. Even at commercial rates for programming and computer time, we had spent under $4,000. We demonstrated the system in several states; instead of trying to sell an idea, we could show a complete working DSS. We kept careful track of the development process up to this stage; we wanted to check our experience with the general conclusions of Ness (1975), Courbon, Grajew, and Tolovi (1978),[8] and Grajew and Tolovi (1978). We agree with Grajew and Tolovi's estimate that the initial system, which will then evolve through usage, can be built for under $10,000 in less than 16 weeks (our experience was $4,000 in 2 weeks). This is an important point, since:

1. It reduces the users' risk and encourages experiment; a DSS becomes more of a research and development effort than a capital investment; and

2. The lead time between the initial proposal and a usable system is short enough that the users' enthusiasm and momentum are not dissipated.

Version 0 was simple but not simplistic. The analysts who saw it were impressed by how easy ISSPA is to use and by its power:

Rule 8. Deliver Version 0 quickly and cheaply. Keep it simple from the start; aim for a few useful commands for Version 0, and evolve a complex DSS out of simple components.

4.3. Phase 2: Soliciting User Reaction

In a sense, potential users of ISSPA were involved from the start. Keen and Clark's (1978; 1980) studies of school finance had included surveys and interviews with analysts, legislators, and administrators in 11 states. They discussed the idea of ISSPA with several experienced analysts who worked with Version 0 and played a major role in the evolution of ISSPA.[9]

We were extremely selective in looking for potential users. Since Version 0 was purposely only a beginning, not the final system, the skills and creativity of the early users would strongly influence the quality of the full system. Adaptive design *relies* on good users. Our first user was a widely-respected senior analyst in a large Midwestern state. He was impressed with ISSPA and, with the help of a subordinate who had some knowledge of computers, began using it after one demonstration. There was no user manual; although this led to occasional problems, ISSPA is largely self-explanatory.[10]

We wanted the initial users to react to ISSPA and to test it. We did not want them to have to debug it. Debugging means finding errors; testing, in our sense, means seeing how well the system works, deciding what needs to be changed or added, and, above all, giving a critique on the quality of the interface. Version 0 was *not* bug-free. We had left the complex issue of data management until last. We had carefully designed the *representation* of the data—how the data looked to the user. As we built the data management routines, we introduced errors; what worked on Monday failed for no apparent reason on Tuesday. In retrospect, we should not have released Version 0 until we had implemented a reasonably complete initial version of these routines. Some users get very unhappy very quickly with an unstable system. However, they are very tolerant of errors in the first release of a new command.

As we expected, we learned much from the early users. One example is instructive. NTILES is a command that identifies the cutpoints that break the distribution of values into equal groups (e.g., 5NTILES REVENUES lists quintiles, 10NTILES lists deciles). This was an obvious command to include in Version 0, since in school finance court cases and legislative reports, a frequent comparison is made between, say, the top 10% and the bottom 10% of school districts. We assumed that the NTILES command would be seen by analysts as helpful, but not unusual. In fact, NTILES was enough in itself to sell the merits of ISSPA. In most states, calculations of deciles were done by hand. SPSS, the standard statistical package analysts use, does *not* allow observations to be reordered (required as part of computing a quantile). In several states, we found instances where COBOL programs had been written to print the 2%, 5%, 10%, 25%, 33%, . . . 95%, and 98% intervals for a distribution, but only for specified variables. The idea that such programs could be generalized and on-line access could be provided came as a surprise to many analysts.

Once the analysts had access to a general routine like NTILES, they used it in new ways and developed new ideas from it. For example, the early users requested and received a WTILES command, which adds an equity measure to the simple deciles or quintiles NTILES provides (WTILES stands for Weighted NTILES). It allows the analyst to answer such questions as "What are the 1978 expenditures for the bottom 10% and bottom 90% of the *students* in the state?" The analyst who defined WTILES used it as the basis for a major report on school finance equity, and he felt that the analysis would not have been practical previously.

The sequence of events summarized above occurred several other times. The general pattern was as follows:

1. The data processing department had provided a specific solution to a specific problem.

2. We identified the *general* verb relevant to the problem.

3. We provided a flexible command.

4. Use of the command stimulated a distinctive new idea or approach.

5. We added the resulting *user-defined* command to ISSPA.

We strongly feel that this pattern is a central aspect of DSS development. Keen (1980a) studied over 20 published case descriptions of DSS and concluded that in many instances the most effective uses of the systems not only were entirely different from the intended ones but also could not have been predicted beforehand (see Section 5). Revision and evolution of system commands are a natural outcome of adaptive design.

More than once early users used ISSPA in ways which were completely unanticipated. Several times the system builder was amazed at the analyses performed using his system. One time he admitted that he would have stated ISSPA could not be used to perform a certain analysis had the user consulted with him in advance. This was a case of the system builder learning from the system user.

Only skilled users can learn to use a tool in new ways. Throughout the second phase of the development of ISSPA, we found the users' role to be central; we had not anticipated their importance in testing. At one stage we had users in five separate states. One of them was of immense value to us; one was close to a disaster. We feel sure that the experience provides a general lesson to DSS builders. Adaptive design provides a working system quickly. *The designer realizes that there will be many things wrong with it and gains immensely from the users' reactions.* If the users are not highly skilled in their own jobs and not actively motivated to use the DSS, advanced imaginative use does not take place, and the designer does not get essential feedback. We paraphrase an old saying to express the importance of a good user: The system and a good user are greater than the sum of their parts.

A "working" system is one that has no *obvious* bugs. *!39VW or SYNTAX ERROR is clearly a bug, but getting a value of $210 instead of the correct $160 is a more subtle error. Because a DSS is intentionally a flexible tool, operated under the user's control, it does not have a set of "correct" inputs, procedures, and outputs. Even in a standard data processing application, it is impossible to test all combinations. Flexibility, generality, *ad hoc* uses, and the variety of inputs, commands, and outputs compound the problem. Only a good user can alleviate it. User A (the good one) provided invaluable feedback. User Z either did not recognize errors or simply complained that "something's wrong"; the credibility of ISSPA suffered as a result. In several instances, legislators were given incorrect reports. The errors were subtle, and only an expert on school finance could spot them. User Z was, reasonably enough, very bothered when errors were revealed but did little to uncover or cure them. User A sought them out.

What we learned from all this was that a distinguishing aspect of DSS development is that it is user-dependent. This leads us to another rule:

Rule 9. Pick a good user. Look for someone who:
   a. Has substantial knowledge of the task the DSS supports,
   b. Has intellectual drive and curiosity,
   c. Will take the initiative in testing and in evolving Version 0, and
   d. Enjoys being an innovator.[11]

During this second phase of development, ISSPA grew in scope and sophistication. Very few commands were left unchanged; many of the improvements were minor enhancements in formatting or ease of use.

4.4. Phase 3: Building a System Product

Phase 3 involved converting ISSPA from a system to a product. Users were now *buying* a DSS. We had to provide technical support, documentation, and training. We were increasingly concerned with costs. APL programs can be expensive to run. We had expected ISSPA to cost $50 an hour on the excellent system we were using. The actual figure was closer to $200 an hour. We found that APL penalizes careless programming very heavily indeed. Unfortunately, however, when we improved the efficiency of the programs, users were able to do more work in a given time, so that our cost per hour *increased*. We hired a group of APL experts who were sure they could halve the cost per hour. They were unable to do so. The revised system, rewritten for CPU efficiency, ran at a 5% premium compared to the original system. From this we could conclude that an inspection of the APL code gives little idea of the computer time needed to run a program.

Efforts to use desk-top and mini-computers to reduce costs were amusing but ineffectual. With an IBM 5100, run time went from seconds to hours. Even with an HP-3000, we reduced costs by a factor of 5 and increased response time by a factor of 20. Every improvement in the cost-effectiveness of hardware improves DSS capability. However, current technology is still inadequate for providing fast *and* cheap *and* easily developed *and* flexible systems.

Whereas in Phase 1 we were concerned with the *process* of developing a DSS, in Phase 3 we had to shift our attention to the system product. The transition is expensive. Over a four-month period, we added few new user commands but spent almost 600 hours on programming. The effort went into:

1. Improved data management routines,

2. Overlaying functions to reduce cost,

3. System commands, such as:
   a. SESSION COST (How much have I spent so far?),
   b. WHAT IS Vxxx (What is the label for Vxxx?),

4. New commands demanded and often defined by users (it is worth noting that in most cases the commands represented *new* ideas and approaches stimulated by ISSPA), and

5. User documentation, including a comprehensive manual.

As we expected, data and data management became a key issue. Policy analysis generally involves both operational data (such as historical figures on expenditures, program levels, and budgets) and planning data (often not available from routine sources). We deliberately limited the data management capabilities in ISSPA, and we required users to overcome this barrier to entry. If a state lacks capability in data collection or if reliable, current historical data are not available, it makes no sense to provide an interactive DSS to process bad data more quickly and in more detail. We learned another useful lesson: Assume the data do not exist, no matter what the data processing people tell you.

Creating an ISSPA data base is technically very simple. Even so, we encountered a variety of irritating minor problems, many of them procedural ones. Even with operational data taken directly from computer tapes, there is some manual link needed. We had to provide a variety of facilities for error checking, updating, correcting, and adding to the data base. Obviously, a generalized data base management system (DBMS) would have helped, especially by reducing the manual work required. However, it was, and still is, an infeasible option for this application area. DBMS requires a maturation in the use of computers, a financial investment, and a level of technical competence that state governments (and, in our experience, many mid-sized private businesses) lack.

We found that most of the complicated programming for ISSPA went into minor functions for data management. Moreover, in this area we were unable to provide the same responsive service to users that we featured for ISSPA commands. If a user wanted a special analytic routine, we could provide it overnight. Whenever there were problems with a user command, the difficulty was invariably localized and therefore easy to resolve. A disadvantage of having data management be "invisible" to the users was that, when an error occurred, they had no idea what was going on—and at times, neither did we. The error often affected several user commands. None of our problems were complex or hard to resolve, but we increasingly found that:

1. Programming effort was diverted from user commands to system functions.

2. Processing time and inefficiencies increased as we tackled data management issues; for example, we often had to keep track of several duplicate copies of matrices in the workspace.

3. Our simple data structure in matrix form (from the user's view) and vector form (the physical structure) was still the best solution.

The dilemma for DSS design is that, since uses are varied and unpredictable (Section 5), there is no optimal physical or logical structure. The complex data management procedures which we required greatly added to system overhead.

The whole issue of data management in DSS is a complex one, and we could find little help that translated into reliable rules of thumb. Carlson *et al.* (1974) describe a methodology for data extraction that is powerful but expensive (see also Methlie, 1980). In general, techniques for *ad hoc* modeling are far ahead of those for *ad hoc* data management, especially with large data bases. In Gerrity's Portfolio Management System (1970) and GADS, a DSS developed at the IBM Research Laboratory (Carlson *et al.*, 1974), most of the programming effort and computing resources were needed for data extraction—pulling from a large permanent data base the relatively small subset of variables manipulated by a given user command. We could not have afforded such overhead; the price we paid was an imbalance between the responsiveness, low cost, and flexibility of our analytic commands on the one hand and the limited, slightly cumbersome nature of our data management routines on the other hand.

Rule 10. Recognize that data management, rather than commands (or models), is a binding constraint on DSS development.
   a. Choose as simple a representation as possible (e.g., a matrix).
   b. Avoid complex data extraction and manipulation.

Some may argue that Rule 10 is highly context-specific. Support for Rule 10 can be found in the DSS literature. Ness (1975) advises against early development of a strong link between the DSS and the data base used in the transaction processing system. During the initial stages of the DSS, let the data be passed in a loose, *ad hoc* manner (e.g., collect data from pieces of paper, monthly reports, statistical fact books, or one-time transaction programming projects). Get the DSS operating, establish its value, and, if justified, make the required investment to define and develop the DSS/DB link.

4.5. Conclusion

ISSPA is now (early 1980) a commercial product. It has to compete in a market that is very cost-conscious. Users also expect instant service. Whereas at the end of Phase 1 we were ready to write a paper on the mythical man-month defeated, now we are not so sure. APL, the middle-out strategy, and a command-driven architecture provide immensely powerful techniques for developing a DSS. However, extending a working system into a system product is a complex process with many hidden costs. For example, there is no quick or cheap way to produce a good user's manual. In Phase 1 we were able to "sell" the system through explanation and hands-on experiment because we were *personally* credible with our users. By Phase 3, the manual was needed to establish the credibility of ISSPA at those locations where we could not personally be present.

The following is a list of our ten rules of thumb for building DSS, with two more added:

1. Design the *dialog* first.
    a. Define *what the user says and sees.*
    b. Define the *representation of data.*
    c. Adopt a system model which matches the user's conceptual model.

2. Identify the user's *special-purpose verbs.*

3. Identify *generic verbs* relevant to this DSS.

4. Translate the *verbs into commands*, and vice versa.

5. Check *public libraries* for off-the-shelf routines.

6. Set priorities for implementing *commands for Version 0.*

7. *Support first, extend later.*

8. Deliver Version 0 *quickly* and *cheaply.*
    a. Evolve a complex DSS out of a simple Version 0.
    b. Version 0 is intended to establish value and to sell itself.

9. Pick a *good user* who:
    a. Has substantial *knowledge* of the task,
    b. Has intellectual drive and *curiosity*,
    c. Will take the *initiative* in testing and in evolving Version 0, and
    d. Enjoys being an *innovator.*

10. Recognize *data management*, rather than commands, *as a main constraint.*

11. Remember that Brooks is *right*—programming *is* 10% of the effort.

12. *Know your user* at all times.

Rule 11 may be restated in several ways:

1. Programming is 10% of the effort.

2. If you want to build a product that will stand by itself, recognize the time and effort needed.

3. Version 0 can be built in weeks.

Rule 12 reflects the whole logic of adaptive design. Of all the techniques for applying computer-based models and information systems to complex decision processes, DSS involve the most attention to the user as a real person. At every single step in the development of ISSPA, our success depended on:

1. Supporting a person, not solving a problem or building a model,

2. Getting feedback from analysts' direct use of the DSS, and

3. Responding to users' ideas and requests.

5. PRINCIPLES OF ADAPTIVE DESIGN

5.1. Introduction

A recurrent theme in DSS research is user learning (see Keen 1980a). A DSS does not solve problems; it lets individuals exploit their own skills in problem solving. The obvious stategy for DSS design is to support first and extend later. The initial system must be close enough, in terms of commands and mode of dialog, to the users' current procedures to be both attractive and easy to use. Clearly, however, if the DSS is to stimulate changes in the decision process, user learning has to occur.

Keen and Wagner (1979) draw attention to a consistent finding in DSS case studies—the unpredictability of system uses. The actual uses of a DSS are frequently entirely different from the intended ones. For example, Gerrity's Portfolio Management System, intended to support the investment decision, became instead a valuable aid for marketing and for communicating with customers. Often, the most innovative and valued uses of a DSS could not have been anticipated by the designer.

Keen (1980a) summarizes this process in a framework that views a DSS as an adaptive development strategy applicable only to situations where the "final" system cannot be predefined. This has substantial implications for the choice of a design architecture and an implementation strategy. The DSS must evolve through the interactions of user, system, and designer. Figure 7.5 shows these adaptive influences schematically. This conceptual framework was developed partly from a review of DSS research and case studies and partly through the process of developing ISSPA. It translates into some very specific design criteria and techniques. Most importantly, it shows user learning as a direct outcome of DSS usage and a contributor to it. The explicit reason for building ISSPA was to help improve policy analysis; learning was viewed as the central issue for design and usage.

5.2. The Cognitive Loop

Each arrow in Fig. 7.5 indicates an adaptive influence. System⟶User, for example, indicates that the DSS stimulates changes in the user's problem-solving process. If an interactive system does not require or aim at such user learning, then the label DSS is superfluous. Keen argues that it is meaningful to label a

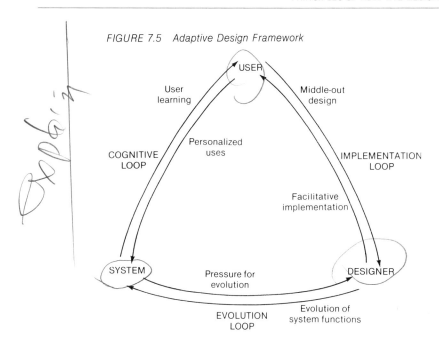

FIGURE 7.5   *Adaptive Design Framework*

system a DSS only if doing so leads designers to a different development strategy than would otherwise have been chosen. Situations where a system cannot be predefined and used independently of the choices and judgments of the user, and where it will be extended and modified, require a distinctive development process in which learning, adaptation, and evolution are central.

The interactions between the user and the system directly relate to learning. The DSS is intended to stimulate changes in user thinking; at the same time, it must be flexible enough to adapt to the user as these changes occur. New tools must shape new uses, *and vice versa*. As users develop a new approach to problem solving, they must not be constrained by the previous one. If a system follows a rigid sequence of routines, learning is blocked. The User→System link thus relies on a design architecture that permits personalized use; without it, any learning stimulated by the DSS cannot be exploited.

Keen (1980a) terms these links the cognitive loop.

5.3. The Implementation Loop

The implementation loop refers to the relationship between the designer and the user. Ness (1975) defined a key aspect of adaptive design—"middle-out" development. This is in contrast to top-down or bottom-up approaches, and it relies heavily on fast development and prototyping. Middle-out design provides a means for the *designer* to learn from the *user* (User→Designer). Although the concept of adaptive design is somewhat broader than that of middle-out design, the latter is at the core of the former.

The implementation process requires a facilitative strategy on the part of the designer (Designer→User). A DSS is not an off-the-shelf product. Building it requires close involvement with the user. Several researchers have commented on the need for an intermediary (Keen 1975) or integrating agent (Bennett 1976) who can act as a crusader, teacher, and even confidant. Adaptive design is a joint venture between user and designer. Each needs to respect and understand the other. The designer's job goes well beyond traditional systems analysis and functional specifications. The designer needs to:

1. Understand the task and user,

2. Be able to humanize and even customize the system, and

3. Be responsive to the user and help stimulate exploration and learning.

In most instances of successful DSS development, the system is associated with a skilled intermediary/implementer. The DSS is as much a service as a product.

5.4. The Evolution Loop

The evolution loop relates to the process by which learning, personalized use, middle-out design, and facilitative implementation combine to make the initial system obsolete and its evolution essential. This is shown in Fig. 7.5 as an adaptive link from system to designer. Evolving the system means adding new commands (Designer→System). Knowing when and how to evolve it requires keeping track of user and usage (System→Designer).

The main value of the command-based architecture used in ISSPA is that APL makes it easy to add new commands. The DSS designer has to *plan* for evolution. Since many of the new commands will be user-defined, they may be very different from the preceding ones. Obviously, however complex or esoteric they may be, it is essential that new commands only involve adding independent modules to the system; they must not require a fundamental restructuring of it. Brooks (1975, p. 6) describes the need for "conceptual integrity" in the architecture of a system:

> The purpose of a programming system is to make a computer easy to use. . . . Because ease of use is the purpose, the ratio of function to conceptual complexity is the ultimate test of good system design. . . . For a given level of function, however, that system is best in which one can specify things with the most simplicity and straightforwardness.

Evolving a DSS is contingent on conceptual integrity. The command-based, top-down structure of ISSPA provides for this. A major postulate of the adaptive design framework is that a DSS is a vehicle for user learning and, hence, that evolution is inevitable and essential.

Knowing when and how to evovle the DSS is often difficult. In the initial stages of development, there is usually close and direct contact between designer and user. Later, however, the designer needs a more formal methodology for tracking usage. The obvious one is a data trap, which records, with users' permission, each command they invoke. These records may be analyzed in terms of the mode of use, the reliance on individual commands, and the stringing together of commands into distinct sequences or sentences. A data trap can provide a wealth of information to the designer. However, there is no easy way of interpreting it. Stabell (1974) and Andreoli and Steadman (1975) do provide one approach, which was used to evaluate Gerrity's Portfolio Management System.

5.5. Adaptive Design in ISSPA

The descriptive mapping of the ISSPA users' decision process was done by Keen and Clark (1978), with a view toward defining ways to improve analytic capability in school finance policy analysis. It was clear that analysts most want, and know how to use, simple, reliable data. Whereas in statistical analysis the focus is on medians, averages, and correlations, in policy analysis additional concerns are with measures of range and variance and with outliers. For example, policy analysts often need to look at extremes, such as the lowest and highest 10% of districts in terms of tax revenue per pupil. Their usual role is to explain issues to legislators and to respond very quickly to legislative requests for analysis.

Descriptive mapping identifies the key issues in making a DSS usable. The prescriptive map defines how to make it more *useful*. Our analysis was similar to Gerrity's (1970) and Stabell's (1974) assessment of the Portfolio Management System. We found that the analysts had fairly simple concepts of policy analysis and relied on only a few techniques, especially ranking and linear regression. The descriptive map for a DSS focuses on how people carry out a task. The prescriptive map looks at the task itself. Gerrity found a lack of analytic concepts among portfolio managers. There is a rich body of financial theory relevant to their job, but they do not use it. They do not base their decisions on analyses of their customers' portfolios; they think in terms of individual stocks, ignoring issues of risk-return trade-offs. The school finance analysts similarly ignore policy research; they think incrementally and rarely go beyond the discussion of the bottom line. They focus on very few overall policy issues. Gerrity built the Portfolio Management System to support the existing process and to move users toward a more analytic one. Stabell found that the intended change did not occur and argued that not enough attention was paid to *how* to stimulate learning.

In an effort to enhance the quality of school finance policy analysis performed with the support of ISSPA, we added several new commands specific to school finances. For example, EQUITY (see Fig. 7.6) provides 11 measures of the equity of an existing or proposed state aid plan. It is derived from a research paper by Berne and Steifel (1979) which has had substantial influence on school finance policy research but little on policy making. Whereas the initial commands sup-

FIGURE 7.6   The EQUITY Command

```
COMMAND: WHAT IS REVPUPIL79

A5    REVPUPIL79    TOTAL REVENUE (ALL SOURCES) 1979

COMMAND: EQUITY REVPUPIL79 BY TOTENRL79
STATISTICS ('ALL','STOP'):?  ALL
ENTER PERCENT FOR 'PERCENT MEAN' CALCULATION:?  50
ENTER 'E' VALUE FOR 'ATKINSON'S INDEX' CALCULATION?  .5
.PP.


                            REVENUE
                            PER PUPIL
                              1979
                            ----------
NO. OBS. (N)                        25
RANGE                          2,566.
RESTRICTED RANGE                 976.
FED RANGE RATIO                0.780
REL. MEAN DEV.                 0.166
PERMISSIBLE VAR.               0.939
WEIGHTED VAR.               126,074.
COEF. OF VAR.                  0.226
STD. DEV. OF LOGS            355.070
GINI COEF.                     0.109
PCT. MEAN                       99.0
ATKINSON'S IND.               0.989

COMMAND:
```

ported analysts' existing processes, EQUITY was specifically intended to support new *analyses*.

Keen and Clark (1980) identified as major shortcomings in existing policy analysis a lack of any real focus on strategic issues, long-term forecasting, and conceptual models. Berne's research on equity measures was too far from most analysts' experience and interests for them to apply it unaided. By embedding the easy-to-use EQUITY command in ISSPA, we could encourage analysts to adopt a broader approach to policy issues. We explicitly viewed ISSPA as a way of bringing policy research to policy making. We did not force analysts to use EQUITY. It is one of many resources available in the DSS. Since it involves typing a single phrase, there is minimal effort involved in trying it out. Keen (1980b) argues that a DSS often provides a way of making useful models usable. We took Berne and

Steifel's 11 measures—the useful component—and made them accessible. Once we had a complete and stable system, more and more of our effort went into commands like EQUITY, which extend rather than support the user.

Three additional commands (BOXPLOT, STEMLEAF, and CONDENSE) were taken from Tukey's (1977) Exploratory Data Analysis (EDA).[12] They required very little programming effort.[13] Some of our users are unaware of their existence; they are an unobtrusive method for stimulating learning. Rule 7 stated that the DSS builder should support first, extend later. For a DSS to be more than a convenience, it obviously must go beyond LIST, RANK, DESCRIBE, etc. At the same time, unfamiliar concepts and routines must be presented in a simple way. We did not define an EQUITY *model* or an EDA *package*. The verb-based architecture provided an easy bridge between usefulness and usability.

Clearly, it is unlikely that analysts subject to organizational traditions and pressures of day-to-day operations will spontaneously adopt these new approaches. We needed some leverage point, and we decided that the key to stimulating learning is to find a really good user. Our assumption, backed up by findings from DSS case studies, was that skilled users, helped perhaps by capable intermediaries (Designer→User in Fig. 7.5), will explore the DSS, find personal ways of using it (User→System), provide the design team with insights and challenges (User——→Designer), and respond to recommendations and training (Designer→User). In this way, users themselves help the system evolve.

We viewed ISSPA specifically as a vehicle for stimulating user learning. We expected that:

1. Initially users would rely on fairly simple commands, reflecting simple user verbs.

2. As they used the DSS and found it valuable, they would string commands together into sentences representing their own methodology for analysis. Once this occurred, we would need to provide for modeling.

3. They would then ask for extensions to existing commands, define new ones, and be ready to try out ones such as EQUITY.

The principles of adaptive design indicated that for this sequence to occur (as it did), we had to ensure that the development process allowed all of the adaptive links to operate:

1. For the cognitive loop:
   a. The interface and dialog were designed to be communicative, responsive, and easy to use. The commands were made directly relevant to the existing process so as to facilitate use and learning (System→User). (We have no formal measures of the quality of these features of the interface; the number of user errors, as revealed by the data trap, and user comments are reasonably adequate for us as indicators.)
   b. The DSS was command-based with minimal constrictions on mode and sequence of use to allow personalized, innovative use (User→System).

2. For the implementation loop:
    a. Middle-out design relied on APL to permit responsive service (User→ Designer).
    b. We required close contact with users, either by one member of the development team or by a technical intermediary from within the user organization who had good knowledge of school finance (Designer→User).

3. For the evolution loop:
    a. A data trap monitored how individual users worked with ISSPA.
    b. New commands were added, especially in response to user requests and ideas (Designer→System).

The weakest aspect of our efforts to apply this adaptive development strategy was in the implementation loop. We frequently did not provide adequate facilitation (Designer→User). Users need "hand holding," not because they are stupid or scared of the system, but because the adaptive links, especially the cognitive loop, *consistently strain the existing system*. There is a continuous state of flux. Users who have been effective for months may move to more complex analysis using the same commands, or they may want to try new ones. The designer has to remain in the loop, and the middle-out process has to continue. We frequently received phone calls from users about new needs, asking for very small adjustments to the DSS. Failure to respond in such situations blocks learning or interrupts the users' efforts to adapt the system to their own problem solving.

We found that personalized usage is, as we expected, the rule and not the exception. Every ISSPA user has an individual style. Some are very visually oriented and rely on graphics rather than tables, and some continuously define new variables, for example:

$$(V101 + V207)/V371 = \text{number of special education students}$$
$$\text{per full-time teacher}$$

Some use ISSPA as a report generator, others as a means for model building. Some are systematic, and others are more divergent in their problem solving. Almost invariably, dissatisfaction with ISSPA comes from a failure to respond to a user's need for an individualized system.

The good users quickly identified new commands they wanted. These commands could not have been defined in advance. We spent substantial time when the initial version was released getting a "wish list" from the first users. However, it was the actual use of the DSS that stimulated demands and specifications.

The success of ISSPA has depended on supporting the cognitive loop and evolving the DSS. We anticipated this, and we conclude that DSS designers should, as we did:

1. Design the dialog first and ensure that it provides an immediately usable, flexible, and responsive system;

2. Think in terms of verbs and commands; and

3. Present users with a simple, clear data representation.

6. COMMAND-BASED DSS AND USER VERBS

The suggestion to focus on verbs and commands is contentious and conflicts with the recommendations of several DSS researchers. Bennett (Chapter 3 of this book), for example, demonstrates the value of a menu-driven approach for interactive graphics. It is easier for users to be reminded of what they can choose than to have to specify it. A menu design minimizes the need for prior knowledge and provides familiar and recognizable options. Artman (1980) shows how a DSS architecture can combine the merits of the menu representation and command flexibility, using an APL-based menu generator developed by Sigle and Howland (1979).

Our choice of a command-driven system was based on both behavioral and technical considerations:

1. Given our concern for stimulating learning and, hence, the use of new analytic methods, we wanted the design structure to be directly related to the users' way of thinking.

2. If the DSS is a collection of discrete, independent functions, APL can be used to great advantage.

    A new function in ISSPA is defined by the user in terms of:

    VERB: NOUN(S): MODIFIER   (For example, RANK V401, V509 by V101)

The verbs are APL functions, and the nouns are data items. There is a minimal amount of translation from the user's concept to the technical implementation. Users understand the idea of commands; specification of commands is bounded by the use of verbs, even though the verbs may not define exact calculations and output formats.

This approach is ideally suited to middle-out design. The designer and user sketch out the dialog, and the designer produces a first cut that can be quickly modified in response to the user's reactions.

Within a command, we use a structured dialog or menu to handle suboptions. The first version of CORRELATE thus asked:

DO YOU WANT PARTIAL CORRELATIONS?
WHICH VARIABLE DO YOU WANT TO CONTROL FOR?

We later broke this into two commands: CORRELATE and PARTIALCORR. The original CORRELATE command contained codes to generate both a matrix of correlation coefficients and selected partial correlations. Thus CORRELATE was really two separate "do somethings." Much of the dialog was clumsy and redundant. The main reason for using the original design was that the function could be taken directly from the public library. However, we have consistently found that APL programmers—and perhaps most programmers—seem to pay very little attention to the connection between the user's way of thinking and the logic of the program. The dialog is often cumbersome, and output formats are visually cluttered and hard to follow. When integrating any function from a public library

FIGURE 7.7 An Example of the User Dialog Provided by
a Typical APL Program

```
        MREG
ENTER REGRESSION PARAMETERS?
YES
ENTER NUMBER OF VARIATES.
0:
      3
ENTER NUMBER OF CASES.
0:
      10
ENTER DATA,ONE CASE AT A TIME.
CASE 1
0:
     23 10 7
CASE 2

     . . .
CASE 10
0:
      19  6  3

      . . .
LIST DATA?
NO
MORE?
YES
STATISTICS?
YES

VARIABLE     AVERAGE         VARIANCE         STAND.
1              17         30.22222        5.49747
2               6          5.11111        2.26078
3               4          2.44444        1.56347

ENTER TITLE.
TYPICAL USER INTERFACE FOUND IN APL LIBRARIES.
ENTER INDEPENDENT VARIABLES.
0:
      2 3
ENTER DEPENDENT VARIABLE.
0:
      1
STEPWISE?
YES

   TYPICAL USER INTERFACE FOUND IN APL LIBRARIES.

INDEPENDENT VARIABLES 2 3
DEPENDENT VARIABLE     1

STEPWISE

VAR.          COEFF.    ST. ERROR     T-VALUE
     ATION
  2          2.49117   0.70289       3.54
        83.15
  3        ⁻0.46643    1.01638     ⁻0.46
        0.49
A=3.91873

REGRESSION
  DEGREES OF FREEDOM   2
  SUM OF SQUARES       227.51237
  MEAN SQUARE          113.75618

ERROR
  DEGREES OF FREEDOM   7
  SUM OF SQUARES       44.48763
  MEAN SQUARE          6.35538

R-SQUARED             83.64
S.E. OF ESTIMATE      2.52099
F-VALUE               17.9
```

into ISSPA, we generally had to do very little to the logic, but we did have to tidy up the dialog. For example, the FREQUENCIES command took 2 hours to integrate and check out, but we spent almost 20 hours redesigning the dialog. Judging from the functions found in public libraries, many programmers seem to have little sense of aesthetics.

Figure 7.7 illustrates the kind and quality of user interfaces found in APL libraries. This composite example shows aspects not well suited to managers' needs. We note the use of artificial, technical terminology (e.g., parameters and variates). The output table is not self-explanatory, the abbreviations seem unnecessary, and the spacing is poor. The presentation is computer-oriented, not reader-oriented. Readers would expect to see the variables named Consumer Expenditures for 1975, Disposable Income for 1975, and Size of Family—not 1, 2, and 3. Finally, the entire DSS is designed around a question-and-answer dialog rather than a command dialog. This imposes a particular analytical structure upon the user that may not match the user's decision-process structure.

Our ideas on verbs and commands were influenced by Blanning (1979) and Contreras and Skertchly (1978). Blanning takes a linguistic approach to DSS design and aims toward a generative grammar. Contreras and Skertchly, following Berry (1977), show how APL allows levels of language that permit a rich English-like dialog to be built up from very simple building blocks. Keen and Wagner (1979) describe IFPS, a FORTRAN-based end-user planning language, well suited to DSS development.[14] IFPS is not command-based, but reflects a focus on specifications being given to the system via a simple syntax based on command/verbs, nouns, and adverbs. This syntax seems to correspond to something in the user's head. Examples are as follows:

1. From Contreras and Skertchly (1978):

   DEFINE 'RESULTS' AS (PRICE × SALES) − (COST × INVENTORY)
   COMPUTE RESULTS
   DISPLAY MEDIAN PROFIT
   COUNT DEMAND > AVERAGE DEMAND

   (DEFINE, AVERAGE, COMPUTE, DISPLAY, and MEDIAN are APL functions.)

2. From IFPS:

   COLUMNS 4
   SALES 109, 115, 1.03 * PREVIOUS SALES
                        .
                        .
                        .
   WHAT IF SALES 110, 116, 1.05 * PREVIOUS SALES

3. From ISSPA:

    DESCRIBE TOTENRL78; AVERAGE; MEDIAN; STOP[15]
    DISPLAY V101 FOR DISTRICTS
    SELECTIF COUNTY = 2

The ISSPA sentences are less rich than the sentences in the other systems. However, this building-block approach is easily extended. The initial version of ISSPA was a simple set of commands. Noise words (e.g., FOR) and adverbial modifiers (e.g., CROSSTAB . . . BY and DISPLAY . . . PER) were added to make the sentences easier to read.

More recently, Gambino has extended the command syntax and developed an ISSPA planning language which provides a model-building capability. Interactive Modeling and Planning System (IMPS) has grown directly out of ISSPA. A DSS for learning and adaptive development in effect provides an end-user *language*, and the verb-based structure is an elementary pidgin-English. Blanning's (1979) richer linguistic formalization and Contreras and Skertchly's (1978) use of APL are a natural extension of our simpler approach.

7. APL AND THE MYTHICAL MAN-MONTH

The preceding two sections discuss aspects of program design rather than programming. DSS do not involve any distinctive technology; they use FORTRAN, APL, display terminals, standard data management concepts, etc., and are frequently small in scale. They imply, however, a particular programming style. The fact that many DSS designers advocate the use of APL reflects their concern for:

1. Fast delivery of the system,

2. The ability to restructure the DSS on short notice,

3. Direct and responsive service to users, and

4. Reducing the fixed costs of program development and making it a marginal cost venture.

The first three of these points follow from the principles of adaptive design. Middle-out design, in particular, relies on fast delivery and fast modifications; all momentum and credibility are lost if users have to wait a month for a response. Case studies of DSS, such as those found in Alter (1980), emphasize these issues, particularly the importance of having a prototype system available at a low cost to demonstrate the feasibility and value of the DSS. Quite often these prototypes are "bootlegged"; the design team spends one or two weeks rushing to get a system up while management is still discussing the business problem and management options. Low cost is essential in such a situation. Management clearly is unlikely to approve a $50,000 investment to try out the designers' ideas; the prototype is after all only a first cut, a hypothesis, and an experiment.

One of the major blockages to the application of computer technology to management decision making over the past decade has surely been the high fixed costs of programming. Data processing departments cannot respond to *ad hoc* requests for small reports or simple analyses. Any COBOL program is likely to take a month to write and test, even when the logic is simple. Similarly, changes to an existing program are surprisingly expensive (surprising to the client, that is). Often they are not even feasible, because they require major changes to the existing program structure.

The cost function for program development is basically as follows:

$$\text{Cost} = F + (PH \times PR) + (MH \times MR) + (UH \times UR)$$

where:

1. F is the fixed cost of logic design, housekeeping, and system set-up (e.g., job control language and ENVIRONMENT DIVISION statements in COBOL); this is basically independent of the application.

2. PH is number of programmer hours, and PR is the cost per hour.

3. MH and MR are the machine hours (for testing and trial use) and cost per hour.

4. UH and UR are the user's time and user's cost per hour.

In traditional data processing applications, F is high, and the costs for machine time and user time are relatively low. The programmer cost per hour for COBOL is also low in relation to the cost for really outstanding programmers working in a marketing staff unit or as consultants. PH is generally high.

The costs are very different in DSS applications. PR is high for the following reasons:

1. Middle-out design and descriptive and prescriptive mapping require an understanding of the decision-making context. The designer has to be able to relate well to and interact with relatively senior managers and professionals; the average systems analyst or COBOL programmer lacks the training or interest for this.

2. If a system is to be built quickly, the programmer has to be far more productive than the average data processing professional.

3. The importance of a clear program architecture, a flexible structure, functional generality, and a responsive interface requires that the programmer have experience with on-line applications and have strong skills in programming techniques. Much of the adaptive development strategy is similar to top-down design, structured programming, and stepwise refinement. These tools for improving software productivity are not easy to learn; *EDP Analyzer* reports that programmers need to be "converted . . . and very likely they will resist the new techniques at first."[16]

If *PR* is high, *PH* needs to be low. Moreover, DSS development requires users to be directly involved. Grajew and Tolovi (1978) found that the number of hours required—using a middle-out approach—is not high (less than 50 hours spread over 16 weeks); but, whereas "users" in data processing applications are generally junior- to middle-level clerical personnel and supervisors, DSS users are higher-paid managers or professionals, who have little time available. Reducing *PH* helps reduce *UH*.

The attractiveness of APL for many designers follows from the trade-offs it allows among components of the cost function. The fixed cost *F* is negligible, particularly if a command-based structure is used; in general, one can "breadboard" a system and get started quickly. APL relieves the programmer of set-up charges such as dimensioning arrays and declaring variable types of data names. *PH* is dramatically reduced; a given piece of program logic can be coded in about one-tenth of the time required with FORTRAN. The language is compact; 1 APL line is equivalent to 6–15 lines of FORTRAN. With APL, the cost function becomes the following:

low fixed cost (*F*) + low programmer hours
(*PH*) × high programmer cost per hour (*PR*)
+ *high machine cost* (*MH* × *MR*) + relatively high user costs (*UH* × *UR*)

If delivery time is a key factor, then obviously users will be ready to pay a premium in terms of *PR* to reduce *PH*.

With APL, one must accept relatively high machine costs per hour for several reasons:

1. APL is an interpretive language.

2. An interactive system must provide good response time. This is often possible only through use of a high-quality, expensive, time-shared system, especially if, as with ISSPA, the program performs operations on large matrices.

3. A good user can do a great deal of work in an hour with a well-designed DSS.

Cheap APL services are available. Too often, however, they are unreliable and overloaded. High-quality service is not cheap.

It is extremely unlikely that we could have built the initial version of ISSPA without APL. Middle-out design implies a fairly continuous cycle:

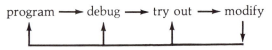

While the process is inefficient in terms of machine usage, with middle-out design every day counts. Much of the interaction between designer and user involves trying out ideas at the terminal. In several instances, we responded to a user's request on the spot. For example, one analyst wanted to know if we could provide a PERCENT function. Ten minutes later—and three lines of APL—there it was. An interpretive language facilitates such development.

The specter of the mythical man-month loomed over us throughout the development process. Brooks's warning for software designers says:

1.   When the code is written, 10% of the work is done.

2.   As program complexity grows by x, programming effort increases by x^a, where the exponent a is estimated by Nanus and Farr (1964) and by Weinwurm (1965) to be about 1.5 (see Fig. 7.8).

3.   Much of the incremental 90% of the effort involves testing and integration.

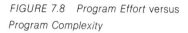

FIGURE 7.8   *Program Effort* versus *Program Complexity*

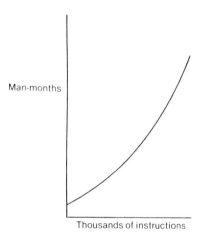

Man-months

Thousands of instructions

We believed that using APL would enable us to:

1.   Reduce the time needed for the 10%,

2.   Borrow from public libraries, thus reducing testing,

3.   Break the program up into small, discrete units so that x^a is close to x,

4.   Integrate new routines easily, and

5.   Reduce program errors.

In general, our expectations were met. We encountered three main types of problems, all of which had a significant impact on development time and costs:

1.   As the *use* of ISSPA became more complex and new functions were added, interaction errors were introduced. (Command A worked perfectly, as did Command B, but used in sequence they generated a bug, often an elusive one.)

2. Far more resources were needed for the user-system dialog than for the logic of the commands.

3. The initial commands permitted us to use simple sentences. Evolution, user learning, and the addition of user-defined commands resulted—intentionally—in more complex sentences. It then became essential to introduce consistent system conventions and to add system commands. These did not add to the functional capabilities of the system, and they diverted resources from the evolution of user commands.

4. Machine costs were far higher than expected, and the code was "opaque."

Brooks is entitled to respond to the first three of these points with "I told you so." He did. We thought we could finesse the problems implicit in Fig. 7.1. Almost certainly, we still saved substantial time and effort by using APL, but the pattern Brooks identifies seems to hold just as much for ISSPA as it does for data processing projects. Coding is still 10% of the effort. This point is not discussed much in work on either APL or DSS. Many, perhaps most, model-based DSS described in case studies either are for *ad hoc* use, in which case there is no need to make them into products, or are worked out by high-quality, low-cost programmers working in universities. Clearly, APL is very effective for *ad hoc* systems.

The interaction errors often related to problems with internal pointers and multiple copies of matrices which were not kept consistent. As we elaborated the "syntax" of ISSPA, several commands were used within other commands. To the user, the structure remained simple; indeed, the whole aim in designing the user-system dialog was to ensure that ISSPA be easy to use even for someone with no prior experience with computer systems. Internally, however, the structure grew exponentially more complex. This was also true for the data management routines.

The interaction errors were sometimes hard to trace. Errors in the logic of a user command were quickly found. As mentioned earlier, users played a key role in locating unobtrusive errors, ones which the programmer is unlikely to spot. Their expertise in school finance combined with their initiative, intelligence, and interest in ISSPA significantly affected the *technical* quality of the DSS. While the use of already debugged routines from public libraries clearly reduced testing time, we had to spend substantial effort in improving the user-system dialog.

Ness (1975) argues that a DSS cannot be made more useful by addition of "cosmetics." Our view is that a useful set of tools needs also to be usable. This seems to be supported by users' reactions. We felt that a DSS should be seen as a personal tool and a mundane one. *Mundane*, as used here, means easily lived with, quickly integrated into one's ongoing activities, and then, in a way, taken from granted. A calculator is personal and mundane in this sense. "Cosmetics" are an important aspect of mundaneness. The quality of the read-out display, the size of the buttons, the location of functions, etc., make a particular calculator easy to live with. An indication of one's satisfaction with it is that it is taken for granted. With some calculators, one's attention is drawn to very minor inconveniences or cosmetic flaws. We felt, and still do, that cosmetics are important for a DSS *product*. The dialog in Fig. 7.7 may be acceptable to a person with a technical bent, but it is not acceptable to most others. We went to great lengths to build a mundane system. For example, the DESCRIBE command produces descriptive statistics, including the standard deviation and the variance of a variable. Initially, if the variance was too large for the output field, we printed asterisks. This is a convention familiar to FORTRAN users, but one that makes no real sense. The variance is not *******. While a policy analyst will get used to asterisks appearing on a report, a legislator will wonder why the computer made a mistake. We decided to substitute the words VERY LARGE. Similarly, if the variable had no mode, we printed NONE instead of 0.

In several states, we did not make any presentation of ISSPA to senior administrators in the users' organization. The users did so; it was their system, not ours. They almost invariably emphasized the "cosmetics," which they viewed as a reflection of our willingness to tailor ISSPA to their needs. To an extent, functional capabilities are taken as a given. Any calculator can multiply and divide; the issue is how well it does so, which translates to how "mundane" it is.

For similar reasons, we increasingly had to commit resources to developing system commands which either increased system flexibility or provided help and information about ISSPA. *All* such commands were developed in response to user requests or problems. The design structure made it easy to integrate them, and they involved small increments of effort. However, at one point we had to hire a junior programmer to handle them, and for some time we were not able to keep up with our users' growing demands for such add-on features.

Despite problems associated not so much with the development as with the consolidation of ISSPA, APL provided the expected advantages. In particular, the programming cost for a new user command is indeed incremental, with an extremely low fixed component. For one user, we developed a major new command based on ideas he gained from using ISSPA. This added an important policy concept to school finance analysis. It was "working" in a day; he estimated that at best it would have taken three months for the state education programming department to implement a similar capability. He was quite willing to put up with minor blemishes in the routine in exchange for such responsive service.

We estimate that about 800 programmer-hours of effort have gone into ISSPA. Of course, the system is much more powerful than the initial version, but even so, the figure is painfully close to Brooks's estimate that the amount of final development effort will equal nine times the amount of coding effort.

From looking at the few case studies which describe the extension of a DSS to a product, we see clearly, in retrospect, that our experiences were fairly typical. For another example, see Alter's (1980, p. 225) discussion of a DSS for media planning.[17] We have given our chapter the subtitle of "The Mythical Man-Month Revisited." Six months ago, we assumed it would be "The Mythical Man-Month Defeated."

8. CONCLUSION: GUIDELINES FOR BUILDING DSS

In Section 1 we stated that one aim in describing our ISSPA experience was to see if the DSS field is now at a point where one can define reliable guidelines for building DSS. Obviously, our experiences are not generalizable. Nonetheless, they confirm many of the often implicit principles of DSS design and the explicit findings of DSS research. We thus feel that we can make some fairly strong assertions:

1. Adaptive design is essential; any systems analyst, programmer, or consultant who wants to build DSS has to know how to:
   a. *Get started.* DSS applications do not come tidily packaged with neat specifications. The middle-out approach provides a means of learning from and responding to the user.
   b. *Respond quickly.* A DSS is equivalent to a system for evolution and learning. The design structure and programming techniques must facilitate this.
   c. *Pay close attention to user-system interfaces and outputs.* A DSS is a set of relatively simple components that must fit together to permit complex, varied, and idiosyncratic problem solving. The designer needs to get a very detailed understanding of the task to be supported and of the people who carry out the task. The natural sequence and order of priority in DSS development is as follows:
      (1) Design the dialog.
      (2) Design the commands in terms of the *users'* processes and concepts.
      (3) Define what the *user* does and sees when this command is invoked.
      (4) Work backwards to program logic and data management.

2. *The architecture of a DSS is critical.* It must be built on the assumption that there will be substantial evolution and that flexibility is essential.

3. The development process must be based on techniques and design structures that *reduce the fixed costs of programming and the time required to respond to users.* The trade-offs are complex. (We suffered badly from the high machine costs we incurred in gaining low programmer costs.)

4. *Data management involves high software overhead* and is the major source of complex program errors.

5. *A good user is essential.* As one ISSPA user stated: " . . . working with a DSS, at a certain point, it takes on a life of its own." The DSS is person-with-machine; the machine alone is not enough.

The final point to be made is a rueful one. There is indeed no free lunch. The demands in time and effort for delivery of a DSS product are as high as for any computer system. The process is more flexible, and early progress is often dramatically and excitingly faster than it is for traditional data processing applications, but the 9X factor observed by Brooks still holds.

ENDNOTES

1. ISSPA is suited to any application where the data consist of a set of planning units (e.g., school districts, employees, buildings, or states) and where the analysis involves aggregating, selecting, and reporting some or all of the units. For example, ISSPA is likely to be used in the near future as a DSS for planning and analysis of personnel data and for tracking and evaluation of federal research grants.

2. Brooks's book is surely the best single discussion of software engineering. There is not room in this paper to do justice to its scope and insight. It covers, among other topics: (1) the distinction between programs and programming systems products (the main topic of this chapter), (2) the nonlinear relationship between program size and development effort, (3) the problems of coordination in large-scale software development efforts, (4) the importance of program architecture, (5) the need for independent certification and testing of software, (6) the need for sharp tools (including APL), and (7) disciplines for debugging and documentation. Brooks was the project manager for OS/360, the operating system for IBM's third generation. Between 1963 and 1966, about 500 man-years of effort went into OS/360, and at one point over 1000 people were working on it. His book is both an analysis of what happened and a recommendation on how to avoid similar programming "tar pits."

3. We have added a third dimension, years, so that future versions of ISSPA will include capability for time-series analysis.

4. Most ISSPA users either work with a subset of about eight variables or begin by pulling in a larger number that they then aggregate or combine, using the DEFINE command. A dilemma for DSS designers is how to efficiently and quickly extract the small number of variables a user wants to work with from what is often a very large data base.

5. The Gini coefficient and Lorenz curves are standard measures of disparity of income or wealth. See Garms, Guthrie, and Pierce (1978).

6. Our colleague David G. Clark joined us in developing ISSPA around this point. He has played a major role in translating ISSPA from a program to a product, especially in the areas of training, documentation, and marketing.

7. David A. Ness, who has probably been the most important single contributor to DSS design techniques, developed the term "middle-out" to describe this approach. Middle-out development (in contrast to top-down and bottom-up) relies on prototyping, "breadboarding," and designing-by-using. Ness's ideas and experience have been a major influence on our work.

8. Courbon and his colleagues have carefully tracked the costs of DSS development and provide detailed data on the time involved for managers and designers.

9. James Phelps, Associate Superintendent in the Department of Education in

Michigan, and William Harrison, Legislative Assistant to the Education Review Committee in Ohio, were invaluable to us. The literature on the need for user involvement in systems development seems so far to assume a more passive role for the user than we required. In adaptive DSS design, the user is active and indispensable. Dr. Phelps and Dr. Harrison became *designers* of ISSPA by being responsive, creative users.

10. There should have been a manual; its absence caused occasional irritating and unnecessary problems (e.g., "Is it CROSSTABS . . . WITH or BY?"). One problem adaptive design causes is that, since the DSS is constantly evolving and Version 0 is designed with change in mind, there is no stable system to document. It is thus essential to build as much of the user documentation into the DSS as possible. One approach we are considering is to store the text of the user's manual on disk so that it can be accessed directly from ISSPA.

11. The literature on diffusion of innovations indicates that "early adopters" are generally part of an elite that is self-confident and willing to break with norms and traditions. One reason for seeking out such people as the first users of a DSS is that they are effective contacts and crusaders within the wider organization. As well as helping design the DSS, they in effect sell it.

12. Tukey (1977) defines a range of innovative, mainly graphical, techniques to aid analysts in looking carefully at their data before committing themselves to analytic methods.

13. McNeil (1977) provides APL and FORTRAN source code for many EDA techniques. His output formats are generally clumsy; here again, we concentrated on making these useful routines more usable.

14. IFPS (Interactive Financial Planning System) is a product of Execucom, Inc., Austin, Texas.

15. The use of semicolons allows users to operate in an "expert" mode in which they do not have to wait for ISSPA to type out the standard instructions or questions. This enhancement was provided in response to user demand.

16. See *EDP Analyzer*, January, February, March (1979).

17. This DSS was built by Ness and a colleague; it illustrates middle-out design in practice.

BIBLIOGRAPHY

Alter, S. L., *Decision Support Systems: Current Practice and Continuing Challenges*. Reading, Mass.: Addison-Wesley, 1980.

Andreoli, P., and J. Steadman, "Management Decision Support Systems: Impact on the Decision Process." Master's thesis, M.I.T., 1975.

Artman, I. B., "Design and Implementation of a Decision Support System for Hospital Space Management." Master's thesis, M.I.T., 1980.

Bennett, J. L., "Integrating Users and Decision Support Systems," in J. D. White (ed.), *Proceedings of the Sixth and Seventh Annual Conferences of the Society for Management Information Systems.* Ann Arbor, Mich.: University of Michigan, July 1976, pp. 77–86.

Berne, R. M., and L. Steifel, "Concepts of Equity and Their Relationship to School Finance Plans," *Journal of Education Finance*, Vol. 5, Fall 1979.

Berry, P., "The Democratization of Computing," paper presented at Eleventh Symposium Nacional de Systemas Computacionales, Monterrey, Mexico, March 15–18, 1977.

Blanning, R., "The Functions of a Decision Support System," *Information and Management*, Vol. 2, No. 3, 1979.

Brooks, F. P., Jr., *The Mythical Man-Month.* Reading, Mass.: Addison-Wesley, 1975.

Carlson, E. D., B. F. Grace, and J. A. Sutton, "Case Studies of End User Requirements for Interactive Problem Solving," *Management Information System Quarterly*, Vol. 1, No. 1, March 1977, pp. 51–63.

Carlson, E. D., J. L. Bennett, G. M. Giddings, and P. E. Mantey, "The Design and Evaluation of an Interactive Geo-data Analysis and Display System," *Information Processing 74.* Amsterdam: North Holland, 1974, pp. 1057–61.

Contreras, L., and R. Skertchly, "A Conceptual Model for Interactive Systems," paper presented at APL Users Meeting, Toronto, September 1978.

Courbon, J. C., J. Grajew, and J. Tolovi, Jr., "L'approche Évolutive dans la Mise en Place des Systèmes Interactifs d'Aide à la Décision," *Papier de Recherche IAE*, No. 78-02. Grenoble, France: Institute d'Administration des Entreprises, Université de Grenoble II, January 1978.

Garms, W., J. W. Guthrie, and L. C. Pierce, *School Finance: The Economics and Politics of Public Education.* Englewood Cliffs, N.J.: Prentice-Hall, 1978.

Gerrity, T. P., Jr., "The Design of Man-Machine Decision Systems." Ph.D. dissertation, M.I.T., 1970.

Grajew, J., and J. Tolovi, Jr., "Conception et Mise en Oeuvre des Systèmes Interactifs d'Aide à la Décision: L'approche Évolutive." Ph.D. dissertation, Université de Grenoble, 1978.

Keen, P. G. W., "Computer-Based Decision Aids: The Evaluation Problem," *Sloan Management Review*, Vol. 16, No. 3, Spring 1975, pp. 17–29.

Keen, P. G. W., "Computer Systems for Top Managers: A Modest Proposal," *Sloan Management Review*, Vol. 18, No. 1, Fall 1976, pp. 1–17.

Keen, P. G. W., "Decision Support Systems: A Research Perspective," CISR Paper. Cambridge, Mass.: Sloan School of Management, M.I.T., 1980a.

Keen, P. G. W., "Decision Support Systems: Translating Useful Models into Usable Technologies," *Sloan Management Review*, Vol. 21, No. 3, Spring 1980b, pp. 33–44.

Keen, P. G. W., "Simulations for School Finance, Survey and Assessment," Research Report to the Ford Foundation, 1980c.

Keen, P. G. W., and D. G. Clark, "Computer Systems and Models for School Finance Policy Making: A Conceptual Framework," Research Report to the Ford Foundation, August 1978.

Keen, P. G. W., and D. G. Clark, "Simulations for School Finances: A Survey and Assessment." Denver, Colo.: Education Commission of the States, 1980.

Keen, P. G. W., and J. Wagner, "DSS: An Executive Mind Support System," *DATAMATION*, Vol. 25, No. 11, November 1979, pp. 117–22.

McKenney, J. L., and P. G. W. Keen, "How Managers' Minds Work," *Harvard Business Review*, Vol. 52, No. 3, May–June 1974, pp. 79–90.

McNeil, D. R., *Interactive Data Analysis*. New York: Wiley-Interscience, 1977.

Methlie, L., "Data Management for Decision Support Systems," *Data Base*, Vol. 12, Nos. 1 & 2, Fall 1980, pp. 40–46.

Nanus, B., and L. Farr, "Some Cost Contributors to Large-Scale Programs," *AFIPS Proceedings SJCC*, Vol. 25, Spring 1964, pp. 239–48.

Ness, D., "Interactive Systems: Theories of Design," *Joint Wharton/ONR Conference—Interactive Information and DSS*. Philadelphia: The Wharton School, Department of Decision Sciences, University of Pennsylvania, November 1975.

Sigle, J., and J. Howland, "Structured Development of Menu-Driven Application Systems," *APL QUOTE QUAD '79*, Association for Computing Machinery, June 1979.

Stabell, C., "On the Development of the Decision Support System as a Marketing Problem," paper presented at the International Federation for Information Processing Congress, Stockholm, August 1974.

Tukey, J., *Exploratory Data Analysis*. Reading, Mass.: Addison-Wesley, 1977.

Weinwurm, G. F., "Research in the Management of Computer Programming," Report SP-2059. Santa Monica, Calif.: System Development Corporation, 1965.

META-DESIGN CONSIDERATIONS IN BUILDING DSS

Jeffrey H. Moore • Michael G. Chang

CHAPTER 8

This chapter focuses on design difficulties encountered in building an effective Decision Support System (DSS), given the organizational and technological constraints inherent in any computer-based development effort. Surprisingly little attention has been given to these issues in the DSS literature. In addressing design and development issues, we contrast the guiding frameworks and recommended procedures commonly associated with the development of Management Information Systems (MIS) with those required by DSS design. The central theme is that, despite the common technological/computer base employed by both MIS and DSS, the design *process* for effective DSS is generically different and necessarily more complex than that for MIS. Both the "unstructured" nature of the user's decision-making problem and the computer's active role as a decision aid in the DSS scenario are the driving forces necessitating this differential treatment. Our key point is that, from a design perspective, the classic MIS development life-cycle approach is insufficient as a prescriptive guide for building DSS.

First, we examine various categorizations of DSS, directing special attention to the semantic difficulties that have arisen in describing DSS development efforts. Then, current MIS and DSS characterizations found in the literature are reviewed and several taxonomies are examined from the standpoint of their usefulness in guiding DSS design. As a focal point for the analysis, several ideas are presented that are intended primarily to help the DSS designer rather than the user.

The discussion addresses *meta-design* considerations. That is, the DSS designer should be aware of certain issues above and beyond the specific details

Adapted, with permission, from "Selected Papers on Decision Support Systems from the 13th Hawaii International Conference on System Sciences," published in *DATA BASE*, Vol. 12, Nos. 1 and 2, and *SIGOA Newsletter*, Vol. 1, Nos. 4 and 5, Special Interest Groups of the Association for Computing Machinery.

of any particular design engagement. The distinction here is subtle but important: this chapter does *not* lay out a step-by-step procedure or even an exhaustive list of topics that are important in designing DSS. Rather, we synthesize ideas from existing DSS design frameworks to produce a meta-design methodology from which individual DSS designers can develop their own design frameworks, appropriate to their particular needs.

Four key ideas will be introduced:

1. *System/problem migration.* Both system design and problem understanding shift over time. Migration results from the intrinsically dynamic nature of DSS implementation efforts. This migration concept highlights the difficulty of predefining system specifications when learning and DSS development occur simultaneously.

2. *Subset evolution.* This design philosophy applies to expansion of system capabilities. It is based on an extensible design approach that is needed to match the decision maker's revealed preferences and growing capacity as a user to handle enhanced DSS options.

3. *"Soft" versus "hard" DSS capabilities.* Soft, initial, generalized system capabilities should eventually be "wired down" into hard, streamlined, powerful operators. This idea is closely related to the "subset evolution" concept. The flexibility to begin with "soft" and move toward "hard" capabilities is gained at the expense of initially higher user investment in learning and potentially greater total development cost.

4. *"Weak-strong" design continuum.* This concept distinguishes between DSS designs that follow the user's current preferences and existing capabilities (weak) and those designs that deliberately attempt to shape or refine the user's decision-making process (strong).

BACKGROUND OF DSS ISSUES

Since Gorry and Scott Morton [1971] coined the term "decision support system" (DSS) in their seminal article, there has been confusion and controversy over the interpretation of this notion. This is unfortunate; the semantic issues surrounding DSS often cloud the discussion in the literature. The origin of the term is clear:

1. *Decision* emphasizes the primary focus on decision making in problem situations rather than the subordinate activities of simple information retrieval, processing, or reporting.

2. *Support* clarifies the computer's role in *aiding* rather than replacing the decision maker, thus including those decision situations with sufficient "structure" to permit computer support, but in which managerial judgment is still an essential element.

3. *System* highlights the integrated nature of the overall approach, suggesting the wider context of user, machine, and decision environment.

In practice, however, this DSS rubric is much too broad to provide any meaningful categorization. That is, almost any system—ranging from a programmable hand-held calculator, through a general ledger system with report-writing capabilities, to a sophisticated interactive decision-modeling system—could qualify as a DSS. Consequently, the DSS school of thought has had trouble in (1) clearly distinguishing its work from previous efforts in MIS development and (2) providing any insightful *prescriptive* guidelines for DSS design and development. The situation is further complicated by the frequent use of ill-defined terminology in building DSS concepts. Three of these—problem structure, bounded rationality, and managerial effectiveness—deserve additional comment before we develop our design framework.

Problem Structure

DSS researchers have used the concept of *problem structure* as a fundamental dimension for categorizing decision situations and hence system type. Gorry and Scott Morton [1971] introduced the notion of "structured decision system" (SDS), which roughly covers the domain of classical MIS, as a complement to DSS. However, this distinction hinges on the definition of problem structure, and therein lies a major source of confusion in the minds of both DSS scholars and designers. Problem structure, as originally interpreted by Gorry and Scott Morton, was simply a relabeling of the programmed/nonprogrammed dichotomy originally proposed by Simon [1960]. Simon's earlier work suggested that a problem was programmed if it had a routine response; that is:

> Decisions are programmed to the extent that they are repetitive and routine, to the extent that a definite procedure has been worked out for handling them so they won't have to be treated *de novo* each time they occur. . . .

> Decisions are non-programmed to the extent that they are novel, unstructured, and consequential. There is no cut-and-dried method for handling the problem because it hasn't arisen before, or because its precise nature and structure are elusive or complex, or because it is so important that it deserves a custom-tailored treatment.

The term programmed in Simon's work was intended to convey the notion of a computer program—a "detailed prescription or strategy that governs the sequence of responses of a system to a complex task environment." Gorry and Scott Morton introduced the "structure" terminology for two reasons:

1. To avoid any confusion about the existence of an actual computer program for solving the given problem, since in a wider decision context there was no *a priori* reason to assume the use of a computer;

2. To suggest the notion of "deep structure" as used in the context of Artificial Intelligence.

DSS scholars, however, have attempted to apply this structured/programmed distinction as a criterion for classifying potential DSS problem areas—the conventional wisdom being that a DSS is appropriate for semi-structured decision problems. This in turn has stimulated an attempt by both scholars and practitioners to classify all decision-making situations by a sort of structured/unstructured criterion, an activity we consider to be largely fruitless and a major source of confusion in the DSS literature. This confusion is also evident in Simon's notation of programmed *versus* nonprogrammed decisions.

As we see it, a problem can only be considered more or less structured *with regard to* a particular decision maker, or group of similar decision makers, and at a particular point in time. In our experience there is simply no structure that can be identified with any decision-making problem independent of the decision maker.

Simon's classification scheme refers to whether or not the organization has a programmed response to a given type of decision problem. A repetitive decision procedure applied to a common class of problems is considered programmed regardless of whether the results of the decision-making process are "good" or "bad" in a larger sense. An unprogrammed decision problem is simply a novel one, in which the decision maker must first develop what may be an *ad hoc* procedure for reaching the decision.

Thus we believe it is both incorrect and misleading for DSS designers to speak of structured or programmed problems in the general case when approaching a DSS design situation. In particular, our perspective implies that DSS design problems must be viewed in terms of *user-specific* problem structures. This requirement in turn emphasizes the need for accommodating individual differences among DSS users or clients and *tailoring* DSS features in response to these differences. In other words, as a result of differences in information, beliefs, or even values among decision makers, a given decision-making procedure cannot be universally accepted as a valid response to a given problem.

To clarify this interpretation of the terms structured and programmed, the following examples are helpful. To say that problems of determining oil tanker fleet size or scheduling are programmed or structured applications means either: (1) there is a generally accepted model for this decision problem among industry practitioners, or (2) a given decision maker has developed a systematic procedure for dealing with the particular problem (i.e., has more than a "naïve" model for dealing with the decision). On the other hand, merger-and-acquisition analysis may be thought of as a relatively unprogrammed or unstructured if either: (1) a given decision maker has not faced the decision before and therefore has no established procedure for dealing with the problem, or (2) there is no general consensus as to which model is "best" (by some accepted criteria), although various individuals may have defined models for this decision. While merger-and-acquisition analysis might generally be considered unstructured, tanker-fleet problems can also be unstructured for a decision maker inexperienced with such problems. More will be said about this later when we present a simple DSS design framework. Since the term structured is now an integral part of the DSS vernacular, it will occasionally be used in this generally accepted sense throughout the chapter. The reader should bear in mind, however, our implicit notion of a user/problem reference when structure is used to categorize decision contexts.

Bounded Rationality

Various DSS researchers have also embraced Simon's notion of *bounded rationality* [1972] when describing decision-making styles of managers. This concept appears to explain observed behavior very well at a macroscopic level. From a DSS design perspective, however, this notion is difficult to apply for two reasons:

1. It is a highly subjective, user-dependent concept.

2. Bounded rationality often represents an *ex post* justification for a particular decision and often does not contribute concretely to the evaluation of trade-offs among alternative decisions *ex ante*.

While the notion of bounded rationality is certainly appealing, its major implication for DSS designers is limited to highlighting the need for care in predicting the range of rationality of potential users of the intended DSS. This process of determining the user's preferred level of analysis and information availability is itself a difficult and highly individualized endeavor. The unique nature of this work underscores the importance of accommodating individual differences, via tailoring, into the DSS design.

Managerial Effectiveness

A third confusing idea often cited in the DSS literature is the intentional focus on improving managerial *effectiveness* rather than managerial efficiency. Keen and Scott Morton [1978] distinguish these terms:

> Efficiency is performing a given task as well as possible in relation to some predefined performance criterion.

> Effectiveness involves identifying what should be done and ensuring that the chosen criterion is the relevant one.

Clearly, this distinction deserves consideration by DSS designers since it reflects the inherent trade-off between strategic, or global, planning and tactical, or local, decision making. However, as before, effective decision making by an individual at one level in an organization is often interpreted as only efficient decision making at another, usually higher, level. Again, the application of the efficiency/effectiveness concept is relative to both the decision context and the individual decision maker. Hence total exclusion of managerial efficiency considerations by the DSS designer during the design process can lead to implementation problems, subsequent system failure, and ultimately *ineffectiveness*. That is, exclusive focus by the DSS designer on improving users' effectiveness may induce unforeseen implementation problems later because the designer ignored the practical advantages of "scoring an early victory" available from embedding simple efficiency-improving options into the DSS.*

In summary, three of the most popular concepts deemed important to DSS research—problem structure, bounded rationality, and managerial effectiveness—are not inherently very helpful to a DSS designer faced with a specific design task. They serve, at best, to sensitize designers to important issues, but they do not offer much in the way of prescriptive guidelines for DSS design. Our intention is to develop a complementary set of concepts relevant to DSS designers. However, before expanding on this theme, we shall review several popular frameworks, interrelating these and other concepts from the literature. These frameworks are attempts to represent the experience of individual designers as they have interpreted the kind of general concepts we have been discussing when they worked on specific problems.

OVERVIEW OF SOME DSS FRAMEWORKS

The TPS/MIS/DSS Framework

The first and most common framework, which classifies computer-based systems, is founded on the simple notion of task structure. The commonly applied definitions of computer-based technology are often variants of this taxonomy:

1. *Transaction Processing System* (TPS)—pure data processing system for gathering, updating, and posting information according to predefined procedures. By "pure" it is meant that little or no managerial decision making is involved; most decisions are clerical and routine. Such decision making constitutes "programmed" tasks *à la* Simon; examples include a basic payroll system or an order-processing system.

2. *Management Information System* (MIS)—a system with predefined data aggregation and reporting capabilities. MIS reports are usually either printed in batch or queried on demand. However, if present, query options normally include only a set of predefined data extraction operators. An MIS is often built upon an existing TPS. An example of an MIS is a payroll system with managerial reports, such as a labor distribution summary.

---

*We have expanded upon this issue elsewhere; see Moore and Chang [1978].

3. *Decision Support System* (DSS)—an extensible system with intrinsic capability to support *ad hoc* data extraction, analysis, consolidation, and reduction, as well as decision-modeling activities. For example, a general ledger-based planning system with both preformatted and user-definable reports or forecasts (loosely interpreted as models) is a DSS.

Note that we view interactive access to a DSS or an MIS as an implementation consideration rather than as an intrinsic part of this categorization.* A batch system with these characteristics, while doubtless less responsive to the user's demands, would nonetheless in principle be a "qualitative" DSS or MIS.

The above taxonomy crudely summarizes the conventional wisdom in defining the differences among computer-based information systems. From a descriptive standpoint, TPS are frequently devoted to routine data processing tasks, involving a high degree of formality, timeliness, accuracy, and efficiency in the processing of comparatively large volumes of data. MIS are often report-oriented in that data are extracted and summarized into predefined formats, often on a periodic basis, for purposes of managerial review, reporting exceptions or deviations from standards, and observing historical trends. MIS reports are often produced during or after transaction processing cycles, and the production of reports frequently requires the prespecification of content. A DSS subsumes some of the features of an MIS (especially summarization and extraction capabilities), but the procedures for presenting information are more loosely defined. This allows the end user to select on an *ad hoc* basis the frequency and, to a limited extent, the content of reports. This usually, but not always, implies the need for an interactive hardware capability in the computer-based information system. Most importantly, the usage of the DSS by the end user is, within limits, not prespecified and is aperiodic in contrast to MIS usage. As indicated above, it is also often stipulated that a DSS should support limited modeling and data analysis capabilities on an *ad hoc* basis. This requirement reflects the future, or planning, orientation of a viable DSS, as opposed to the historical, or management control, focus of an MIS.

We consider the *ad hoc*, "as needed," nature of DSS usage to be essential, since planning is largely an unstructured activity, with procedures which are difficult to prespecify. Often, the currency, accuracy, and precision of the data incorporated into a DSS are deemphasized on the grounds that planning activities should not be sensitive to minor discrepancies in data. This notion implies a less regimented system whose usage is not subject to external audit or other formalized review. The goal is improving managerial effectiveness (in some sense) as opposed to improving the operational efficiency of data processing.

---

*Any attempt to distinguish among these alternative computer-based information systems exclusively by means of the hardware and software used to implement them is completely misdirected and is also a source of considerable confusion in the literature. As we see it, such distinctions confuse means with ends.

Despite these obvious task differences, the key factor which distinguishes a DSS from other systems is the extent to which the information processing task can be prespecified by the user of the system. In the above taxonomy, a TPS is by definition prespecifiable, while a DSS is by definition *not* prespecifiable. That is, from a design standpoint, the categorical difference among these three types of systems is unrelated to the technology or even to the mode of use, but rather is related to the degree to which the specifications of the information processing tasks are known or knowable prior to actual implementation. Note that this is a necessary, but not a sufficient, condition for classifying a proposed computer-based information system; prespecification of a task is not the only condition for classifying a system as transaction-oriented. Note further that specification setting is usually a nontrivial process, arising out of a review process prior to development of the computer-based information system. Furthermore, these specifications can meet the acid test of obtaining consensus by the clients of the information system prior to implementation. As will be further discussed below, this is not the case for a DSS. This notion of system prespecification underlies the now classic framework for systems design, which provides a starting point for our discussion of DSS design.

The Life Cycle Framework

Several review approaches for developing computer-based information systems have been prescribed in the MIS literature; the most popular is called the "systems development life cycle." The steps in this process as succinctly summarized by Davis [1974] are shown in Table 8.1. This framework for developing systems grew out of nearly twenty years of experience by many practitioners in the development of computer-based information systems. The phases in the development cycle are theoretically sequential, which presumes that sufficient foreknowledge and consensus are available to permit, for example, feasibility assessment and in-

TABLE 8.1   Systems Development Life Cycle from Davis [1974]

Life Cycle Phase	Comments
Feasibility assessment	Evaluation of feasibility and cost/benefit of proposed application
Information analysis	Determination of information needed
System design	Design of processing system and preparation of program specifications
Program development	Coding and debugging of computer programs
Procedure development	Design of procedures and writing of user instructions
Conversion	Final test and conversion
Operation and maintenance	Day-to-day operation, modification, and maintenance
Post audit	How well did it turn out?

formation analysis to be carried out. Once the specifications are obtained in this process, systems design and the other development activities can proceed.

As every practitioner who has actually designed a computer-based information system knows, the life cycle approach is an idealized abstraction, based upon an essentially top-down design philosophy. The limitations of this approach are immediately apparent in the development of those MIS systems for which prespecification is difficult because consensus among the users concerning the characteristics of such an information system is difficult to achieve. Practitioners recommending the use of the development life cycle framework are, therefore, quick to caution that its application over time in the development of a particular computer-based information system is iterative, embodying a certain amount of bottom-up design activity. That is, one will cycle through some of the feasibility assessment, information analysis, systems design, and even programming stages several times before converging on a final specification. The purpose of the iterations is to resolve inconsistencies and ambiguities, to evaluate trade-off subtleties, and to permit the end user to reveal "true" preferences (a surprisingly difficult task). Although the systems development life cycle approach, with its iterative modification, has proven to be the single most useful approach to developing transaction systems and most MIS-oriented systems, we hold that its focus and purpose are inadequate for the task of building and implementing successful DSS.

Loosely speaking, the reasons for this inadequacy are related to the previously described notion of problem structure. The development life cycle approach presumes that the structure of a decision-making problem to be addressed by the information system is known or, in the case of iterative development, knowable. The problem setting, managerial preferences, decision-making procedures, and managerial environment are, at least for the purposes of the framework, assumed to be largely unchanging. The iterations, if necessary, "scrape away" ignorance on the part of the designers in order to more clearly reveal the intended nature of the computer-based information system. In the experience of the authors, this presumption is simply untenable in the context of building an effective DSS. Ignorance on the part of the designers is not the only issue; the problem setting, preferences, and the decision-making process of the client managers are all changeable and changing throughout the DSS design process. It is this absence of constancy which renders the life cycle viewpoint inadequate.

In summary, there are at least three distinct problems in applying the design implications of the three-way information system taxonomy and the development life cycle approach:

1. The three-way taxonomy of TPS, MIS, and DSS provides an important starting point for distinguishing among computer-based information systems and is especially useful in describing alternative information systems from the viewpoint of the *end user*. Unfortunately, the taxonomy is descriptive and provides little in the way of guidance to the systems designer.

2. Lacking operational definitions, the terminology itself has been subject to overuse; we have seen almost any interactive computer system called a DSS. Thus it is comparatively easy to generate examples of systems which have some of the attributes of a DSS but which have no discernable purpose other than to provide summarized data—a characteristic attributable to MIS.

3. The development life cycle approach tacitly assumes that the decision-making problem faced by the end user is essentially static, so that successive iterations within the life cycle phases are convergent. This is not true for a DSS. We will return to this issue in the next section after discussing yet another popular DSS framework.

The Gorry and Scott Morton Framework

The Gorry and Scott Morton [1971] framework synthesized two ideas proposed earlier by Anthony and Simon. Anthony's [1965] framework identified three levels of organizational decision making: Strategic Planning, Management Control, and Operational Control. Anthony's classification is essentially a loose description of decision-making task structure in a hierarchical organization, and he developed at length the attributes of decision making for each of the three levels. In contrast, Simon [1960] focused upon a mode of decision making, independent of organizational structure, in his characterization of programmed and unprogrammed decision making. As mentioned previously, considerable confusion surrounds the notions of problem structure and programmed decision making.

The Gorry and Scott Morton framework combined both of these approaches into a matrix, as illustrated in Fig. 8.1 in simplified form. Naturally any attempt at making distinctions of this sort is somewhat artificial. However, the Gorry and Scott Morton framework has been widely referenced, presumably because of the insights that it provides. Presented also in Fig. 8.1 are some examples of the kinds

FIGURE 8.1   Gorry and Scott Morton DSS Framework (Simplified)

	Operational Control ◄---►	Management Control ◄---►	Strategic Planning
Structured (Programmed) ⋮	Accounts receivable	Production scheduling	Financial management
Semistructured (Nonprogrammed)	Joint costing	Plant location	Mergers and acquisitions

Institutional DSS ◄----► *Ad hoc* DSS

of decision-making situations that might be classified within the matrix. Some of these classifications are debatable because of the aforementioned differences of opinion in defining structured *versus* unstructured decision making. Nevertheless, there is a distinction between the kind of decision making required in the upper left-hand cell of Fig. 8.1 and that in the lower right-hand cell. Problem focus, task structure, and design approach are held to be radically different for these two cells, and similarly so for the other cells. The conventional wisdom is that most transaction processing systems fall in the upper left-hand cell and, most importantly, that the procedures for successful design in that cell do *not* necessarily generalize to the other cells.

Other authors—for example, Donovan and Madnick [1977]—have attempted to refine the Gorry and Scott Morton framework. Donovan and Madnick introduced the labels of "institutional" and "*ad hoc*," which are applied to the DSS itself. They define an institutional DSS to be one utilized for repeated decision-making tasks. An important example of this is the Portfolio Management System (PMS) reported on by Gerrity [1971]. The PMS system involves the use of a computer-based information system by several portfolio managers within a bank, each addressing the portfolio management problem in a different and unique manner. In contrast, an *ad hoc* DSS is developed and utilized to address the class of problems which are nonrepetitive. As the name implies, it is used for support of decision making in infrequent but important situations—particularly those in which the DSS can aid in both development of the problem definition and evaluation of alternatives on a "one-shot," high-payoff basis. An example of this is a corporate merger decision.

Shortcomings of Traditional Design Frameworks— The Migration Effect

Like the threefold taxonomy of TPS, MIS, and DSS, the Gorry and Scott Morton framework has proven useful in describing alternative information systems from the viewpoint of the *user*. However, neither the taxonomy nor the framework is prescriptive, and thus they provide little in the way of guidance to the DSS *designer*. In contrast, the development life cycle approach is prescriptive, but it implicitly assumes that the decision-making problem requiring the capabilities of a computer-based information system is essentially static so that successive iterations within the life cycle phases are convergent. We maintain that this is not true for a DSS; the decision context itself modifies and is modified by the very attempt to obtain these specifications for the purpose of DSS design. That is, the decision problem itself is migrating in the minds of both the decision maker *and* the DSS designer; both are groping for a satisfactory approach. There is, therefore, no guarantee that successive iterations through the development life cycle will be convergent. As a result, while the iterations might be rewarding as a learning experience, they can be time-consuming and may not lead to improvement ultimately in either decision-making effectiveness or design cost-effectiveness of the resulting DSS.

At the risk of oversimplification, the traditional life cycle approach, even if iterated, has as its ultimate goal the "freezing of the specs" to permit the actual design and software development to proceed in an efficient manner. That is, the purpose of feasibility and requirements analysis is to develop the specifications for the information system. This permits subsequent design effort to be decoupled from the rest of the organization and enables the designer to "tie down" the technological requirements of the information system. This approach is, of course, eminently reasonable and is frequently utilized in engineering development efforts. However, the formalization of procedures necessary for these steps to be carried out is not possible in unstructured settings without: (1) intimidating the decision makers themselves, (2) forcing premature closure on problem-solving approaches, and (3) inhibiting the important learning and search processes that managers must go through when addressing the less structured and more planning-oriented cells in the Gorry and Scott Morton framework.

In other words, the problem is that the development life cycle approach has as its very goal the *decomposition* of the problem into a sequence of steps. Specialized approaches are then utilized in carrying out these steps. The resulting sequence of activities with the attendant formalities of "signing off," cost estimates, and organizational "boiler plate" prematurely imposes a *developmental* structure upon the decision-making situation. Note that we consider this to be independent of the usual human relations or communications problems between decision makers and systems analysts which often interfere with the production of effective information systems. These problems, rightfully, are the source of numerous warnings in the MIS literature. The dilemma we refer to is, rather, a systemic problem brought on by cooperating, well-intentioned, and knowledgeable analysts who tend to fall back on the very procedures that have proven successful in TPS or MIS design, applying them to unstructured planning activities with which they are inherently incompatible.

We believe that attempts to apply these or similar methodologies often lead to what we call the *migration effect*:

> Over time the initially unstructured or semi-structured planning issue that originally motivated the DSS project migrates in the minds of both the user and DSS designer. This occurs when the traditional life cycle design methodology begins to enforce premature closure on the original problem definition so that the specifications can be "frozen." The resulting DSS system design, therefore, also tends to migrate over the development time interval. This migration is invariably toward the upper-left, structured/operational cell in the Gorry and Scott Morton framework.

That is, the DSS finally developed is in reality an efficiency-improving MIS utilized for relatively structured administrative problems, rather than the originally envisioned planning system to be utilized for improving decision effectiveness. Of course, the migration effect is not inevitable, but the tendency for it to occur is increased if rigid application of traditional life cycle design methodologies is made.

In light of this migration effect (brought on by design methodologies incompatible with decision styles and learning of the user and the designer), what DSS design methodology *is* compatible with unstructured decision making in the planning arena? Unfortunately, there is not and may never be any set of pat answers to this question. Our ability to generalize beyond the few specific instances that we and our fellow workers have studied is extremely limited. Before we attempt such generalization it is important, therefore, to understand several of the key factors, both organizational and design/technical, which interact with decision making and the DSS design process. After these notions have been developed in a simple design framework, two illustrative cases based on actual DSS design engagements will be offered to exemplify our ideas concretely.

A DSS DESIGN FRAMEWORK

We regard the migration effect as the driving force that makes the traditional life cycle design approach only partially adequate in the design of a DSS. Our belief is that the DSS designer must be aware of the potential for migration of the problem definition and that this migration is likely to occur during the design and development interval. Furthermore, the designer must, therefore, introduce additional flexibility in preliminary designs to "track" the migration, or in some cases must resist its occurrence. As our response to the migration effect we introduce three additional key concepts—evolving system capabilities, "soft" *versus* "hard" capabilities, and "weak" *versus* "strong" design—which comprise our framework.

An important characteristic shared by all computer-based information systems is the need for periodic restructuring, updating, or expansion activities unrelated to simple maintenance and error-elimination functions. For a variety of reasons—changing needs, earlier misspecification, revised context, change in capacity, newer technology, etc.—all systems periodically undergo such redirective activities. Without such activitites, the system's usefulness would decline rapidly—hence these changes are essentially mandatory. We believe that the *periodicity* of these redirective operations is *shorter* for DSS than for any other type of computer-based system. In particular, a TPS might be rewritten or undergo major modification every five to ten years to synchronize with changes in the underlying operational hardware or to accommodate substantial change in specifications. An MIS might be expanded or revised every one to two years to handle new requirements and regulations. A DSS could change every few days or weeks, particularly during early phases of implementation and use. Thus demand for flexibility at moderate cost (in terms of both time and money) is the rationale behind the extensibility requirement posed for good DSS designs.

This interpretation contrasts with the usual justification of extensibility, which sees it as a panacea or remedy for misspecification or limitations in design. Expanding on this theme, we recognize three agents to be integral to the development of a DSS:

1. The *client*, who initially solicits the development of a DSS, determines the overall performance criteria, and often pays for the system;

2. The *decision maker* or *user*, who actually interacts with the DSS and for whom the support aspects are to be tailored*;

3. The *designer*, who specifies the detailed structure and capabilities of the system and is responsible for its implementation.

In some cases the client and user are the same individual, while at other times one person may play all three roles. However, in situations involving three or more distinct individuals, the DSS designer must be aware of potential conflicts in values and beliefs, particularly concerning the intended role of the DSS.

Evolving System Capabilities

The classical view of MIS design considers the manager to be both client and referent in defining the requirements for an essentially static problem. The underlying *decision context*—problem definition, managerial preferences, decision-making procedures, and managerial environment—is treated as unchanging. The alternative model for DSS proposed here is that the decision context as seen by the client/user is constantly evolving in a *decision space* whose dimensions include the problem setting, the manager's preferences and skills, the procedures for decision making, and the managerial environment. In addition, the designer must append certain dimensions, such as hardware and software technology, relevant to design interests, thereby producing a higher-dimensional *design space*. One of the designer's responsibilities, therefore, is to continuously monitor the movement of the decision context as it migrates through the decision/design space. This awareness is needed as the designer seeks to minimize the discrepancy between the current DSS as implemented and the currently perceived or anticipated needs of the user.

The proposed approach to DSS design involves the implementation of *expanding subsets of system capabilities* based on an initial nucleus of extensible features. At any point in time, the DSS provides a subset of capabilities to be realized in the future, which includes all earlier capabilities and is sufficient to handle at least a reasonable portion of current requirements. This philosophy permits the designer to start with a limited design scope sufficient to satisfy the user's preferences for support and allowing preferences to be revealed in the context of the decision situation itself (i.e., by actually using a rudimentary version of the system). Again, the inherent extensibility of the recommended DSS nucleus facilitates this evolution in design within the time frame of days and weeks suggested earlier.

Although a modular software approach has been commonly incorporated into the design of computer-based systems, subset evolution is a larger concept.

---

*The client-user distinction is not necessarily identical to nor should it be confused with the manager-chauffeur distinction (see Bennett [1976]) that is often drawn in the literature.

Modularity is usually introduced by designers to facilitate their own software development and maintenance. The resulting system as seen by the *user*, however, is often neither modular nor extensible. Subset evolution, in addition to being modular, permits the easy definition of new operators, data constructs, or reports by the user without redesign or even reprogramming. This is accomplished by building upon the existing operators, constructs, etc., in an extensible fashion. In other words, the DSS must appear modular from the user's viewpoint, not just from a software development viewpoint. An example of a modular software system which is not extensible from the viewpoint of the user would be an applications package made up of many subroutines driven by a "main" program. This would be modular from the designer's perspective. However, if the program involved predefined sequences of calls to the subroutines in a path not modifiable by the user, then the system would certainly not appear modular (hence extensible) from the user's viewpoint.

Clearly, the provision of such extensibility is a substantial requirement to impose on DSS designers. This viewpoint sees DSS software as implementing a form of extensible high-level "command" language. This is in contrast to the traditional question-and-answer prompting characteristic of simple applications packages.

This approach also addresses two other issues in DSS design which Keen has pointed out*:

1. Starting a new DSS design is always a problem—once the ball is rolling and the user gains some results, it is easy to get feedback on both system enhancements and user acceptance.

2. Development *and* implementation of a working DSS for the same cost as a traditional MIS feasibility study is crucial to preempting the conventional formalized approach to system design.

It is important to note here that subset evolution is quite distinct from traditional system prototyping; the latter presumes that the system specification is fairly well defined and that the chief role of the prototype is feasibility analysis and final resolution of the system design. In subset evolution the intial requirements analysis is geared to providing sufficient information to build only the nucleus of a system. That is, *the first implementation is itself the feasibility study*. Any further hardware and software enhancements or refinements are rolled into the continuing process of system extension as the decision context migrates—as it will—in the minds of the user and designer.

"Soft" versus "Hard" Capabilities

Two important assumptions often characterize DSS design guidelines found in the literature: (1) the user's needs are supreme; and (2) all capabilities must be in-

---

*In informal conversations with us.

stantly and easily accessible as well as bug-free on delivery. In part, these notions justify an extensive design process prior to actual prototyping and implementation. However, our subset evolution approach is not compatible with such rigid requirements, and this suggests the need to reevaluate these assumptions.

In practice the DSS designer encounters a continuum of user preferences in terms of willingness to trade off additional work for enhanced capability. The *"soft"* capability approach suggested here involves the development of a core of generalized, but possibly *inefficient capabilities* in early versions of the system, which can subsequently be specialized into "hardened," easy-to-use, efficient system operators. Thus the decision maker reveals individual preferences for aids through use of the system. For example, an initial DSS design might require the user or a "chauffeur" to rekey certain limited amounts of data or to employ imagination in combining calculation operators to achieve particular modeling results. A subsequent set of system capabilities might provide a new data extract option or a primitive operator that addresses these respective needs when use and feedback from users justifies it.

This "soft" capability approach permits the designer to work with an initially smaller set of requirements which should, in turn, contribute to a simpler conceptual design. In addressing this, it is important that one consider whether or not a given capability has positive net payoff relative to the cost and time required for its development and implementation. That is, it is sometimes necessary to make hardware efficiency changes to ensure proper and timely system operation; on the other hand, a small loss in managerial efficiency in system usage, necessitated by a "soft" design, may often be parlayed into potentially significant future system enhancements given a limited support staff—a trade-off which the conventional DSS literature does not generally recognize. Ultimately, as the system evolves, these "soft" capabilities may also be replaced by off-the-shelf packages or programs with greater power and lower operating costs as they become available.

"Weak" versus "Strong" Design

Although the designer is traditionally viewed as a neutral party in the designer-client-user relationship, there is, in fact, considerable opportunity to influence the user's decision-making process. The *"weak" versus "strong"* design dimension distinguishes those designs that follow the user's preferences and personal decision-making style from those that conciously attempt to manipulate or refine the user's approach to problem solving. In situations where the client and user are distinct individuals, their opposing needs and views with regard to the role of the DSS as a training or educational tool must be considered. Two important propositions arise from this analysis:

1. A *weak design* is appropriate whenever the client elects not to influence the user's decision-making style. In such cases, the system design may either migrate into an information retrieval and control system (higher efficiency)

or else, in the case of a self-motivated user, may expand into a sophisticated support system for improved decision making (greater effectiveness).

2. A *strong design* is appropriate in a situation where more effective decision making is required by the client, but the user is (passively) resistant to changes in the decision-making process demanded by the client (i.e., the user is not motivated to expand personal decision-making capabilities).

It is not unusual for a DSS to be a strong design, since a major motivation in its development is the desire by the client for an improvement in the user's planning process. Strong designs require considerable attention to phasing the introduction of the system, to user training, to overcoming implementation resistance in users, and to other motivational issues. In strong designs the DSS characteristics are often shaped more by the need to deal with these problems of implementing the use of the DSS in the organization (associated with "unfreezing" the users) than by any new planning capabilities offered by the DSS itself. That is, the designer in these cases must carefully emphasize those features of the DSS which will capture user enthusiasm while at the same time providing and encouraging use of those DSS capabilities which are new to the user's experience.

In order to illustrate the ideas developed above more concretely and to prevent the discussion from becoming too abstract, two examples will be presented in some detail. Both are based upon actual DSS design projects; the company names have been disguised.

THE FIRST DSS EXAMPLE:
THE EASTERN MANUFACTURING COMPANY

Background

Eastern Manufacturing Company is a large producer of heavy machinery used by other manufacturers in production and transportation. With an annual sales volume of approximately $4 billion, Eastern Manufacturing faced a procurement problem involving some $1.5 billion worth of materials for its domestic plants and another $0.8 billion overseas. As early as 1975, management at Eastern Manufacturing had perceived the need for some type of computer-based information system to assist in procurement planning activities. The key problems identified were as follows:

1. The number of items and amount of information involved were far beyond the range of human memory and processing capacity;

2. There were delays in obtaining data and inaccuracies in available information; and

3. There was a failure to disseminate accumulated information and experience within the organization.

After preliminary brainstorming discussions by senior management, a year was spent developing an integrated data base system with built-in constraints and controls that would monitor purchases and automatically flag deviations from policy for approval by corporate staff. However, prior to implementation of the resulting system, the project was abandoned largely because of its emphasis on central decision making, which ran counter to Eastern Manufacturing's corporate philosophy. This initial failure, however, did not dampen management's enthusiasm for a corporate purchasing strategy. In fact, centrally coordinated procurement of fasteners had already realized savings of several million dollars out of the $30 million in annual fastener purchases.

Revamping its view of support, Eastern Manufacturing management focused on two key issues—(1) maintenance of the decision-making power at the local or plant level, and (2) sharing of information and experience among buyers—as a basis for ultimately refining the local, tactical procurement decision into a corporate, strategic one. The idea for a Procurement Decision Support System (PDSS) was approved by Eastern Manufacturing's top management as a two-year project with target savings of at least one-tenth of one percent on one-fourth of purchased items, or roughly $500,000 annually. With this goal in mind, a project supervisor/designer and two programmer analysts were hired to do the actual project development. Although PDSS fell behind schedule, preliminary results were still sufficiently impressive to win budget support for yet another year. By June 1978 a working version was available at corporate headquarters for access by the system design staff and limited use by buyers. Field and plant installations began shortly thereafter and continued into 1979.

PDSS Design

Before we describe the design process and the difficulties encountered in system implementation, a short technical description of PDSS is warranted. PDSS was implemented in COBOL using IBM's hierarchical Information Management System (IMS) to manage the data base structure. Seven related data bases—parts, contracts, supplies, purchase orders, buyers, master commodity list, and a supplier–Eastern Manufacturing part number cross-reference—were used, each containing information updated weekly or monthly from some 30 field and corporate source files. Using the Eastern Manufacturing part number as a key, the buyer could access and display such information as all locations using or stocking a part, their projected requirements, and purchase orders, contracts, and price for that part. With some 500,000 parts in inventory, efficient data management by the system was a significant issue. Eventually, the effect of this computer efficiency consideration was felt in terms of constraints on IMS processing strategy imposed by the corporate data center, which reduced the system performance as seen by the user. In fact, a fair percentage of user complaints concerning PDSS were related to system response time, which was slow enough to interfere with the buyer's decision-making process.

Because of the diversity of the targeted user community—from plant clerk to corporate buyer—PDSS was designed around a menu format. By moving through a hierarchical menu structure, the user was able to submit requests and receive preformatted displays of information. Although the system was ultimately intended to answer "what if" questions, as of mid-1979 no analytical or modeling capabilities were available.

From the beginning PDSS followed essentially the standard development life cycle process. Since it was justified strictly on the basis of projected cost savings, the next obvious steps in its development were to assess the users' information requirements, to design potential screen layouts, and then to iterate to satisfy user demands. Following this, detailed programming and testing were done in isolation prior to system release. As a result of considerations of both convenience and timeliness, the system was actually developed and released to users in increments—a group of screens or capabilities at a time. While this approach might be justified on the basis of the size and diversity of the user community, in fact it reflected the bias of the designer toward immediate usage and the overriding demands of data organization and computer efficiency. It is interesting to note that the designer adequately treated the technical system details but failed to address the problem of system introduction—identifying key interests and objectives and obtaining management commitment to the specific design—and was subsequently transferred to another project after the design work was completed.

Discussion of the Eastern Manufacturing Company Case

Several meta-design issues considered earlier can be tied directly to the PDSS design effort in the Eastern Manufacturing case. First, the overall design problem can be viewed as having migrated from a strategic policy determination problem into a management control and tactical decision-making problem, which we believe was foreseeable given the design and development process utilized in this case. At the strategic level it might be expected that the attention to computer efficiency considerations mandated by the large data bases could have been relaxed by use of aggregated files or statistical abstracts. Focus would then have shifted from the purchase of specific parts to the procurement of commodities or classes of parts, such as molded rubber parts or fasteners. One of the problems encountered by the design team in planning for this capability involved unifying the Eastern Manufacturing internal part-numbering code and reclassifying parts so that an easy and efficient aggregation procedure could be developed. While it is tempting to develop a DSS with fully integrated access to existing large-scale corporate data bases, this vision can lead to misdirected and costly software development efforts and to premature hardening of the DSS design. As the Eastern Manufacturing example illustrates, an early concern for access to large volumes of historical information is incompatible with the overall planning orientation of DSS and often precipitates a demise or early migration from decision-oriented systems toward operational/administrative control systems. Even with the presence of off-the-shelf, high-level data base management systems, delays associated with integrating access to such data into the DSS design may unnecessarily postpone initial prototypes of the DSS, during the crucial early learning and feedback phases.

Although the incremental introduction of newly developed IMS screens in this example can be viewed as a sort of expanding subset approach, very little attention was actually given to feedback and clarification of requirements once the initial design specifications were developed. Hence the evolution was not user-driven as we insist it should be. This incremental approach actually failed in practice, since no notification was ever given to users that new screens were available or that existing ones had been updated to correct bugs or provide new capabilities.

Finally, the PDSS design effort can be viewed as a weak design process. Some training and introduction to the system were offered, but no attempt was made to establish new performance criteria or force new procedures on potential users. Nevertheless, given the diversity of the targeted user community, it was inevitable that some percentage of users would modify their decision-making styles to accommodate a more formalized and informed review of purchases. At some field sites new local procedures were developed to mandate the use of PDSS printout as background documentation for purchase arrangements. As a result tighter controls were instituted, although none of the decision-making responsibility was actually relocated downward in the local management hierarchy. Those individuals who formerly made purchasing decisions continued to do so; however, clerks and assistants were able to reduce the information-gathering load for the buyers through use of PDSS. It was consistent with Eastern Manufacturing's decentralized management philosophy that purchasing staff members were free to accept or reject PDSS, with the understanding that corporate headquarters monitored the bottom line on material costs. Because PDSS was funded by the corporate purchasing group and constituted the accepted performance benchmark, user resistance to the system was low. Within the corporate procurement staff, some resistance to the system was felt, largely as a result of the performance characteristics or of perceived difficulty in operating the system. Since PDSS clearly dominated other alternative information sources, it was readily accepted as a good idea in principle. As at the field sites, shifts in decision-making styles resulted primarily from improved information rather than from overt control or reeducation on the part of the system design staff.

As we emphasized previously, our notion of DSS focuses on the provision of *ad hoc* analysis and modeling capabilities by the computer-based system. Hence, even though an MIS reports essential information for decision-making purposes, it is the intrinsic focus on decisions rather than on efficient information retrieval that helps distinguish a DSS from an MIS. In the Eastern Manufacturing example, the client's original intent was to develop a corporate-wide, coordinated procurement strategy. To this end, a sophisticated, on-line information retrieval system tying together inventory, purchasing, and engineering data was implemented. It was expected that such a system would provide both the level of control and the requisite data for corporate planning activities. In our view, however, the resultant system evolved into a structured MIS, with its attendant focus on efficient access by a diverse range of users to detailed information stored in large, tightly coupled data bases. This migration effect is illustrated in Fig. 8.2. Moreover, this case illustrates several of our key points:

1. The system was conceived with decision support in mind. The fact that a DSS, as defined here, was never implemented provides some insight into the migration of the problem in the minds of the participants.

2. The modified development life cycle approach used in designing and implementing the system contributed to the unforeseen migration of the projected DSS toward an MIS utilized ultimately for routine tactical control.

3. The system did not incorporate evolving subsets of capabilities based upon user experience. The evolution was driven almost totally by development priorities.

FIGURE 8.2   *Migration Effect in Eastern Manufacturing Case*

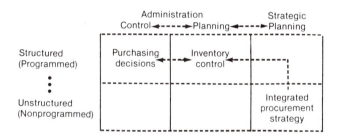

As the discussion indicates, the system was clearly not a *personalized* DSS. Neither the tailoring activities nor the tight user-designer coupling that we believe must characterize DSS development efforts was apparent. Although PDSS was somewhat modular in design with an emphasis on menu-driven modules, it did not incorporate our concept of evolving system capabilities. For example, there was no provision for the user of PDSS to extend the system by adding new operators or commands or to define new reports. This lack of extensibility reflects the designer's essentially static view in specifying the features of PDSS—an approach we believe follows naturally (but not inevitably) from the traditional life cycle development framework.

Furthermore, PDSS was for reasons of hardware efficiency and cost essentially a "hard" design from the start. The size and variety of the data bases employed, the large user community, and the need for rapid response time on heavily loaded computers mandated efficient computer programs. This forced PDSS designers to restrict flexibility in the design in order to achieve software run-time efficiency. In other words, the designers adopted a "hard" design before calibrating, via actual use, the features of PDSS suited to the managerial environment, user preferences, and decision-making procedures of Eastern Manufacturing. Only actual experimentation and learning by both designers and users can help the designer determine these features. The initial "hard" design of PDSS precluded such learning. The "hard" design approach actually taken follows quite naturally from the assumption that the desired features of PDSS would be determined via the system-specifications phase of the life cycle.

Because migration always occurs during DSS development, the "hard" design approach used at Eastern Manufacturing in fact did not address the planning function originally contemplated. The PDSS design ultimately delivered addressed "what *is*?" issues (structured administrative control—MIS) instead of "what *if*?" issues (administrative or strategic planning—DSS). The migration away from planning-centered features was quite predictable. The migration effect is strongest when DSS design procedures encourage "hard" as opposed to "soft" capabilities and when they fail to allow the tailoring and evolution of system capabilities via extensible designs.

Was PDSS, therefore, a complete failure? Certainly not—PDSS was technically a success in improving the efficiency of procurement at Eastern Manufacturing; the resulting cost savings were undeniable. The PDSS design was relatively "weak," requiring only modest change in managerial decision-making styles. This aspect, coupled with the migration effect encouraged by the life cycle approach, produced a useful, efficiency-improving MIS for the company. The failure in this case was the lost opportunity for decision support in less structured, planning-related areas of procurement, which was precluded by the nonextensible, "hard" design of PDSS.

THE SECOND DSS EXAMPLE:
WESTERN ELECTRONICS

Background

Western Electronics manufactures computers and other high-technology equipment. It is a large, diversified company with annual revenues in excess of $2 billion, and it employs in excess of 20,000 people. One of the advantages that Western Electronics has over its competitors is that it designs and fabricates many of its own customized, highly specialized, integrated circuits. When these integrated circuits are incorporated into Western Electronics's equipment, the company is able to offer features which are not available in competing products. In achieving this advantage Western Electronics has committed substantial capital to the creation of nearly one dozen integrated circuit production facilities. These facilities required investment of $2 to $10 million each and necessitated the specialized training of technicians, assemblers, and design engineers. The technical demands placed on managers of such facilities are considerable, and the company has deliberately followed a policy of "promotion from within" in selecting managers for its integrated circuit facilities.

The following is a description of the environment we saw at Western Electronics as we began our DSS design. Normally the best qualified design or production engineer was selected to be the general manager of an integrated circuit (IC) facility. The managers of these facilities reported directly to the corporate engineer, who in turn reported directly to the president. The corporate engineer was well trained in both engineering and management, having graduate-level degrees in both disciplines. However, this was not true of the IC facility managers. Generally speaking, the IC facility managers were younger and less experienced, with little or no formal managerial training. Quite understandably, most of these managers devoted much of their time to dealing with major technical problems faced by their staff in meeting design and production deadlines. As a result the corporate engineer was generally unhappy with the managerial planning (cost and productivity forecasting, scheduling, asset and capital budgeting, etc.) as opposed to the technical performance of the IC facility managers. In addition, despite the company's emphasis on controlling costs, there was no managerial staff support and very little managerial accounting support available to the IC facility managers.

The existing MIS system for IC facilities reflected the accounting definition of a cost center and provided only a monthly report of expenditures and account balances, similar to that produced by a general ledger system. The reports were extremely detailed, showing all transactions, and they were produced in batch from the company-wide financial accounting system. A typical report comprised 100 to 300 pages of computer output; this was not normally used by the IC facility managers for any purpose other than resolving expenditure disputes. The absence of planning by the IC facility managers and the emphasis on the minimal stewardship function in the MIS reporting led not surprisingly to the IC facility managers' adopting an informal, "fire fighting" approach to facility planning and to their paying relatively little attention to the administrative aspects of formalized managerial planning. The corporate engineer recognized this deficiency and championed the development of a DSS for use by these managers to facilitate IC facility planning activity.

DSS Design Process

The designers of the IC facility DSS project recognized from the start that its success would depend on considerable attention to implementation issues. Motivation, education, and participation of the IC facility managers became integral aspects of DSS design and development. A phased development and implementation scheme, spanning slightly more than two years, was decided upon by the corporate engineer and two of the most senior IC facility managers. These managers also agreed that their facilities would serve as trial test sites, and they would evaluate and critique early versions of the system. In addition, an outside management educator-consultant undertook to provide a phased series of educational presentations to the IC managers, as a group, on a quarterly basis over the two-year period. The purpose of the presentations was to introduce elementary planning and management control topics, such as ratio analysis and forecasting, to the IC facility managers so that they would understand the concepts embedded in the DSS technology. Examples utilizing "live" data from IC facilities were presented, along with demonstrations of preliminary DSS offerings. During these quarterly meetings progress reports on the DSS design effort were given. Despite misgivings of some about the value of planning models, active and enthusiastic participation by the IC facility managers in the DSS project was generally observed.

The DSS itself was designed to offer the capabilities inherent in what are now called financial planning systems. These systems commonly employ programmed operators or commands—to extrapolate or project financial time-series data, such as revenues, material and labor costs, etc., or to calculate various performance measures, such as internal rate of return—without the requirement of any conventional programming by the user.

The particular DSS design for the IC facilities evolved (migrated) over time, but it included from the start a perspective based on financial planning. It was this aspect that had been commonly ignored by the IC facility managers and that was most critically needed. The company's internal demand for customized integrated circuits was growing at that time by 40% annually, and this mandated additional attention to financial matters related to capacity expansion. The features of the DSS, as developed with the IC facility managers and their boss, the corporate engineer, included:

1. An elementary data base management capability to support data collection, categorization, and manipulation of IC facility data;

2. A simple report generator to permit extraction, consolidation, and summarization of data into user-formatted reports on an *ad hoc* basis;

3. High-level routines for data analysis (forecasting, extrapolation);

4. Column and row-oriented arithmetic operators (for running cross-footing, ratio analyses, etc.);

5. Extensive graphics (both CRT display and hard copy, including four-color plotting);

6. User-defined models utilizing a very high-level command language to support financial-planning; and

7. Analytic commands ("what if" operators, sensitivity analysis, etc.).

In addition the resulting system offered a simple and novel "documentation-by-example" feature for the *automatic* generation of documentation for user-specified models. The examples served as handy memory aids. Finally, extensibility functions were designed into the DSS to permit the addition of new commands, definable by the user without programmer support, and new primitive operators, requiring programmer assistance.

It was assumed throughout the design effort that the IC facility managers would personally utilize the DSS. This dictated development of interactive software with "failsoft" and menu features wherever possible. Also, all user reference documentation was on-line, accessible by HELP commands. Fortunately, all of the IC facility managers had had previous computer experience, and this minimized the usual difficulties associated with introducing new computer-based systems into a managerial environment.

The hardware for the DSS design was a stand-alone, desk-top computer system, incorporating a CRT with graphics capability, magnetic tape cartridges, floppy disks, a four-color XY flatbed plotter, and a letter-quality printing device. It was intended that each manager would be provided with such a computer system.

Since it is often difficult to develop major systems on small computers, all early DSS software was developed on a medium-scale computer system, utilizing the APL language in an interactive mode. The APL language was chosen because it offers very powerful interactive operators for the data handling, graphics, and report generation requirements of the intended planning system. Furthermore, an APL-based financial planning system was available commercially, and this, combined with the inherent modularity of the APL language, greatly accelerated the initial design and programming effort. Developing customized procedures for adapting the existing package for IC facility purposes was a comparatively straightforward task, and concrete demonstrations of intended capabilities could be made quickly on an *ad hoc* basis. All early demonstrations utilized this APL-based system, and feedback from the IC facility managers was often quickly incorporated into the DSS.

The first version of the enhanced APL-based planning system was produced within six months by a single part-time programmer. The second version, incorporating design changes based on feedback from several IC facility managers, required another three months of effort. All design work was oriented from the beginning toward the eventual translation of the package into a form suitable for use on a desk-top computer, and the transliteration of the system into the BASIC language required by the small computer was implemented without difficulty during about four months of work by a single part-time programmer. The entire DSS design and development project was remarkable in that no major or unexpected software development pitfalls materialized. For example, the software was generally delivered early, and it often contained "hidden" features inserted by the DSS designers. These hidden features were usually advanced analytical or graphical functions that would not be made known to the IC managers until they had more training and experience with the DSS. The hidden features could, at an appropriate future time, be announced as new enhancements when (and if) demand for them developed. The first version of the desk-top DSS system had just been made available to one of the IC facility managers for actual field testing and usage when the entire DSS project was abruptly cancelled.

Discussion of the Western Electronics Case

Before summarizing the factors that led to the project's cancellation, we must first review the design issues that were incorporated into the development effort and their relationship to the frameworks developed thus far in this chapter. First, the need for early user involvement was recognized; important feedback to the design process was provided by active user participation and early availability of software packages for selected IC facility managers. Second, adapting an existing application package and utilizing an existing mini-computer time-sharing system greatly accelerated the production of a demonstrable system. The preferred features could then be quickly transliterated to the target hardware. A *de novo* attempt to develop the software on the desk-top computer would have delayed demonstrations and lengthened feedback loops from the managers on design enhancements. Third, the system was designed to be modular and extensible to permit addition of *ad hoc* and unforeseen features without complete system redesign. Fourth, the DSS incorporated common and elementary concepts of quantitative analysis for management. Advanced analytics, such as optimization and simulation, were a part of the initial design, but they were postponed (or "hidden") in the initial phases to speed early development and to assure that early systems would not provide more sophistication and abstraction than the intended managerial group could profitably utilize. Fifth, managerial training and education were recognized as being critical to the success of the DSS. Repeated seminars on managerial decision making, reports on design progress, and live demonstrations took place concurrently with the ongoing development. In fact, much of the planning and development effort by the DSS designers was focused upon the phased production of those system features considered to be essential for supporting the educational efforts. Sixth, the system produced met the necessary strictures for a DSS. It was interactive, friendly, suitable for *ad hoc* usage, and produced without the usual delays and bureaucratic tangles commonly associated with MIS development projects. Finally, the development effort did not become ensnarled in the problems which often plague traditional MIS projects: the management of large teams of programmers, the integration of new software with existing software systems, the need to handle large volumes of data efficiently, and the requirement that the system support a widely diverse user community.

Using the terminology developed earlier, we can say that the system incorporated expanding subsets of capabilities, based on an extensible design approach. Features were routinely added throughout the design/evaluation process as feedback was received from the trial IC managers and the demonstrations. The subset evolution approach meant that this could occur without system redesign. The tendency of the migration effect to occur was minimized by focusing the development of DSS features on planning and by repeated emphasis, via training and demonstrations, on "what if" planning issues. The design process was admittedly "strong," and considerable attention was directed to avoiding the inadequate-education-and-training and solving-the-wrong-problem pitfalls that can plague "strong" designs. Furthermore, the initial software capabilities were implemented "softly" on a larger mainframe in a language noted for its flexibility in data handling and analysis. The DSS was later "hardened" by transliteration to a less flexible, but more efficient language on the streamlined target hardware. This step was taken only after much feedback and learning by users and designers as the potential uses and desired features of the system emerged. This approach caused initial user-designer overhead to be high. The system began operation initially on a remote time-shared computer, and execution was inefficient; the designers were required to develop two systems on two different machines in two different languages. However, the resulting DSS incurred few user-implementation problems and incorporated many unforeseen options.

In light of the careful preplanning and successful technical development that went into the DSS design, why was the project cancelled? Without question the project had indeed met its goal of producing a useful DSS system, carefully developed and implemented in a phased manner for a receptive group of users, while staying within planned budget and development time guidelines*. However, this DSS development was subject to a set of political forces which are in many ways unique to DSS development efforts and which must be carefully considered during the design phase. Unfortunately, they were not recognized by the designers of the IC facility DSS. Cancellation of the project was in some respects unrelated to the particulars of the DSS itself. Nevertheless, some lessons relative to the DSS design process may be gleaned from this example. The precipitating event in the unexpected cancellation was the sudden resignation of the corporate engineer to accept the presidency of another company. The duties of the corporate engineer were reassigned to other corporate officials. The assistant to the corporate engineer, who had served as a critical liaison between the IC facility managers and the development group, was also reassigned to other duties and to a new boss. This left the project without executive leadership, thereby leading to its demise. Clearly, any development project can be sabotaged by sudden and unexpected reversals of this sort, and this is not in itself a reflection on the DSS design or the DSS planning effort.

A more systematic inquiry into the demise of the project was undertaken by one of the authors nearly a year later. Several subtle but important conclusions can be drawn. Without question, the immediate cause of the failure was the departure of the top executive who legitimized the effort in the eyes of the IC facility managers and who performed the all-important function of crusader in urging its adoption and use. More fundamentally, however, the DSS designers

---

*In fact, nearly two years later the test case IC manager received the first (and last) micro-based DSS continues to use the DSS routinely for facility planning.

did not adequately consider the need to develop a larger political base for legitimizing the system; the rapid winding down of the project after the crusader's departure was evidence of this.

Large-scale MIS development projects, in contrast to this DSS effort, require many months of formalized planning, review, and "selling" throughout the traditional management bureaucracy of a firm. As we discussed previously, this development life cycle process is often unsatisfactory and unwieldy from the standpoint of getting useful DSS systems designed and built quickly. But the life cycle approach does have the desirable side effect of building momentum, which the resignation of a single executive may not easily deflect. The conventional wisdom concerning DSS is to eschew rigid, formalized systems analysis and design procedures out of concern for inhibiting the process of managerial learning and system evolution. The DSS goal is to get useful and extensible software into the hands of the users quickly. The unfortunate side effect of this is that the informal and *ad hoc* design approaches, so desirable from a design and implementation standpoint, highly personalize the DSS design process and the DSS itself, thereby subjecting the DSS designers and users to greater buffeting, whipsawing, and other organizational turmoil.

Why were the IC facility managers as a group not a significant political force in continuing the project? Although the reasons are not entirely clear, in retrospect it appears that the DSS was fundamentally too ambitious from an organizational standpoint. In our parlance, the design was too "strong." That is, successful implementation of the DSS admittedly involved a substantial change in the managerial style of the IC facility managers. Most of them were open to this change; however, because of their very lack of managerial training, they could not be prime movers in effecting it. In addition, the DSS design was not without its detractors outside of the IC facility setting. In particular (and this was not known by the designers at the time), accounting officers at Western Electronics viewed the project as subverting their traditional purview. This negativism was successfully blunted by the corporate engineer, but it became manifest after his departure. As a result, the superficial enthusiasm of the IC facility managers gave way quickly under the criticism of more senior accounting executives within the company.

Finally, the DSS designers failed to deal with the conventional computer mentality of the senior executives at Western Electronics, who naïvely viewed the DSS as "just another software development project." Once the first desk-top computer version of the DSS was delivered, the new management felt that the project was essentially complete and that further training, documentation, and other supportive or evolutionary growth activities were unnecessary.

In summary, it is clear from the Western Electronics example that, where substantial managerial change is involved (a "strong" design is warranted), a well-designed DSS free of the usual hardware-software development problems can, nevertheless, fail if the designers do not initially devote energy to establishing a viable and enduring political base. The "stronger" the design, the greater the importance of establishing political ties and of having a mentor.

SUMMARY OF META-DESIGN ISSUES

It is useful to reexamine the meta-design framework we have proposed in light of the two DSS cases. Although the two cases were not the complete successes originally envisioned by their respective designers, they were not complete failures either. We believe the insights offered by the simple framework we have proposed allow one to understand more clearly the issues brought to the surface by these cases.

The migration effect was most obvious in the Eastern Manufacturing case; we believe this result was fostered by the "hard" design approach and the rigid application of traditional MIS life cycle design principles. The migration effect was effectively blunted in the Western Electronics case by the designer's recognition of the possibility of its emergence and by the attention to educational and motivational-training issues early in the design process. The use of an initial "soft," extensible design in this case allowed flexibility in the designer's initial response to unforeseen requests for additional options. This was precluded by the nonextensible "hard" design that essentially characterized the PDSS in the Eastern Manufacturing case.

On the other hand, because the Eastern Manufacturing design was relatively "weak" and the design migrated into a relatively structured, efficiency-improving MIS, there were fewer implementation problems. The absence of tailoring features was not, therefore, as critical a shortcoming as it might have been if the PDSS had been utilized for its originally intended planning function. In contrast, the Western Electronics design was quite "strong," and despite early recognition of this fact by the DSS designers it was a proximal cause of the premature failure of the project.

In contrast to the Eastern Manufacturing approach, the Western Electronics design utilized a series of small, single-user systems with only limited communications and data base capability. Each Western Electronics system allowed support of planning operations using a highly aggregated data base. Several factors favor such a configuration: (1) rapidly falling hardware prices, (2) stand-alone system reliability and decoupling from other corporate data processing operations, and (3) responsiveness to the user. Interactive system access is not a prerequisite for decision support, but it does allow users to explore the problem space as part of their thinking processes rather than forcing them to separate thinking and data access processing. Low incremental hardware costs, the availability of CRTs, and locally attached printers and plotters make this approach feasible at comparatively little financial sacrifice.

Management of the user's information is an essential aspect of decision support. However, an implicit trade-off opportunity exists between decreased managerial efficiency in information access and the expenditure of resources in utilizing and supporting a sophisticated data base management capability. Premature concern with efficient access to the underlying corporate data base may lead to a more restrictive system design, as it did in the Eastern Manufacturing case, and inevitably sap the development effort of scarce design resources, which further encourages the migration effect. The designers in the Western Electronics case avoided this particular pitfall by not tying the DSS into the corporate data base, relying instead upon aggregate data input manually into the DSS.

In addition, the *ad hoc* usage that is characteristic of a DSS suggests that housing the DSS on the same centralized mainframe hardware employed for transactional processing, as was done in the Eastern Manufacturing case, is risky if the mainframe is heavily loaded with other work. The DSS users are often unwilling to schedule their DSS usage to conform with resource availability from the central data processing (DP) site and are intolerant of the slow responsiveness often associated with running interactive software on heavily loaded DP systems.

Standardized DSS packages for financial planning are now readily available both for use on remote time-sharing services and for operation on a local processor. While it is tempting to develop each new DSS "from scratch," standardized packages reduce entry time by providing, early in the design cycle, a well-developed base for user feedback to the designer. This was convincingly illustrated in the Western Electronics case, and this early feedback greatly affected the ongoing design process and the learning by the intended users. Furthermore, despite the potentially higher total development cost resulting from the tailoring or recoding/extension of a package, overall project risk may be reduced by this early user involvement. Also, the highly competitive nature of the market for financial planning systems means that available systems are well documented, debugged, and equipped with powerful features. Hence a packaged system may satisfy the user's immediate needs, thereby freeing design resources for the implementation effort or for other high-payoff projects.

The two cases also nicely demonstrate the distinction between "soft" and "hard" designs. There appears to be an analogy here to the classic dictate of language designers in computer science: Postpone binding of variables until program execution time whenever possible. We would propose that DSS designers postpone hardening of the DSS design until final implementation whenever possible. Indeed, unless there are unavoidable contingencies, such as the requirement that the software be made available on a small micro-computer in the Western Electronics case, a DSS designer might be wise never to harden the DSS design and to live with the (potentially substantial) software/hardware efficiency losses thereby incurred in order to maintain flexibility.

Even though many DSS designers favor a particular high-level modeling language, no single choice has proven to be sufficiently powerful, portable, cheap to run, and extensible to satisfy all potential DSS requirements. In our view an extensible design is absolutely fundamental to the success of a DSS. It may be obtained from the inherent modularity of the underlying programming language, such as APL in the Western Electronics case, or it may be achieved through the design of a special user language or through the proper integration of modular application packages. The approach taken in the Western Electronics case involves developing the initial software in a powerful, compact, highly modular language—in that case, APL—and recoding the resultant system for the final target hardware in the appropriate language—in that case, BASIC. Although this technique incurs the added cost of transliteration, it maximizes design effectiveness by providing immediate user feedback. Also, it is extremely flexible during the early project phases when problem definition is most dynamic and difficult and when it is critically important that the DSS designer quickly establish credibility by scoring the "early victory" mentioned previously.

Finally, the connection between design strength and the need for training and tailoring is obvious. In the Western Electronics case we see an unmistakable interaction between design strength and the need for political sovereignty. In particular, design of a DSS must be viewed as the design of a *process* for supporting managerial decision making rather than as the mere construction of a "thing" or product, as it is often described in the literature and as it was, unfortunately, viewed by senior executives in the Western Electronics case.

CONCLUDING REMARKS

We have demonstrated how several points of confusion in the literature can relate to DSS design. Specifically, while problem structure, bounded rationality, and managerial effectiveness are important issues, they are easily misapplied in practice and provide almost no prescriptive guidance for the DSS designer. The three meta-design ideas—evolving system capabilities to accommodate migration effects, "soft" *versus* "hard" DSS functional capabilities, and "weak" *versus* "strong" design—as presented here provide a basis for defining an alternative to the standard development life cycle design approach for MIS.

The designer's conscious awareness of system and problem migration is essential for preventing premature closure on system design. In particular, the faster pace of problem/decision evolution that is characteristic of DSS settings and the consequent need for periodic restructuring are the driving forces behind the extensibility requirement imposed on DSS designs. The proposed design approach involves developing expanding subsets of system capabilities from an initial extensible nucleus. To this end generalized, "soft" capabilities are initially developed to provide the "flavor" of future system revisions, focus attention on the central decision-making process issues, and facilitate revelation of the user's preferences.

A majority of these remarks have been framed in the setting of *personal* DSS or at least in situations where *cooperative*, or team, behavior is assumed among relatively homogeneous colleagues. In an organizational setting with conflicting goals, multiple decision makers, and adversarial proceedings, similar design prescriptions might apply. However, the DSS designer must be aware that in these settings the risk of implementation failure or misuse of the DSS is higher. Ultimately, the DSS may become the scapegoat for unfavorable outcomes of a given decision. In such cases, the DSS may actually lead to a degradation in the quality of the resultant decision-making process.

Finally, we note that, even though the system designer is traditionally held to be a neutral party in the designer-client-user relationship, the available opportunities for influencing the user's decision-making process cannot be ignored when one is designing a DSS. Often a change in this process is a hidden motive of the client who has opted for DSS development. In such cases, a "stronger" design process is necessary. This means the designer should include more extensive user training and education and should pay more attention to implementation and other situational and political considerations than may be necessary for more traditional EDP or MIS design. Neglect of these considerations is likely to result in strong migration effects during the design process or outright implementation failure of the DSS. Unfortunately, in the eyes of the client it is the DSS designer alone who will be held responsible for such failures.

REFERENCES

Anthony, R. N. *Planning and Control Systems: A Framework for Analysis.* Cambridge, Mass.: Harvard University Graduate School of Business Administration, Studies in Management Control, 1965.

Bennett, J. L. "Integrating Users and DSS," in J. D. White (ed.), *Proceedings of the Sixth and Seventh Annual Conferences of the Society for Management Information Systems.* Ann Arbor, Mich.: University of Michigan Press, 1976, pp. 77–86.

Davis, G. B. *Management Information Systems: Conceptual Foundations, Structure and Development.* New York: McGraw-Hill, 1974.

Donovan, J. J., and Madnick, S. E. "Institutional and *Ad Hoc* DSS and Their Effective Use." *Data Base,* Vol. 8, No. 3, Winter 1977, pp. 79–88.

Gerrity, T. P., Jr. "Design of Man-Machine Systems: An Application to Portfolio Management." *Sloan Management Review,* Vol. 14, No. 2, Winter 1971, pp. 59–75.

Gorry, G. A., and Scott Morton, M. S. "A Framework for MIS." *Sloan Management Review,* Vol. 13, No. 1, Fall 1971, pp. 55–70.

Keen, P. G. W., and Scott Morton, M. S. *Decision Support Systems: An Organizational Perspective.* Reading, Mass.: Addison-Wesley, 1978.

Moore, J. H., and Chang, M. G. "An Implementation Paradox of Decision Support Systems," in *Proceedings of the Eleventh International Conference on System Sciences.* Los Angeles: Western Periodicals, January 1978.

Simon, H. A. *The New Science of Management Decision.* New York: Harper & Row, 1960.

Simon, H. A. "Theories of Bounded Rationality," in C. B. McGuire and R. Radner (eds.), *Decision and Organization.* Amsterdam: North Holland, 1972.

ARTIFICIAL INTELLIGENCE RESEARCH AND DECISION SUPPORT SYSTEMS

G. Anthony Gorry • Rand B. Krumland

CHAPTER 9

INTRODUCTION

Definitions of Decision Support Systems (DSS) place different emphasis upon their conceptual and technological aspects, but all acknowledge that the primary function of such systems is to aid one or more people in making decisions. As evidenced in the other chapters of this book, there are a number of important ideas about DSS. These ideas arise in the main from work done on specific systems, and few general principles have been firmly established concerning those aspects of computer systems which best augment the ability of people to solve problems.

In a paper written several years ago [1] it was noted that information system development in industry had been concentrated within the operational control setting, and within this setting the focus of this development had been on so-called structured problems [2]. On balance this judgment holds today, despite progress in the intervening years that has brought computer technology to bear upon those less structured managerial activities termed by Anthony [3] "managerial control" and "strategic planning." Successful DSS, by bringing structure to at least part of managerial decision-making processes, shift the line dividing structured from unstructured problems so as to encompass more in the former domain. To this end some systems primarily store and retrieve data, and they leave to the user the important procedural aspects of decision making. Others embody decision-making algorithms but leave to the user the task of collecting and distilling the data that must be provided for these algorithms. The use of the term "structured" may hide a certain degree of progress, since a problem that at first seems intractable may yield at least in part to analysis. When it does, it moves into the domain of structured problems, leaving the class of unstructured problems still apparently unaffected by analysis and computer technology. Still,

205

on the whole, the penetration of DSS into higher management functions has been neither rapid nor deep. It seems unlikely that a satisfactory general theory of DSS design and implementation will be developed within the near future.

In view of the many efforts to develop DSS and the interest which has centered upon them in recent years, this state of affairs is disquieting. One senses a lack of cohesiveness in those efforts. Examples of DSS, even when they are successful in their own ways, do not collectively lead to much of an understanding of a coherent field of endeavor, much less to a general theory. To the casual observer, this situation bears considerable similarity to that which exists in the area of computer science known as artificial intelligence [4]. As we shall see, this similarity is more than superficial. Efforts to build artificially intelligent machines have been underway for more than twenty years, and in certain respects the progress made and the problems encountered during that time may be harbingers of similar progress and problems in research on DSS.

MODELS AS PUZZLES

To a large degree, the success of a DSS depends on the recognition of a structure suitable for the intellectual task in question or on the creation of such a structure. The imposition of structure upon aspects of managerial problem solving rather than the discovery of a manager's preexisting mental organization of a task has been the mode favored by most designers of DSS. It is as the English Platonist Weldon suggested: There are *troubles* which we do not quite know how to handle; there are *puzzles* whose clear conditions and unique solutions are marvelously elegant; and then there are *problems* which we invent by finding an appropriate puzzle form to impose upon a trouble. In management science, models are the puzzles to which attention is directed, and much of the work in DSS constitutes the imposition of those models on various aspects of managerial decision making.

There is much to recommend such efforts. Models for use in production scheduling, inventory control, crew scheduling, and the like have a value that has been amply demonstrated in industrial settings. Many of the models share certain features. Each was derived from a problem that differed from the one to which it was ultimately applied. It was imposed on the later problem, generally on the grounds that some analogy existed between that one and the original problem for the solution of which the model had shown some merit. It is interesting that the problem in question often fails to dictate the use of a particular model, and so one may find the same problem solved in different situations through the use of decision analysis, systems dynamics, linear programming, or some other method. The use of any of these methods may have a decidedly positive effect on the solution of the problem, because such models make a clear distinction between descriptive knowledge and procedural knowledge. The former, comprising an explicit view of the problem expressed in terms of state variables, logical expressions, or probabilities, grows to encompass more of the problem domain.

Procedural knowledge, encapsulated in an implicit and generally monolithic inference mechanism, remains fixed. This distinction enables the researcher to concentrate on the collection of descriptive information, which is initially easy to obtain.

Much the same is true of models commonly encountered in DSS. The procedural aspects of problem solving are embedded in a program that remains fixed. Only descriptive information is varied. The bulk of the interaction between the user and the system is devoted to the specification of the values of parameters in terms of which the decision-making situation is to be described. The separation of descriptive knowledge from procedural knowledge can facilitate shared problem solving. The manager may have a clear comparative advantage in providing descriptive information (but may also have some difficulty casting it in terms of the parameters in the model) and may delegate to the system the manipulation of that information. DSS succeed most often when this separation does little violence to the true nature of the problem.

Choosing a single puzzle to impose upon a given trouble has another virtue. The puzzle or model clearly defines the nature and extent of the needed knowledge of the problem domain. For example, if we choose decision analysis as the framework in which to view a problem of managerial decision making, then we know that the problem domain must be described in terms of states, actions, probabilities, and utilities—and in these terms alone. Such a strict categorization of descriptive knowledge can bring order to an otherwise confusing picture of a problem-solving task. This idea is effectively exploited by the management science consultant who repeatedly uses a few models to guide information gathering in various managerial settings. As Forrester has noted [4]:

> . . . many persons discount the potential utility of models of industrial operations on the assumption that we lack adequate data on which to base a model. They believe a first step must be an extensive collecting of statistical data. Exactly the reverse is true . . . a model should come first. And one of the first uses of such a model should be to determine what formal data needs to be collected. . . . Before we measure, we should name the quantity, select a scale of measurement, and in the interests of efficiency we should have a reason for wanting to know.

Many of the more structured management problems are good examples of the development and successful application of puzzles. For example, in every large manufacturing company there used to be an expert who managed the inventories using "a sense" for when items should be ordered, an ability to associate current stock levels with anticipated demands, and a way of incorporating intangibles such as rumors of strikes into the reckoning. For the most part such people were dinosaurs of the industrial scene. They were well adapted to a certain niche within the organization. However, management scientists using mathematics and the computer produced the computer-based inventory system, an artificial intelligence expert that was superior in this particular domain to the person who had previously held the job. In other functions in industry, similar encroachments of artificial intelligence expertise into intellectual territories formerly held by humans have been seen; warehouse location decisions and quality control decisions in production processes are notable examples. Such incursions are most apparent in the operational control functions of organizations, and they have led to some of the major successes of operations research and management science.

But in contrast to such relatively well-defined problems, many of the most important problems of an organization are less structured and less directly amenable to prescriptive approaches derived from management science. Although a number of important problems in the operational control arena can be completely "solved" by the judicious use of models, many problems in operational control and most of the problems in management control and in strategic planning are much less approachable through the use of mathematical models. Indeed, in spite of the advances in management science, there are few situations in which mathematical models can completely solve managerial problems. At best, a model may approach only a few aspects of a complex problem, and a manager who believes a model does not treat important factors can hardly be expected to use it in an important problem-solving activity. The question of the extent to which a model is relevant to a particular problem is further complicated by the difficulties managers may have in expressing their thoughts with respect to the problem or in understanding the nature of the model itself. Thus, although certain formal methods are sometimes useful, for most real management problems more factors than a typical puzzle treats must be considered and more knowledge than a typical puzzle accommodates must be applied.

Much of the progress in DSS derives from the structure formal models bring to decision-making tasks. Progress may continue to come through the gradual accretion of successful modeling efforts and the embedding of new models in computer programs to support managerial decision making. Such progress, however, is not apt to lead very rapidly to a better understanding of DSS in general. That understanding will come only from the development of systems in direct response to the less well-structured aspects of managerial decision making. We now turn our attention to this more difficult problem.

THE DECISION SUPPORT SYSTEM AS A CONSULTANT

By taking a broad view of what constitutes a DSS, we may see a way to proceed with the development of a more powerful system and of a more comprehensive intellectual foundation for the field. Many information systems and computer programs are not used directly by higher-level managers. Instead they are used through an assistant or a staff person, an intermediary who exercises a program in the service of the manager. Such an extended DSS gains much of its power and flexibility from the human intermediary. Generally the computer program is rather rigid, and the view of the world it embodies is quite limited. One of the principal roles of the intermediary is to convert the manager's problem description into a form suitable for the computer program. The interpretation of the results of the computer analysis in terms that the manager can understand is another vital function of the intermediary. An even more flexible kind of extended DSS is the management science consultant who at best has, in addition to a facility for defining problems and explaining solutions, an ability to develop models specifically suited for the problem at hand.

If we could glean from the activities of intermediaries or consultants the principles and strategies they employ, and if we could codify this knowledge, then we could build DSS that would have a substantial impact on unstructured managerial problems. Unfortunately, at present relatively little is known about the exact nature of the cognitive skills that consultants use. For the most part knowledge about management science consulting is embodied in rather general statements that provide little illumination of the strategies involved and of how these strategies are applied in various managerial settings. Still, with such statements as general guidelines, it may be possible to move to more specific hypotheses about intelligence and problem solving and to incorporate them in computer programs for testing.

It is here that the interests of DSS developers may intersect those of researchers in artificial intelligence. For if the latter identify principles of mechanized intelligence or if they define procedures for equipping computers with extensive and diverse knowledge, then construction of a new generation of DSS can proceed. These programs could be distinguished from their predecessors in their flexibility, interactive capabilities, and potential power. It is appropriate then to consider the state of affairs in artificial intelligence research to see to what extent principles and techniques of knowledge engineering have been developed.

PROGRESS IN ARTIFICIAL INTELLIGENCE

The purpose of research in artificial intelligence is to produce computer programs that exhibit behavior that would normally be termed intelligent if such behavior were that of a person. For approximately twenty years, researchers in this field have been trying to build computer programs to accomplish such tasks as understanding English, making sense of visual scenes, and controlling the operations of robots. Although some of these tasks seem far removed from managerial concerns, the conceptual and technical problems involved in equipping computer programs with even rudimentary abilities in these areas are the same general problems which must be overcome in order to create more useful DSS.

The field of artificial intelligence currently stands at the confluence of several streams of research. The most apparent of these is computer science; but psychology and linguistics are two other fields from which artificial intelligence research draws and to which it contributes. Because of the expansive nature of its endeavors, artificial intelligence seems a somewhat protean field, and a description of its boundaries and interests in very specific terms is apt to provoke debate and criticism. Various subdivisions of the field can be recognized, and the distance between some of them may be greater than the distance from them to related, more traditional disciplines. Thus research on natural language conducted by workers in artificial intelligence is intimately related to many of the concerns of linguists, even though the differences in the tools and methods used may obscure this fact. On the other hand, despite the common use of the computer as an experimental tool, the work on natural language may, in a cursory view, be seen as quite different from attempts to automate aspects of medical decision making. Yet both efforts fall within the domain of artificial intelligence, related as they are through their common concerns with knowledge and the nature of intelligence. For us to describe the current intellectual and technological state of affairs in artificial intelligence, then, we must use a broad brush, hoping to portray the major features of a developing and shifting activity but knowing that in the process we shall lose some interesting details. Those concerned with DSS who find the main ideas sufficiently interesting can investigate the issues alluded to here in other sources (e.g., [5], [6], [7]).

One of the major realizations which has come from twenty years of research in artificial intelligence is that a theory of "knowledge" is important. That such a theory is important in intelligent activities seems axiomatic, but it is only recently that this recognition has had a profound effect on the nature of research in artificial intelligence. (Parenthetically, the importance of knowledge seems to be recognized to a lesser extent in DSS.) To understand why knowledge was so persistently ignored in artificial intelligence, one must consider the appeal of aesthetically pleasing theories of intelligence.

Researchers in artificial intelligence made notable progress in a relatively short time by emphasizing the use of puzzles such as cybernetics and perceptron theory. Those elegant puzzles can be studied outside the context of a particular problem until they are well understood, and then they can be brought to bear upon the trouble in question. In a number of instances the results of this approach were surprisingly good. Computer programs were able to solve problems and to perform "intellectual" tasks with a facility that was quite remarkable at the time [8]. Unfortunately, the bright promise extrapolated by some observers from those early successes was not fulfilled. The difficulty lay in the seductive nature of the puzzles themselves. They encourage one to view problems in restricted terms and to address only those problems which are most amenable to the puzzles. Soon the issue is less one of finding an appropriate puzzle to impose upon a trouble than it is one of finding troubles to which a favorite puzzle does the least violence. To the extent that this view held sway in artificial intelligence, many vital aspects of intelligence, most clearly knowledge, were slighted.

This slighting was, perhaps, unavoidable, because the techniques and methods used to produce the first successes in artificial intelligence were suited only to highly structured problems. The formal methods of cybernetics, mathematical logic, information theory, and the like were used to address well-defined and highly constrained problems such as chess, symbolic integration, and logical deduction in question-answering systems. Much of the early enthusiasm concerning the ultimate capabilities of computers to perform intellectual tasks stemmed from the presumption that most interesting problems—understanding language, doing mathematics, seeing—were susceptible to the same structuring and thus would yield to the formal methods then in use. To date, however, developments have tended to follow a different path from that foreseen. With few exceptions, a problem area has been selected, a particular puzzle applied, and a computer program has been developed to produce reasonable "answers" to the problem in question. However, attempts to "scale" the program to deal with a more extensive and complex problem domain yielded diminishing returns, and finally the effort was abandoned short of the goal formerly envisioned.

A rather simple problem in artificial intelligence has often proven to be quite revealing of the limitations of a particular theory of knowledge and problem solving. Of the numerous examples of such problems, consider one that arose more than ten years ago during the development and testing of a program to solve calculus word problems [9]. The program accepted English statements of problems requiring a determination of certain rates of change. For example, one of the problems solved by the program was the following: "A ladder 20 feet long leans against a house. Find the rate at which the top of the ladder is moving if its foot is 12 feet away from the house and moving at the rate of 2 feet per second."

The program attacked such problems in several stages, which bear at least a superficial resemblance to those one would expect in certain advanced DSS. First, it analyzed the English sentences to extract the essential components of the problem statement. The program's linguistic ability stemmed from its use of a small dictionary of words and some carefully thought-out sentence patterns provided by its designer, which it used to decompose the English statement of the problem into a set of simple declarations. Second, the program built from those declarations a model of the situation about which it was being questioned. The model, as we shall see, was quite restricted, but it did permit the program to link together the components of the problem and to identify those features of the situation which it needed to analyze. In the example cited, in the model-building process the program identified the ladder as the principal object in question and recognized that the problem requires the determination of the rate of change of the position of the ladder with respect to a vertical surface. Using this knowledge the program in the third phase selected appropriate symbolic equations from those it knew and then associated variables in the model with those in the equations. A final stage involved the algebraic manipulation of the equations so that the desired differentiation could be performed and the answer calculated. The program was an impressive accomplishment. Its success resulted from the designer's cleverness in structuring the problem domain, programming skill, and no small amount of chicanery. The latter is what is most important here.

The nature of calculus word problems is such that the exact natures of the entities involved are often irrelevant. In the above example, if we had asked about the movement of a barber pole instead of a ladder, the analysis would have remained the same. The program (or more properly its designer) took considerable advantage of this fact in the construction of the pattern-matching rules that were the basis of the program's linguistic ability. Thus the program was able to solve problems in which were mentioned objects about which it knew very little.

However, consider the following problem: "A barge whose deck is 10 feet below the level of a dock is being drawn in by means of a cable attached to the deck and passing through a ring on the dock. When the barge is 24 feet from and approaching the dock at ¾ feet per second, how fast is the cable being pulled in?" The program analyzed this problem by the method described above and calculated an answer. This time, however, its answer was wrong. If you were to solve this problem, you might well draw a diagram of the situation. Interpreting the phrase "approaching the dock," you would invoke your knowledge of gravity and boats to sketch the boat moving at the level of the water. Lacking that knowledge, the program solved the problem as though the boat would move along the line of the cable by which it was being pulled toward the dock!

It is difficult to see how one could correct this problem simply. The addition of a new pattern, for example, would probably cause an error in a problem in which a kite was being pulled in on a string. The more one thinks about this problem, the more one sees that the program must know about kites and boats and gravity much in the way that we know about them. And we know a great deal about such matters.

Despite the fact that this program was written ten years ago, it has a direct relevance to DSS in that it revealed the danger of illusory intelligence. The program appeared to understand the problems it was given, and it solved many of them correctly. Indeed, the answer it gave to the problem cited above was not obviously wrong. Calculation shows the program's answer to be incorrect, but it does not immediately reveal the reason for the error. Only a detailed investigation of the problem-solving path taken by the program and a careful explication of the underlying assumptions brings the reason for the error to light. The error, of course, resulted from the program's lack of knowledge about gravity, but the error might just as well have stemmed from ignorance of some other aspect of the world.

The program embodied certain techniques for building models from English descriptions of situations, and in that regard it was a notable technical achievement. But once the rigidity of a fixed model is abandoned, the sharp circumscription of the requisite knowledge is abandoned as well, and the realm of the so-called small infinity of facts is entered. This self-contradictory term is used by researchers in artificial intelligence to suggest that knowledge about a given subject—say, boats—comprises a collection of "facts," which, although extremely large, can be enumerated and codified. The correctness of this hopeful assertion has yet to be demonstrated convincingly, but one can defend a related proposition quite readily. To solve problems one generally employs a great deal of knowledge, much of which may not be recognized without a careful explication of the problem-solving process. The reader can undoubtedly identify many instances of managerial problem solving in which large bodies of diverse kinds of knowledge play a central role. It is difficult to see how DSS can substantially affect decision making in such cases without the embedding of large portions of that knowledge in the computer itself.

In the last few years the focus of artificial intelligence research has shifted significantly, with the realization that no single formal approach presently known can accommodate the amount and diversity of knowledge required for activities such as understanding a sentence, making sense of a scene, or solving calculus word problems. Instead, some mixture of the knowledge of "first principles," experience, common sense, and guesswork is needed, but even these terms are not as yet well defined. In the search for better organizing principles and a clearer understanding of exactly what knowledge is required in various problem-solving activities, many artificial intelligence researchers have turned to a serious study of human problem solving. People have an obvious competence to do that which formalisms cannot do. Although there has always been such a stream of research in artificial intelligence, primarily in the work of Newell and Simon [10], the need for such investigations has recently become much more apparent. So the study of *natural* intelligence has become an activity of artificial intelligence, and an important experimental method of the field now emphasizes the use of the computer as a laboratory in which theories of human problem solving can be represented and tested.

The history of artifical intelligence strongly suggests that the intelligent behavior exhibited by a consultant cannot be achieved in a program through the use of a single formal approach as the basic organizing and management principle. If computer systems are to be vehicles for supporting managerial decision making on important problems, they must be armed with diverse and powerful information storage capabilities and problem-solving strategies. They must possess the ability to properly assimilate new information as well as the ability to explain their reasoning processes, the bases and limitations of their conclusions, what unanswered questions remain, etc. Further, although formal approaches to clearly delineated and sharply constrained problems are successful in some instances, there remain the problems of *integrating* these strategies into a coherent approach to less well-defined problems. The administration and orchestration of the several components of any particular problem-solving strategy will be of paramount importance in any sophisticated consulting system. As Minsky and Papert have noted [11]:

> One cannot really use "facts" unless they are accompanied by information on how to use them. Some facts serve to warn against using other facts for certain jobs. A person's most important kind of information, perhaps, is about thinking itself; how to break a problem into subgoals, deciding when certain kinds of analogies are appropriate, when certain kinds of plans are realistic, etc. Much of what one knows, then, will not appear on the "factual" level at all, but will concern when and how to use other parts of the information store, and especially, when not to.

Such capabilities are beyond the reach of any of the formal approaches now in use, and no systems, aside from some experimental systems in laboratory settings, currently can do such things. But there are some important reasons for us to try to equip programs that support managerial decision making with the "self-awareness" implied above. If the program is unable to explain the bases for its conclusions, to make clear the way in which the facts presented bear upon its recommendations, and the reasons for its rejection of other approaches to the matter in question, a shared problem-solving process cannot be truly realized. Without those capabilities, then, a program would be useful only in a setting in which the solution of a very specific and highly constrained problem is desired. Few examples of such problems exist in the domain of unstructured managerial decision making.

DSS also need explanatory capabilities to avoid subtle, but potentially serious, errors. An egregious mistake on the part of such a program may be less of a danger than an ostensibly minor one. The former may cause the program to make a recommendation so at odds with the user's plan or intuition that the user will recognize immediately the existence of some defect in the program's reasoning. A less remarkable mistake by the program is apt to be overlooked if its effect on the immediate recommendation is less pronounced. The error may have a persistent effect, however, ultimately causing the program to wander far from the best problem-solving path. In view of the complexity of many managerial problems and the great diversity of the settings in which they arise, it is reasonable to expect that even very good programs will make errors when confronted with new situations. By explaining its reasoning to its users, such a program may prevent them from taking an ill-advised action.

A program's ability to examine its own reasoning may play a crucial role in its evaluation and 'refinement. In many managerial settings, only programs possessing large amounts of knowledge can be successful. Generally, when such a program is tested, new problems are identified which can only be attacked through the expansion of the program's store of knowledge or problem-solving strategies. With such additions, the size of the problem domain, as measured by the amount of knowledge required to perform effectively in that domain, increases rapidly. The difficulties of coping with large collections of facts are heightened by the diverse nature of the facts themselves. When a program fails to deal adequately with a case, the attribution of that failure to inadequacies in its knowlege will be extremely difficult, unless the program knows what it knows and can explain how it applied its knowledge to the problem in question. Only in this way can the program be evaluated properly, for an assessment of its recommendation without an assessment of the basis for that recommendation will be of little use. A thorough evaluation is a prerequisite for the further refinement of the program.

In those computer programs in which some simulation of the cognitive abilities of experienced consultants is attempted (in contrast with programs based on formal methods manifestly different from the methods used by humans), self-awareness assumes additional importance. At a minimum, an ability to reconstruct a process of reasoning is required, and this implies that some way must be found to make a program's knowledge accessible to it. In the long run such a program should give persuasive explanations and also should accept suggestions as to ways in which it could expand or modify its store of knowledge.

For a program to recapitulate the steps it took to solve a given problem, it must in some way retain information about the facts and strategies it used. Here a balance must be struck. For the program to derive again its entire problem-solving process in order to respond to a user's question is too cumbersome. For the program to remember every detail of its reasoning in anticipation of questions from the user is equally inefficient. Further, neither extreme really meets the need the user has for a cogent explanation. Somehow the proper level of abstraction must be realized in the program's recounting of what it knows and what it did.

Until recently computer technology has not allowed the development of systems with the capabilities implied by this brief discussion. Consider the use of basic computer science tools in the representation of certain problem-solving strategies derived from the introspection of consultants. Often a flow chart is constructed to represent the way in which a particular problem is to be handled. Sometimes the flow chart represents the opinion of an expert as to the perceived thought process. In other cases it is based on a mixture of introspection and more formal modeling. In any event, the resulting flow chart is an encoding of a decision procedure, deemed to be a good one to follow when faced with a particular problem.

Little success has been achieved with this approach, however, insofar as complex managerial problems are concerned. A rigid definition of the logic to be used in a given situation may be impossibly cumbersome. Even if such flow charts can be constructed for subproblems of a managerial problem, decisions as to how and when they should be combined, modified, and applied to a given situation remain. The representation of knowledge in flow charts makes these latter decisions exceedingly difficult. Knowledge about the particular managerial situation is *implicit*, not explicit, in a decision flow chart. For instance, because the reasons for a particular branching are not available to the program, in general it cannot make even simple deductions about them. Thus, unless the situation matches exactly a series of branches in the flow chart, the program is helpless. Its lack of underlying knowledge prevents it from adjusting its approach to a variation of the managerial problem.

These problems typify those that arise when an attempt is made to model cognitive process with conventional computer programming languages and data structures. Conventional technology places severe constraints on the complexity of the problem-solving theories that can be simulated. Fortunately, recent advances in computer science and technology, especially those in areas of artificial intelligence, have ameliorated some of these problems. We can now construct and test complex systems which embody a broader range of tasks for supporting decisions. The increase in the power of computer programming tools and the rapidly decreasing cost of computer hardware have combined to allow the consideration of "unaesthetic" theories of cognition. Greatly improved systems have been developed for managing very large collections of facts, and new "goal-directed" programming languages have been designed for utilizing these facts in the solution of difficult problems [4].

One example of the use of this technology is a program developed to deal with the medical problem known as taking the history of the present illness. The program is discussed in detail elsewhere [2], so here we will describe it only in general terms. The program uses the facts at hand, particularly the patient's chief complaint, to generate hypotheses about the patient's condition. It actively seeks additional information about the patient to accomplish a number of different tasks, including testing hypotheses and eliminating untenable ones. These activities may spawn further tasks, such as checking the validity of newly discovered facts or asking about related findings. The program develops its problem-solving "strategy" from the complex interaction of many different procedures, pieces of advice, guesses, and the facts it is given. The particular selection of methods and the way in which these methods are assembled are controlled by various pieces of advice stored in the program's associative memory. Each piece of advice is keyed to some specific situation; when that situation arises, the relevant advice "comes to mind" for the program.

The difference between this mode of behavior and that provided through conventional subroutine calls is that in the latter case the supervisory program must explicitly invoke a given procedure by its "name." In the case of the history of the present illness program, the invocation of methods is goal-directed in that no explicit call of a particular method is made. Rather, the program activates procedures by indicating a need for a procedure with a particular purpose, and any number of procedures may be activated in response to a particular goal statement. This facility enables the program to access advice about particular situations without having this advice structured in great detail in advance.

Programs written in the new languages tend to reflect a particular programming practice called "heterarchical" in the artificial intelligence community [7]. Through the extensive use of procedures associated with particular goals, programmers create a rather diffuse locus of control wherein modules interact not in a hierarchical fashion, but more or less as a community of specialists or experts [7]. A great emphasis is placed on equipping a problem-solving program with knowledge about itself—the facts it possesses and the procedures it uses. While many of the notions of heterarchical programming are commonly accepted as principles of good programming practice, recent efforts in artificial intelligence research have produced technical improvements in programming languages which facilitate adherence to those principles. Such facilities may ultimately prove important in the development of more flexible and powerful DSS, but many difficult problems must be solved by workers in artificial intelligence before those benefits can be fully realized.

THE CONTRIBUTION OF ARTIFICIAL INTELLIGENCE RESEARCH TO DSS

Recent intellectual and technological developments have, through their synergy, created a particular excitement for workers in artificial intelligence. The recognition of the importance of knowledge in problem solving has sharpened the study of the intellectual topography of problem domains. The study of the knowledge involved in tasks such as analyzing a scene or understanding a sentence has in turn stimulated the development of representational schemes and new programming languages for the organization and marshaling of different kinds of knowledge in problem-solving programs. In this way, a range of problems are being attacked with renewed vigor by researchers in the field.

But it should be recognized that many of these problems are perennial in the field. The goal of artificial intelligence research continues to be the production of computer programs exhibiting intelligent behavior. Therefore in broad terms the subjects of the field remain unchanged, and to an outsider progress may seem to be limited. The lessons learned have, in a sense, been largely negative; various formalisms have been found to be inadequate as general bases upon which to build sophisticated problem-solving programs. However, individual successes have been achieved. For example, complex programs have been developed for solving difficult problems in mathematics, chemistry, and medicine. Other programs have been developed which behave competently in such tasks as conversing about a limited subject. What may obscure this progress is a lack of a single approach or set of principles.

The most notable successes in artificial intelligence, judged in terms of performance alone, have resulted from a "performance orientation." That is, the knowledge that was embedded in the program, the way in which that knowledge was represented, and the methods by which the program availed itself of the stored knowledge were developed in the light of particular problems to which the program was adressed. In his book Weizenbaum [3] asserts that the achievements of artificial intelligence research "are mainly triumphs of technique" despite certain "spinoffs, such as refinements in higher-level programming languages, that were initiated by artificial-intelligence concerns and that have entered the mainstream of computer science." DENDRAL, a program that interprets mass spectrometer readings, and MACSYMA, a program that performs symbolic mathematical manipulations are two exceptions to this assessment. Both programs are extremely powerful, and both owe a significant debt to the artificial intelligence movement. As Weizenbaum notes (p. 231):

> . . . when the design of these programs was initiated, the theories on which they are now based were not sufficiently well-formed to be modeled in terms of effective procedures. . . . The initial versions of these programs were a mixture of algorithms incorporating those aspects of the problems that were well understood and encodings of whatever heuristic techniques could be gleaned from experts. As the work progressed, however, the programs' heuristic components became increasingly well understood and hence convertible to enrichments of the relevant theories. Both programs were thus gradually modified until they became essentially completely theory-based.

These programs are distinguished from most other artificial intelligence programs by virtue of their theoretical maturity, a maturity gained over ten to fifteen years of development. Most research efforts in artificial intelligence have been far less sustained. They have produced programs which are largely heuristic in that their construction is based not on a theory, but "on rules of thumb, strategems that appear to 'work' under most foreseen circumstances, and on other *ad hoc* mechanisms that are added from time to time" [3]. Perhaps theories of problem solving will eventually be constructed for the problem domains in question. The present state of development of those programs does not permit the easy or direct inference of general principles of mechanized intelligence by designers of DSS. Researchers in the field can infer from these successes the emergence of "knowledge engineering" [4], but these successes are at best the harbingers of such a field—the field of knowledge engineering cannot be said to exist yet in any commonly accepted sense.

For researchers interested in the development of DSS, the implications of this situation are several. First, a theory of knowledge is soon apt to prove as important a subject of study for them as it has been in recent years for researchers in artificial intelligence. Second, although artificial intelligence research may provide some technological innovations to benefit DSS design, the solution of the substantive intellectual problems of artificial intelligence will not come in the near future. Therefore the *ad hoc* development of DSS for particular applications will remain the rule. More interesting and substantial DSS can be expected from the gradual expansion of the knowledge bases upon which systems are built, but it is unlikely that any detailed theory of DSS will emerge in the near future. In his discussion of artificial intelligence as the exploration of intellectual functions, Newell [15] suggests that the development of the field seen in that light has become "an exploration in which one function after another is broached and conquered—or perhaps resists all attempts at mechanization." And insofar as the fruits of that exploration are concerned, he concludes: "There need be no real rhyme to the geography of the mental functions, anymore than there need be rhyme to the geography of a new continent. Each valley and mountain range must be attained, explored, and settled; exploration can then push on into new country." Similar explorations are likely to characterize work in applying artificial intelligence techniques to DSS for the foreseeable future.

REFERENCES

1. Gorry, G. A., and Scott Morton, M. S., "A Framework for Management Information Systems," *Sloan Management Review*, Vol. 13, No. 1, 1971, pp. 55–70.

2. Simon, H. A., *The New Science of Management Decision.* New York: Harper & Row, 1960.

3. Anthony, R. N., *Planning and Control Systems: A Framework for Analysis.* Cambridge, Mass.: Harvard University Graduate School of Business Administration, Studies in Management Control, 1965.

4. Forrester, J. W., *Industrial Dynamics.* Cambridge, Mass.: MIT Press, 1961.

5. Winston, P. H., *Artificial Intelligence*. Reading, Mass.: Addison-Wesley, 1977.

6. Schank, R. C., and Colby, K. M. (eds.), *Computer Models of Thought and Language*. San Francisco: W. H. Freeman, 1973.

7. Winston, P. H. (ed.), *The Psychology of Computer Vision*. New York: McGraw-Hill, 1975.

8. Feigenbaum, E. A., and Feldman, J., *Computers and Thought*. New York: McGraw-Hill, 1963.

9. Charniak, E., "Carps, A Program Which Solves Calculus Word Problems," Project MAC-TR-51. Master's thesis, M.I.T., July 1968.

10. Newell, A., and Simon, H. A., *Human Problem Solving*. Englewood Cliffs, N.J.: Prentice-Hall, 1972.

11. Minsky, M., and Papert, S., "Research at the Laboratory in Vision, Language, and Other Problems of Intelligence," Memo No. 252. Cambridge, Mass.: M.I.T., Artificial Intelligence Laboratory, 1972.

12. Pauker, S. G., Gorry, G. A., Kassirer, J. P., and Schwartz, W. B., "Towards the Simulation of Clinical Cognition: Taking a Present Illness by Computer," *American Journal of Medicine*, Vol. 60, June 1976, pp. 981–96.

13. Weizenbaum, J., *Computer Power and Human Reason: From Judgment to Calculation*. San Francisco: W. H. Freeman, 1976.

14. Shortliffe, E. H., Buchanan, B. G., and Feigenbaum, E. A., "Knowledge Engineering for Medical Decision Making: A Review of Computer-Based Clinical Decision Aids," in *Proceedings of the IEEE*, Vol. 67, No. 9, September 1979, pp. 1207–24.

15. Newell, A., "Artificial Intelligence and the Concept of Mind," in R. C. Schank and K. M. Colby (eds.), *Computer Models of Thought and Language*. San Francisco: W. H. Freeman, 1973.

A DECISION-ORIENTED APPROACH TO BUILDING DSS

Charles B. Stabell

CHAPTER 10

INTRODUCTION: A DECLINE OF THE D IN DSS?

This chapter presents ideas on how to build Decision Support Systems (DSS) in accord with a decision-oriented approach that was originally outlined by Scott Morton (1971) and Gerrity (1971). Although the ideas have evolved as the result of work over several years (Stabell, 1974; 1975; 1978; 1979), some of the main points that I want to develop here were sharpened in the process of reviewing and commenting on the other chapters of this book. As a consequence, the first part of this chapter is to a large extent organized as a comment on and critique of some major themes in the analyses, propositions, and guidelines developed by my fellow authors. The comments should, however, also be relevant to the work of a much larger set of both researchers and practitioners (Fick and Sprague, 1980; Young and Keen, 1981).

This opening analysis motivates and delineates the decision-oriented approach that is presented in the next two sections of this chapter. The form might give the impression that we are dealing with alternative and opposing approaches. To a large extent, however, the ideas should be viewed as an attempt to complement and complete the material covered in the other chapters. My discussion is most certainly open to a similar critique of being incomplete and inconsistent. The aim, however, is that the material be both of practical value and a stimulus for further work.

As will become apparent, both the thrust of the comments and the approach to building explored in this chapter rest on a particular view of DSS. Many

I received many valuable comments from a number of persons on earlier drafts of this chapter. However, I am particularly indebted to John Bennett, who has gone far beyond the role of editor in providing continuous encouragement, constructive criticism, and detailed suggestions.

authors begin their discussion with a definition of DSS. Thus some general comments on the issue of definitions seem appropriate here.

The discussion of definitions is often quite sterile. The analyses proceed as if there is a correct definition to be found. It is as if the goal of the discussion is to discover the right definition (or to show that the right definition has been found). As I see it, definitions are created. Definitions are therefore neither correct nor false. They can be more or less useful. Usefulness, however, implies a context. Different definitions of DSS can be more or less useful in different contexts.

Embracing a relativist position does not mean that any definition will do. Rather, it emphasizes the need to define the concept of DSS within a larger framework. That many find the concept of DSS nebulous and superfluous does not mean that we need yet another definition. Instead, I think it suggests the need to restrict in order to sharpen our terms. What we thereby lose in scope might be amply compensated for by increases in what we are able to say. Thus an important role for a conceptual framework is that it should identify the limits of the applicability and the relevance of the concept of DSS.

The concept of DSS is essentially a view of the role of computers in management (Keen, 1980). Therefore the context for a definition of DSS cannot be merely technological, but must address where and why the technology is developed and how the technology is used. It is thus conceptually not very meaningful to try to distinguish DSS from other computer-based systems merely by looking at properties of the technological components in isolation. For example, as is apparent from the chapters in this book by Keen and Gambino, Hurst *et al.*, and Moore and Chang, a number of the more significant features of DSS are bound to characteristics of the system development process.

The wide scope of a framework for DSS makes it imperative to ensure that the key concepts are both necessary and sufficient. Or stated differently, it is important to establish which concepts in the framework are key. What is key will obviously depend on the intended reader—researcher or practitioner, user or builder. For the builder, even though the concept of DSS that is presented is not technology-oriented, there should be links to the what and how of using the technological building blocks. The practical significance of the concept should also be apparent in the features that distinguish DSS from other systems.

Reviewing the different chapters in this book on building DSS, I find that it is the concept of support that has been most influential. The proposals in the literature to distinguish between personal support systems, group support systems, and organizational support systems (Keen and Hackathorn, 1979) and to rename the field executive support systems (Rockart and Treacy, 1980) or mind support systems (Wagner, 1981) and the frequent references to office support systems in the context of office automation (see, for example, Uhlig, Farber, and Bair, 1978) suggest the same: *support* is the common theme.

The concept of support systems is important. It represents a significant advance in our idea of the role for computers. Stated simply, it captures major requirements for computer-based systems in a context where the user is always in charge: both the extent and the nature of system use are at the discretion of the user. Issues for the technology of support have much in common with human-computer interactions and human-computer interface design in general. These issues are of increasing importance to the field of computer science and the design of computer systems (see, for example, Guedj *et al.*, 1980; Shneiderman, 1980; Smith and Green, 1980) as computers proliferate and become directly accessible to ever larger user communities. The potential unique contribution of the DSS field is to focus attention on requirements for computer-based systems that are to be used as aids in complex and ill-structured tasks.

A Limited Role for D in DSS

If we agree that the emphasis on support is helpful, then we need to establish what it is we want to support. It is the *decision* in the concept that should define the unique context of DSS, and the *decision* should have implications for the why, how, and what of building such systems. However, in much of the literature I find that the decision is not really in focus. In many discussions very little would be altered if we were to exchange the decision label for another term (management, executive, personal, mind, or whatever).

Consider the most common uses of the D in DSS: to identify who is the intended user, to motivate the goal of support, and to identify the need for adaptability. In its most trivial use, the D in DSS indicates that the intended users of such systems are decision makers. However, decision maker is often merely a synonym for manager. The terms are used interchangeably, and the implications of building DSS for the manager-as-decision-maker-as-user are seldom explored.[1]

The key use of the word decision in DSS is to motivate the need for systems that support rather than replace decision makers. Historically this concept provided a much needed corrective to the information systems field. Prior to decision support the field was laboring with an undifferentiated view of the role of computers in management and was implicitly working with the assumption that automation was the long-term goal. However, to a large extent the concept of decision support remains ill-defined. This is perhaps particularly apparent when decision support is applied to the building of DSS. The concept is frequently defined obliquely. If the computer-based system is interactive, user-controlled, and easy to use, and if the manager is assumed to use judgment in arriving at a decision, then we have decision support. There is little explicit specification of the *kind* of use necessary for support of decision making. It is as if *any* use is decision support.

Decision processes vary a great deal both across the population of decision makers and, for a given decision maker, across decision situations. Systematic and coherent patterns in individual differences are often referred to as cognitive styles (see, for example, McKenney and Keen, 1977; Mason and Mitroff, 1973). In response to such differences it is frequently proposed that a DSS must be adaptable to a variety of decision processes[2] (Carlson, Chapter 2 of this book).

However, the argument seldom identifies any limits to the need for adaptation. There is not much explicit concern for possible dysfunctional impacts of alternative system designs in terms of inevitable changes in decision processes that will occur even with the most "adaptable" system. The argument does not tell us why we should introduce any system in the first place, for complete adaptability of the support tool implies that no one decision process is "better" than any other. The argument implies instead that the major system benefits are increased efficiency through reduced consumption of manager time and effort and through access to higher-quality inputs. In practice, the adaptability argument frees the designer/builder from the need to specify explicitly how system features provide decision support in a specific decision situation. The position is in part an attempt to give the user complete control over system use. However, any design must imply some choices as to how to use the system, as in practice the design must necessarily limit use along a number of dimensions.

Having indicated the limited emphasis on the decision in current DSS, let us extend the analysis by considering where and why we need a more decision-oriented approach. The discussion addresses the design of the user-system interface and the process of system development—two major topics for the building of DSS that are also covered elsewhere in this book, primarily by Carlson (Chapter 2), Bennett (Chapter 3), Hurst *et al.* (Chapter 6), Keen and Gambino (Chapter 7), and Moore and Chang (Chapter 8).[3]

Interface Design

As noted by Keen (1976), the user-system interface is not a "cosmetic" issue: to the user, the interface is the system. However, we need to recognize that the interface is not merely a question of general hardware and software features (such as terminal type, screen layout, command language, and data representation). How the user should (is expected to) perceive and understand the system—its uses and limitations—in the context of the user's particular decision situation is also an important aspect of the interface architecture.

Following Meador and Ness (1974), we can distinguish between passive and active understanding of a system. Passive understanding refers to the mechanics of system use—how to get started, what functions are available, the syntax of the different commands, etc. Active understanding refers to how to use the system in the task at hand. For a DSS active understanding covers how to use the system for decision making—for example, knowing the meaning and the uses of the different DSS functions in terms of the different stages of the user's own decision process.

Proposals for a representation-centered design (Carlson, Chapter 2; Bennett, Chapter 3) and a verb-oriented design (Keen and Gambino, Chapter 7) emphasize general features of the user-system interface. Both approaches say little about how to map the general approach into a specific decision situation. What representations (or verbs) should be chosen? What data should be included? What is the relationship between functions unique to the primary decision problem and functions solely relevant to the use of the DSS (for example, the system commands in Keen and Gambino, Chapter 7)? The arguments for a representation-centered (or, alternatively, verb-oriented) design emphasize the value of features that minimize the amount of mental energy consumed by attention to system mechanics. Such features simplify passive system understanding. The analysis, however, has little to say about design features that maximize the effectiveness of the user's expenditure of mental energy in dealing with the primary decision problem. It is not clear what to do to amplify the user's problem-solving capabilities.

Increasing decision-making effectiveness through changes in how decisions are made should be a principal objective for DSS development. However, the guidelines for the design of the user-system interface seldom identify features that might direct changes in decision behavior and that might facilitate user learning in terms of how decisions are made. There is little reference to the distinction between an existing and a desired decision-making process. Changes in decision making are instead primarily seen as an issue for the internal architecture of the DSS. The system should be easy to modify to accommodate requirements for new functions, commands, models, and data as the use of the system evolves. Triggering or securing the evolution of decision making is, however, not addressed as an issue for interface design.

Development Process

Proposals for an evolutionary (Moore and Chang, Chapter 8), middle-out (Hurst *et al.*, Chapter 6), or adaptive (Keen and Gambino, Chapter 7) approach do emphasize the process of DSS development, but they say little about the direction or content of the changes to be achieved. The guidelines presented are consistent with the view of the DSS builder as an agent for nondirected change. It is the user who is responsible for defining the content of the change. The builder is merely a facilitator for user-directed change.

Reviewing a number of DSS cases, Keen (1980) concludes that systems often have unanticipated impacts. He proposes that this suggests the need for an adaptive approach to DSS development (see also Keen and Gambino, Chapter 7). Overstating the point, we arrive at the truism that a completely adaptive development process obviously has no unanticipated impacts, as none were anticipated in the first place. I would like to suggest that the unanticipated impacts also indicate the need to expend greater effort trying to specify and to obtain the intended impacts of the system development effort. The builder-as-engineer of a DSS might not care whether uses and impacts are unanticipated as long as the system "works." However, the unintended impacts on the decision process might equally well be undesirable and could imply unnecessary development costs. Unanticipated impacts can be a signal that a system does not "work."

Let us briefly review two examples that illustrate my argument. The cases cover systems designed, respectively, to support production/marketing decisions (Scott Morton, 1971; also in Keen and Scott Morton, 1978, pp. 16–31) and to support portfolio investment decisions (Gerrity, 1971; Stabell, 1975; also in Keen and Scott Morton, 1978, pp. 101–126). The impact on decision processes has been well documented in these instances.

Example 1: Production/Marketing Decisions

Consider the need to coordinate the marketing and manufacturing operations of the laundry equipment division in a very large corporation. The operations are run as independent profit centers. A marketing-planning manager (MPM) is responsible for coordinating sales and production plans by establishing specific production targets. The MPM has to balance expected demand (partly a function of merchandising campaigns) with production capacity, inventory, and work in progress. In the decision process, the MPM confers with both the marketing manager and the production manager.

A graphics-based, interactive computer system (ICS) was developed to support the MPM's decision process. ICS included data on production inventory and sales (previous year, year-to-date, and forecast). It could be used to evaluate the consequences for inventory (decision criteria) of different production schedules (decision variable) given changes in targeted sales.

A major anticipated impact of ICS was a dramatic reduction in decision time (both elapsed and consumed); this is not surprising given a system designed to remove "bottlenecks" observed in the decision process before the system was installed. We note in addition a significant *unanticipated* shift in the focus of the decision-making process. Production decisions must ultimately be made in terms of approximately ten specific products within each of three product categories (washers, tumblers, and agitators). In the old decision process, aggregate sales for the three product categories were first determined, and then the individual products were processed. In the new process, the managers worked first (and also foremost) with the detailed figures for the thirty different specific products.

Scott Morton argues (1971, pp. 112–114) that working at the detailed level of the individual products is more effective. It is the production and sale of the specific products that ultimately can be controlled by the manager. I might argue that the disaggregate focus is less effective decision making, as it perhaps distracts attention from some of the global trade-offs between major product categories. This global view might be particularly relevant for decisions concerning activities toward the end of the planning period: plans for the last months of the twelve-month planning period might be less detailed. There are probably greater opportunities for rearranging both marketing and production activities. Furthermore, the shift in focus in the decision process possibly reflects an unwarranted trust in detailed plans.

The issue of whether the shift in decision making is or is not an improvement cannot be resolved here. The main point is to suggest that the unanticipated impact might represent a misuse of the DSS.[4]

Example 2: Portfolio Investment Decisions

Consider the decisions involved in buying and selling assets for portfolios managed by the trust department in a large bank. Each portfolio manager (PM) is responsible for, on the average, 40 (the range is from 20 to 200) accounts that might be individual investors, trusts, or pension funds of large corporations. Most of the investment decision making is focused on the purchase and sale of stocks traded on the major security exchanges. Making portfolio investment decisions is very much an information game. A PM daily attends to a mass of data on the security markets, on more fundamental developments in the firms and their industries, and on prospects for the economy as a whole. The information sources are internal reviews, external reports, and personal contacts with both analysts and traders.

A graphics-based, interactive computer system was developed to provide each PM with a facility to store, access, and process data on both individual securities and portfolios. A key objective was to move the individual security-oriented decision process toward a more portfolio-oriented process.

An unanticipated impact of the portfolio management system (PMS) was its use as a tool in marketing and client communication. More important here, however, was that the introduction of PMS apparently did not lead to a shift toward a more portfolio-oriented investment decision process. As a consequence of an investment decision process that remained oriented toward individual securities, a limited set of PMS functions were actually used. Of the ten major functions on the system in 1974, two accounted for more than 80% of total system use, and several of the portfolio-oriented functions were never used by a number of the PMs.

PMS was primarily used in the process of implementing decisions concerning individual securities (for example, to find accounts that have cash available for the purchase of a security or accounts that have a particular security that is to be sold). The typical session lasted five minutes and involved obtaining on the average three reports (interactions). The system was, however, designed for interactive analysis at the terminal. The first time the PM accesses information on a particular account, all available account information is loaded from a relatively slow secondary store to a faster working store. The system is then very responsive on all subsequent interactions involving that particular account. The underlying design concept was that the large overhead incurred for the first access would be "covered" by the low "cost" of the subsequent interactions. With the actual pattern of a very limited number of reports per session, the overhead is not "covered."

PMS thus illustrates how unanticipated impacts may involve unnecessary computer costs and a waste of resources. In this particular case it should be possible to develop a system for a fraction of the cost of PMS that would satisfy most of the needs reflected in the pattern of actual PMS use.

These two cases illustrate an obvious but important point. Both the interface and the internal architecture of a DSS must necessarily embody some idea of system use and system impact. A decision-oriented approach can be viewed as an attempt to provide a basis for making explicit choices between design alternatives in terms of use in decision making and impact on the decision process. As the examples also illustrate, a decision-oriented approach will not produce designs that invariably secure the intended uses and the desired impacts. The need for an adaptive development process as advocated in this book is therefore genuine. However, a decision-oriented approach should provide a direction to system development by indicating what impacts to monitor and what choices to make in order to direct the evolution of both decision making and system.

The proposals for an adaptive approach to DSS development emphasize changes in the system. The intent is primarily to secure system use, and little is said about how to secure useful uses of systems. If there is no clear idea of the content and direction of the changes to be achieved, an adaptive approach can fall into a "usability trap," the development of systems that are usable and used, but not very useful (see, for example, Stabell, 1975).

Will systems that are not useful be used? The answer obviously depends on what is meant by "useful." If we assume that the manager-user always knows best, then use and useful are synonymous terms. However, if we accept that managers vary in the quality of their decision making, then they probably also vary in their ability to judge the usefulness of a decision aid. A DSS can be viewed as being very useful even though it leads to further entrenchment of the existing, ineffective decision-making process that it supports. In order to avoid the usability trap, it is necessary to have an explicit goal for system development beyond the goal of getting the system used. The goal must serve as a referent for the development effort for both user and builder—which does not exclude adjustment as the process unfolds. In a decision-oriented approach the goal is expressed in terms of how decisions should be made.

Keen and Gambino (Chapter 7) suggest that it is important to find a "good" user. This guideline can be interpreted as a strategy for avoiding the usability trap. However, introducing the concept of a "good" user begs the question of how one defines (and finds) "good" users. In a decision-oriented approach this is seen as an issue of defining and finding effective decision making.

Why Not a Decision Perspective?

The concept of a decision-oriented approach is not new. It is instructive to explore why the approach has had such limited influence. To conclude this introductory discussion, we will consider three points. First, some find the approach inappropriate. Second, it is difficult to apply in practice. Finally, this book in particular provides a context that downplays the issues addressed by a decision-oriented approach.

The essence of arguments against a decision perspective is that it is not consistent with the actual nature of managerial work. Studies (most notably by Mintzberg, 1973) are cited to document that *managers seldom make decisions as part of a deliberate, coherent, and continuous decision-making process.* Instead, the manager's workday is characterized by brevity, variety, and fragmentation, with, on the average, less than five minutes continuously spent in any single activity. *Managers are much more than decision makers.* In addition to their decisional role, they often need to attend to a number of other roles: figurehead, leader, liaison, entrepreneur, resource allocator, and negotiator.

The context of managerial decision making is important. It defines both the potential for and the limits to decision support. The critique of the decision perspective reminds us that the Intelligence, Design, and Choice model (Simon, 1977) is too narrow. We need to consider the whole decision cycle that includes decision implementation, evaluation, and control. However, this does not necessarily imply that we cannot focus on decision activities. It does not necessarily exclude looking at managerial activities using the conceptual lens of a decision-making perspective.

The amount of time apparently consumed in decision making depends on how we define decision making. For example, nondecisions might be viewed as an important aspect of decision making. Nondecisions (Bachrach and Baratz, 1962) are problems that remain unrecognized, decisions that are taken by default, and actions that are performed with no conscious attempt to consider explicitly the relevant objectives and alternatives. Furthermore, the amount of time consumed in actual decision making is not necessarily a good indicator of its relative significance. Using the time spent in decision activities to motivate a lesser emphasis on decision making is analogous to arguing that we should not waste attention on managers since there are fewer managers than clerks. Rather than try to select between them, it is necessary to attend to both decision making and other managerial activities.

Arguments based on the "true" nature of managerial work are frequently prone to the fallacy of confusing what is with what ought to be. For example, the brevity, variety, and fragmentation of managerial work (Mintzberg, 1973) might be viewed as an indication that managers cannot find time to interact directly with computer-based systems. This is probably a correct description of the current situation. It does not necessarily follow that it is a valid (or the only) prescription for effective use of computer-based systems. Current behavior can in part be seen as the result of a situation where managers do not have direct and personal access to computer-based decision aids. Managers must delegate information and analysis requests. While waiting for a response from the appropriate staff function, managers attend to other activities. The hectic pace of managerial work also reflects the fact that managers spend a great deal of time resolving crises and unforeseen problems. They are constantly "putting out fires." This can be seen as the result of inadequate analysis and planning. The brevity, variety, and fragmentation of managerial work is thus in part a symptom of the ineffective decision making that a DSS is trying to remedy.

The development of a DSS should be viewed as an attempt to focus greater attention on the decision-making aspects of the task of managers. The D in DSS is thus used in a prescriptive sense. It implies more explicit consideration of the decision making that commonly is overshadowed and driven out by the other requirements and roles in managerial work.

Applying a decision-oriented perspective requires both describing and understanding current decision-making behavior in order to define what processes should change and to see how to change them. This will be reviewed in greater detail in the next section. At this point, we need only note that it is hard to obtain the necessary information and understanding. Managers find it difficult to tell how they make decisions (see, for example, Clarkson, 1962; Braybrooke, 1963). They appear to be more comfortable discussing what they decide. Part of the problem is that managers are not used to thinking about how they decide. They often prefer to act. Managers are seldom evaluated in terms of how they decide, but are often evaluated in terms of the consequences of the actions that they have chosen. They are rewarded in terms of outcomes (Stabell, 1978). As a result, although managers most often are aware that their decision making can be improved, they do not know how to improve it. In addition, even though they are receptive to assistance and advice, they do not know what to expect from a builder of a DSS. The interaction between managers and builders is most often focused on what the manager thinks is the area of expertise of the builder, that is, computers. Issues such as inaccurate and inaccessible data are common topics. What the manager-as-decision-maker does with the data is rarely addressed.

The problems encountered underline the need for providing the system development process with methods that can help focus and structure the dialog between manager and builder in terms of decision making. There is a need to establish a basis for the description and diagnosis of decision making in terms of how decisions are made—the procedural aspects of decision making—as distinct from the substantive aspects of decision making.

The distinction between substance and procedure is important. It is used in the sense first introduced by March and Simon (1958, pp. 178–79; see also Simon, 1981). The substantive aspects relate to the *what* of decision making, while the procedural aspects relate to how decisions are made. Consider the purchase of a computer. Characteristics that might distinguish between alternative systems (for example, speed of hardware, amount of software, and price) from a part of the substance of the decision problem. Procedural aspects of the decision process are how the decision maker moves to find out what are relevant characteristics and where a decision maker seeks out information on how the different alternative systems perform in terms of the characteristics. In a nutshell, a basic problem in describing and diagnosing decision behavior is that procedure and substance are highly interdependent. It is apparently quite difficult to say anything very useful or insightful about how decisions are made (procedure) in a specific decision situation that is divorced from the what of decisions (substance).

The problems in applying the decision-oriented approach, however, also motivate the approach. The problems suggest that managers alone and unaided are not likely to be able to systematically improve their decision making. The problems suggest that there is a need to pay more conscious attention to dimensions of effective decision making than is implied by, for example, a "support now, extend later" system development strategy.

Improving decision making involves defining effective decision processes. Because effectiveness is a relative concept (see Stabell, 1978), we must compare and contrast decision makers and decision processes. However, DSS efforts have frequently tackled single users in isolated settings. This context does not provide a basis for comparative analysis of decision processes. The development effort is easily led to focus exclusively on getting into the primary decision problem, the substance of the decision situation. Thus in single-user settings scant attention is devoted to the procedural aspects of decision making.

Proposals for how to design and build computer-based DSS are often concerned about the architecture of systems for use in a large number of decision situations. They consider general-purpose, multiple-user systems. This applies to several of the proposals outlined in this book (see Carlson, Chapter 2; Bennett, Chapter 3; and Keen and Gambino, Chapter 7). The argument is that the costs of developing the system must be amortized or recovered across a large number of users. It is a line of reasoning that probably is more relevant to the DSS industry than to DSS users. The result, however, is that the proposals are more relevant to the architecture of DSS generators (Sprague, 1980) or a DSS product (using the terminology of Brooks, 1975). The proposals are less concerned about what to include in, and how to develop, a system that is both necessary and sufficient for a specific and delineated decision situation. They have little to say about customization—how to tailor a system to a specific decision situation. The proposals therefore also necessarily do not emphasize links to decision making in a specific task.

Finally, given a book with a focus solely on building—that is, on designing and assembling DSS—it is almost inevitable that the role of decision making will be secondary. The decision perspective can have the most influence on design and implementation largely in the analysis phase of the system development process. Analysis defines the objectives for the development effort in terms of both the existing and the desired decision processes in a specific situation. The analysis phase specifies the DSS requirements. In short, most of the decision-oriented aspects of DSS development enter before the system development process tackles the design and building of a DSS.

Outline of a Decision-Oriented Approach

This introductory section has attempted both to motivate and to define issues for a more decision-oriented approach to building DSS. The discussion has primarily positioned the approach relative to other proposals for how to build DSS. The aim of the following two sections of this chapter is to provide a constructive outline of methods and principles for a decision-oriented approach.

In this book we want to emphasize the actual building of DSS. However, as already noted, analysis and diagnosis prior to design are key activities in a decision-oriented approach. Therefore, to provide a perspective on a decision-oriented approach to building DSS, the second section of this chapter first outlines the whole process of system development. The section then focuses on the activities of analysis, what I have labeled *decision research*—the description and diagnosis of decision making in organizations. The "how to" of decision research is reviewed, but the emphasis is on what kind of results the analysis and diagnosis can (and should) provide for DSS design. Some general guidelines, codified in part in the concept of a decisional imagination, are presented in the context of a case on investment decisions in shipping.

The third section of this chapter explores principles and guidelines for building DSS by reviewing both why and how a decision-oriented approach must also enter into the process of translating the diagnosis of decision behavior into the specification of both system functions and a system architecture. The discussion deals with the scope of the system and the design of the user-system interface. A key concept is that the builder seeks a design that channels the decision process of the user.

In the final section of this chapter, I attempt to isolate the essence of the decision-oriented approach by contrasting it with a technologically related, but otherwise quite different, approach.

I do not claim that a decision-oriented approach is the only approach to the development of support systems. Rather, I am attempting to define and explore both the potential and the limitations of decision support as distinct from support of other types of processes and activities (such as analysis support, bargaining support, and communication support).

However, I find a number of arguments that make a decision focus particularly significant. The approach provides a basis for development of management systems that are explicitly linked to the larger context of the organization's goals.[5] In the spirit of Ackoff's classic paper on Management Misinformation Systems (1967), the decision-oriented approach is meant to counter the tendency for information systems to be developed as an end in themselves. The approach is meant to focus attention on how system development can be a vehicle for improving decision making. It is also important to develop systems that are compatible with the existing decision behavior. The challenge is thus to provide a behaviorally grounded, but normatively oriented, approach to building DSS.

DECISION RESEARCH: DESCRIPTION AND DIAGNOSIS OF DECISION MAKING IN ORGANIZATIONS

Although it is beyond the scope of this chapter to either motivate or explore the implications, it is useful to identify at the outset key postulates for the particular decision-oriented approach presented here. Briefly, I assume the following for DSS development efforts:

1. The long-term goal is to improve decision-making effectiveness;

2. Effectiveness is defined in an organizational context; but

3. The focus is on the decision process of the individual manager;

4. The decision situation cannot be structured;

5. The development of a computer-based DSS is but one alternative means to improve decisions; and

6. The DSS is to be used directly by the manager as one of several (computer- and noncomputer-based) decision aids and information sources.

The short-term (immediate) result of a DSS development effort might not necessarily embody much of the long-term aims. For example, the DSS might be used through an intermediary and might primarily affect the efficiency of the existing decision process. The result is, however, viewed as a step in a longer-term adaptive development process.

Development Process

We can now outline the process in an effort to develop a DSS for a specific decision situation. Figure 10.1 provides an overview of the main activities. In this section we highlight aspects of predesign analysis. It is beyond the scope of this chapter to provide a complete guide to analysis. Instead, I attempt to present analysis activities, methods, and principles that are particularly important for a decision-oriented approach to DSS development. A main point is to establish how a decision-oriented analysis is expected to influence DSS design through the definition of system purpose and the specification of system functions.

As indicated in Fig. 10.1, the diagnosis of current decision making and the specification of changes in decision processes are the activities that provide the key inputs to the design of the DSS. Diagnosis is the identification of problems (or opportunities for improvement) in current decision behavior; it involves determining how decisions are currently made, specifying how decisions should be made, and understanding why decisions are not made as they should be. Specification of changes in decision processes involves choosing what specific improvements in decision behavior are to be achieved and thus defining the objectives for the development of a computer-based DSS. The choice of improvements to be achieved reflects a trade-off between: (1) the benefits of resolving/removing the different problems identified in the diagnosis of current decision behavior, and (2) the costs of the necessary changes in the decision situation. It means considering not only what is desirable, but also what can possibly be achieved.

A computer-based DSS is not necessarily the appropriate, or the only possible, vehicle for improving decision making in a specific decision situation. Here

FIGURE 10.1   *Decision-Oriented DSS Development Process*

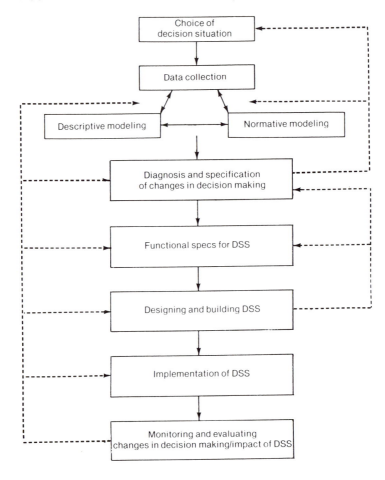

we will assume, however, that such a DSS is required in order to achieve the specified improvements in decision behavior.

Specifying changes in decision behavior involves exploring the benefits and costs of alternative system designs. In the third section of this chapter we will consider some general principles for choosing among alternative DSS designs. For the remainder of this section the focus is on the diagnosis of decision behavior that defines the range of alternative improvements to be considered.

Decision Research

A completed diagnosis results from the following three activities that define what I have labeled *decision research* (see Stabell, 1979):

1. Collecting data on current decision-making using techniques, such as interviews, observation, questionnaires, and historical records;

2. Establishing a coherent description of the current decision process;

3. Specifying a norm for how decisions should be made.

Decision research helps define DSS requirements in a fashion similar to the way that information analysis is the predesign activity in the development of information systems. However, it is perhaps more useful to think of the activity as quite analogous to marketing research. Decision research is not a particular theory of decision making or a specific modeling language; rather it is a broad conceptual basis and a variety of measurement procedures for describing and evaluating decision-making behavior in unstructured decision situations.[6]

As indicated in Fig. 10.1 the three activities of data collection, descriptive modeling, and normative modeling are highly interdependent. We describe by distinguishing current practice from sometimes explicit (or more frequently implicit) norms; for example, a statement that only a few courses of action are currently considered is implicitly telling us that the decision norm is to consider a larger number of alternatives. Similarly, data collection is guided by indications of problems; data are sought to elaborate on and substantiate a tentative diagnosis. By separating the three activities, I primarily want to emphasize that any attempt to improve decision making should be based on a statement of both "what is" and "what ought to be."

The activities outlined in Fig. 10.1 are quite general. They are applicable to any system development effort that involves changing a part of an existing and ongoing social system (as opposed to the development of completely new systems). The unique property of a decision-oriented approach to DSS development is that both description and norm should be expressed in terms of the process of decision making. The principal means to achieve this orientation is through the analytical models and measurement methods that are used to sample and diagnose managerial behavior.

A key principle for decision research is to use models and empirical methods from research on human decision-making behavior. The principle reflects the assumptions that the human decision maker will always be the dominant actor in the decision situation and that improvements in effectiveness can be achieved solely through changes that affect the individual manager and managerial behavior. By relying on basic research aimed at describing and understanding broadly defined human choice behavior, decision research ensures that the methods used have been designed for and thoroughly tested in the field.

A second important principle is the use of multiple models, along with the methods for applying them. The principle reflects the belief that no single, coherent theory can provide the necessary basis for describing and understanding human behavior in unstructured tasks. Through the use of a number of different models and associated methods, we can compensate for some of the limitations of each model. Thus different perspectives on decision making and different empirical procedures enable us to "triangulate" the decision situation.

Consider the structured observation technique used by Mintzberg (1973) in his study of managerial behavior. Structured observation is an activity analysis technique that focuses on recording all events that describe the process of a manager interacting with the organizational environment. Examples of events are "starts reading report," "picks up telephone," and "is contacted by subordinate." Events are identified through observation. They are time-stamped and labeled according to duration, medium, context, and apparent purpose. Structured observation is typically a data-intensive approach that can provide detailed statistics on activities covering a time period of intermediate length (from a couple of days to a week). The method can, for example, be used to produce a good description of what information sources the manager uses. It can provide estimates of the relative frequency and extent of information source use. However, the method as such provides little basis for describing the cognitive processes of the manager that are involved in and that link activities. The method cannot "see" aspects of decision making that extend over activities separated in time. Brevity, variety, and fragmentation of managerial behavior (Mintzberg, 1973) are to a large extent built into the interaction model of managerial work implicit in the measurement technique used. Stuctured observation alone can therefore seldom provide a sufficient basis for description and diagnosis of managerial behavior in a DSS development effort.

Table 10.1 lists a set of alternative models with methods that I have proposed as a possible "tool kit" for decision research (Stabell, 1979). It is beyond the scope of this chapter to attempt a more detailed description of the "tool kit." Instead, let me provide elements of the rationale for the choice of this particular set of models with methods.[7]

TABLE 10.1   Models and Methods for Decision Research

Cognitive	**Organizational**
Simple algebraic model / regression approach	Role model / role episode method
Belief attitude model / Q-sort	Interaction model / structured observation
Problem space search / thinking aloud *problem* protocol	Communication model / sociometrics
Explanatory calculus / thinking aloud *event* protocol	

All the models and methods in Table 10.1 are relevant to decision making broadly defined. The set has been chosen to provide a number of perspectives on managerial decision making in an organizational context. A major distinction is that between cognitive and organizational perspectives. Certain models are primarily for investigating the divergent, open, and thus to a great extent socially influenced phases of decision making, such as problem finding. Others are more relevant to the closed and more convergent phases of decision making, such as problem solving. An important concern has been the identification of methods that, when applied, use terms relevant in a given specific decision situation.[8] This identification is needed to assure high face-validity for the methods so that they are meaningful and understandable to both manager and decision researcher.

The models and associated methods for decision research listed in Table 10.1 do not provide a formula or recipe for translating a description into a diagnosis or for translating a diagnosis into DSS requirements. A single, coherent model-with-method might provide the basis for a more formalized and convergent analysis. However, application of a single model-with-method implies a clear choice for how to decide, for what should be the specific definition of effective decision making. The principle of multiple models-with-methods allows for alternative views on decision making that can serve as a basis for the user and organization to choose, in a specific instance, how to define effective decision making. The principle allows the user to choose how to decide.

An organizing perspective for the diagnosis and evaluation of decision making is needed. Both Scott Morton (1971) and Gerrity (1971) used the IDC model of the decision process—the distinction between the Intelligence (problem finding), the Design (problem solving), and the Choice phases of decision making—as a framework for both describing and prescribing decision behavior. However, the IDC model fits all decision processes; therefore the model does not provide an operational basis for distinguishing between description and norm. Use of the IDC model alone produces very vague prescriptions, such as "There is a need for more intelligence activities" or " . . . more design" or " . . . better choices."

A useful framework for diagnosis should identify how managerial decision making in organizations, in a descriptive sense, differs from effective decision behavior. The work of Cyert and March (1963) provides a comprehensive statement—theory with empirical support—on decision making for such a perspective. Their four major concepts of "local rationality," "uncertainty avoidance," "local search," and "simple learning" describe decision making as it differs from the prescriptions of rational choice models. Each concept summarizes a number of both organizational and cognitive characteristics of decision behavior: satisficing (as opposed to optimizing) is an example of local rationality; reliance on short-run feedback (as opposed to contingency planning) is an element of uncertainty avoidance; search in the neighborhood of the current alternative (as opposed to global search) is an aspect of local search. Table 10.2 is a summary check list of the concepts and the relevant aspects of the decision situation. For decision research these concepts provide a guide for what to look for when diagnosing decision-making behavior.

In many DSS-development projects it is not feasible to perform a full-scale decision research study prior to the design and implementation of the first version of a system. Such a study might be difficult because of problems of access—

TABLE 10.2   *Check List for Diagnosis
of Decision-Making Process*

Aspect of Decision Situation	Common Characteristic
Goals	Local rationality
Uncertainty	Avoidance
Information	Local search
Learning	Simple

managers feel uncomfortable, and it takes too much time to develop the trust
required for use of methods that sample the cognitive dimensions of decision
making. As a consequence, the DSS builder needs a well-developed *decisional
imagination*, an ability to produce a working diagnosis after only limited ex-
posure to a decision situation. The builder has to be able to imagine how decisions are made and to see how decisions might be different based on a few traces
of decision processes. The general dimensions for evaluation (Table 10.2) outline
a framework for imagining both a description and a possible diagnosis of decision
making in a specific decision situation. For example, we would expect to find that
the decision maker relies on point estimates of future events, which is an aspect of
uncertainty avoidance. The diagnosis might imply introducing system capabilities that support a move toward an exploration of the consequences of a range of
possible future events.

This description has neither fully delineated the issues in the field of decision
research, nor told the reader how to do decision research. In an attempt to provide the reader with a better understanding of decision research, of what it might
mean to diagnose decision making, and of the role of a decisional imagination,
we conclude this section with an example dealing with investment decisions in oil
tanker shipping. The same case will be used to illustrate some of the principles for
building DSS discussed in the next section of the chapter.

The case is an example of a relatively brief effort to describe and diagnose
decision behavior. Nonetheless, it is beyond the scope of this chapter to give a
rigorous and complete description of the situation. In the general area of decision
research, a premium is put on the means to summarize the data collected. A
number of figures and tables are used here for this purpose. They should be reviewed carefully.

Case: Investment Decisions in Shipping

Consider the decisions to build, buy, rebuild, store, or sell ships in a medium-
sized Norwegian shipping firm, Starship. The firm has a fleet of gas, product/
chemical, crude, and bulk carriers, offshore drilling rigs, and cruise ships. The investment decisions can involve substantial commitments of funds. Building a

very large crude carrier (VLCC) in excess of 200,000 deadweight tons (dwt) represents an investment of nearly $50 million.

Although investments in ships have much in common with investments in plant and machinery, the decisions are uniquely shaped by the existence of active markets for secondhand ships. There is always the option to sell (or buy). A second important aspect of the investment decision situation in shipping is the nature of the market for the transportation services provided. Carriers and rigs are chartered. Starship is most often involved in either time charters or voyage charters. In a time charter the vessel is chartered for a specified period (for example, five years) at an agreed-upon rate per dwt of capacity per calendar month. Operating costs for crew, stores, maintenance, insurance, etc., are paid by Starship, while voyage costs, such as fuel, port, and cargo charges, are paid for by the charterer. In voyage charters the vessel is chartered for a specified number of consecutive voyages (a single voyage is commonly known as a spot market charter) among specified ports. The charterer pays an agreed freight rate per ton of cargo lifted on each voyage. All expenses are paid by Starship.

Obviously, voyage charters (particularly spot market charters) are more risky than time charters. An owner that has vessels available when there is a surge in demand (such as happened for crude oil carriers when the Suez Canal was closed as a result of the 1967 Middle East war) can obtain very high spot rates. However, when demand slumps, the spot rate can fall well below operating expenses.[9]

A DSS Effort

Starship had been using computers for several years when (in the fall of 1979) a small effort to explore the potential of DSS was initiated. The internal backer was the vice-president (VP) for corporate planning. He had recently attended a two-day DSS seminar and saw a DSS project as a lead-in for a review of the planning and decision processes in the firm. It was decided that investment decisions in the crude carrier division (CCD) might be a good place to start. At the time the demand for tankers was relatively firm. However, the CCD had been a problem spot for several years. The current fleet of five crude carriers (four of which were VLCCs) was down from twenty ships prior to the 1974–75 slump.

Collection of data on the decision situation and the current decision process took place over a one-month period in December of 1979. In this period there were four meetings (see Table 10.3). The first meeting provided a background briefing on Starship. As it is in most Norwegian shipping companies, decision making is highly centralized. Major decisions are finally made by the board of directors with the owners as the key actors.

The firm had established a rather comprehensive procedure for investment project review. Although the general guidelines were followed in most cases, investment decisions often had to be made with such short notice that it was not possible to provide all the prescribed material. The VP for planning felt person-

TABLE 10.3   *Predesign Data Collection*

Meeting	Participants	Purpose/Content
1	VP for planning DSS consultant	General background on Starship, on planning and control procedures, on Crude Carrier Division (CCD)
2	VP for planning VP of CCD Analyst for CCD Analyst for planning DSS consultants	Presentation of DSS effort, goals, methods; set up meeting 3
3	VP of CCD Analyst for CCD DSS consultant	Review of recent problem/decision process
4	VP of CCD DSS consultant	Follow-up to meeting 3

ally that a major weakness in the current decision process was the lack of explicit links between the firm's overall long-range planning and decision making at the level of individual projects. There was apparently little or no systematic analysis of the risks and exposures in the portfolio of projects. The analysis of competitive moves and of developments in the economy or markets was apparently seldom used explicitly in the evaluation of individual investment projects. However, when pressed to elaborate on how market developments were in fact considered, the VP for planning noted that he had only a very vague idea of the details of the decision process.

In a second meeting, contact was established with the target decision maker, the VP of the CCD. The third meeting took the form of an interview focused on a recent investment decision.[10] The purpose was to review how investment decisions were made by identifying process triggers, information and information sources, analysis methods, judgmental inputs, etc. At the time of the third meeting, the VP of the CCD was busy preparing material on an investment program in new engines for Starship's VLCCs. The material had somewhat unexpectedly been requested the previous day for a board meeting the next day. It was agreed to use the new engine project as a reference case.

New Engine Decision Problem

The underlying issue was the dramatic increase in the cost of tanker fuel. While the price per ton of fuel was $13 in 1971, it was $89 in September of 1978, $175 at the time in December of 1979, and was expected to be close to $200 by the end of the first quarter of 1980. As a consequence, fuel costs had become a significant portion of total voyage costs.

Starship's crude carriers all have turbine engines. This was appropriate when fuel costs were low and demand for tankers was high. Since demand slumped in 1974–75, tankers have been steaming at reduced speed in order to conserve fuel and reduce the supply of tonnage. Three additional means to reduce fuel consumption were to be considered for the board meeting:

1. Revise optimal service speed: a low-cost adjustment in engines and VLCC operating procedures.

2. Upgrade turbine engines: a $2 million investment per ship to alter the existing engines and improve fuel efficiency.

3. Reengineer: a $12 million investment per ship to replace turbine engines with diesel engines. The retrofit requires one year to plan, and the VLCC needs to stay four months in dry dock.

Procedural Aspects of New Engine Decision

Table 10.4, which I have labeled a DEAP diagram, presents a chronological overview of the decision process in terms of key events, actors, and process stages. From the table we see that the issue of new engines for the VLCCs was first considered when fuel costs rose toward the end of 1978. The event that triggered the chairman of the board's request for an evaluation of alternatives was apparently Mobil's decision (November of 1979) to retrofit two of their VLCCs.

The decision alternatives were developed over a six-month period by Starship's engineering department, the engine manufacturers, and the shipyards. The VP of the CCD was actively involved for shorter periods of time throughout the

TABLE 10.4   DEAP (Date-Event-Actor
Decision Process) Diagram

Date	Event/Action	Actor	Stage in Decision Process
Dec. '78– Jan. '79	Jump in price of bunker oil	——	Problem finding
June '79	Initiate review of turbine replacement with diesel engine	Technical department; shipyard; diesel engine manufacturer	Alternative generation
Aug.– Sept. '79	Proposal for upgrade of turbine engine	Turbine manufacturer	Alternative generation
Nov. '79	Mobil orders reengineering of two VLCCs	——	Problem finding
Dec. '79	Review of alternative; prepare for board meeting	Board; VP of CCD	Alternative evaluation

FIGURE 10.2   Information Sources

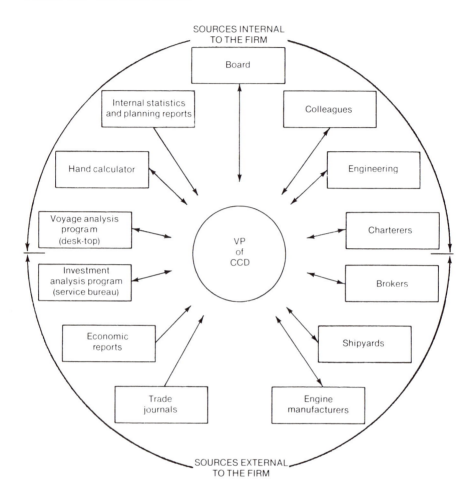

whole decision process. Figure 10.2 summarizes the major information sources used from the perspective of the VP of the CCD. The computer-based programs and calculator in Fig. 10.2 were used in preparing material for the board meeting. At this stage in the decision process the emphasis was on evaluating the economics of the investment alternatives. Net present values (NPV) and net rate for servicing debts ($/ton/day) were the main decision criteria considered.

The evaluation procedure used three different systems or calculators (see Fig. 10.2). The investment analysis program (IA program, run on an external service bureau) provided a standard report with estimates of cash flow, but it did not provide an estimate of NPV. A hand calculator was therefore used to transform the cash flow into an estimated NPV.

The inputs to the IA program were estimates of investments, charter rates, operating costs, and financing costs. There were no provisions for the specification of voyage costs; the program was designed (in the early 1970s) for the analysis of time charter contracts. The IA program could therefore not consider directly the effect of alternative levels of fuel consumption.

A voyage analysis program (VA program) transformed voyage costs (such as fuel, port, and cargo charges) and a spot market rate into an equivalent time charter rate. This is the time charter rate needed to cover the voyage costs and the voyage rate. To perform the calculation, the VA program (originally developed as an aid for chartering decisions) required detailed specification of the voyage and the ship's operating characteristics.

The effects of alternative trades (for example, Persian Gulf to continent, Persian Gulf to Japan, etc.), of alternative fuel costs ($175, $200, and $250/ton), and of alternative spot market rates (world scale 50, 60, and 70) were also explored. Table 10.5 is an example of how the VP of CCD summarized the different runs for a particular ship and trade. These summaries, together with an overview of technical and operating issues, formed the main body of the material prepared for the board meeting.

After the Board Meeting

The attempt to sample the current investment decision process ended with a brief follow-up meeting (see Table 10.3). Most of this last meeting was spent making sure that the substantive part of the problem and the analysis performed had been understood (for example, interpreting the different inputs to the VA program and IA program). Some probing was attempted in order to map what was unique about the new engine decision process relative to other investment decisions. The VP of the CCD noted that projects often involve new and unfamiliar transportation markets. Such a project review would include a much more detailed market analysis than in the new engine case. However, the comments were very general, and there was not time to pursue specific cases to elaborate on the exact nature of process differences.

The result of the board meeting—the output of the decision process at that point—was a decision to proceed with the low-cost alternative of revising the optimal operating speed. No final decision was made on the two other alternatives; the decision was to search for more information and await further developments in the spot market for tanker tonnage.

On the Decision Research Used in This Case

The case is an example of a quick-and-dirty decision research effort. The models and methods of the decision research tool kit were used only to a very limited extent. One simple, but very helpful, methodological principle was the focus on a specific decision case. The main model used was the distinction between problem

TABLE 10.5 *Summary of Alternative Evaluation*

Ship: Golar Nichu   Trade: Persian Gulf–Continent
Sale "as is" *versus* revised speed, upgraded turbines, and reengineering

Rate Level	Revised Speed			Upgraded Turbines			Reengineering		
	50	60	70	50	60	70	50	60	70
Fuel cost: $175/ton									
Eqv. time charter rate	.84	1.60	2.36		1.84	.95	.95	.95	.95
Oper. expenses	.95	.95	.95		.95				
Net investment servicing	− .11	.65	1.41		.89				
Net present value	− 1.7	9.1	19.8		10.5				
Fuel cost: $200/ton									
Eqv. time charter rate					1.87				
Oper. expenses					.95				
Net investment servicing					.92				
Net present value									
Fuel cost: $250/ton									
Eqv. time charter rate									
Oper. expenses									
Net investment servicing									
Net present value									

finding and problem solving; this leads to a probe for decision-process triggers. Managers seldom offer to tell about or recall when a problem (or opportunity) was first brought to their attention. This is a common feature of ill-structured tasks.

The case illustrates quite well how difficult it is to separate the substantive and procedural aspects of decision making. For example, it would be difficult to understand the use of the VA program and the IA program (Fig. 10.3) without some understanding of the distinction between voyage charters and time charters.

FIGURE 10.3   Programs (Calculators) Used to Evaluate Investment Alternatives

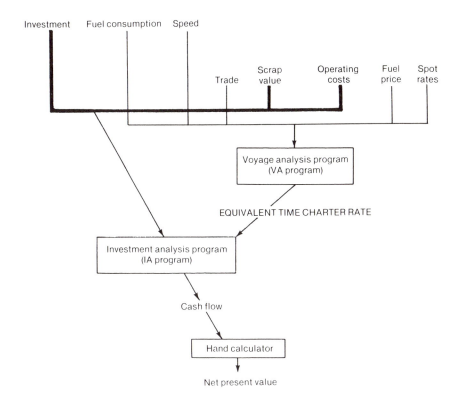

Finally, the case raises the issue of to what extent the investment decision process actually was sampled. The material suggests that the final choice was made at the board meeting. This would seem to imply that the focus should have been on the decision process of the board. However, the approach taken was an attempt to develop support for the decisions made by the VP of the CCD, given the organizational context of the decision situation. The organizational context defines both the limits to and some of the opportunities for improvements in decision making.[11] A possible diagnosis of the decision situation can therefore also include the need for a redefinition of the organizational context.

Diagnosis of Decision Making

Diagnosis must necessarily depend on the level and scope of the analysis of decision processes. Diagnosis also depends on what is taken as given in the decision situation and on what is defined as the range of available remedial actions. A diagnosis that avoids premature closure must move between different levels of analysis and must explore the implications of different changes in a decision situation. Good diagnosis is therefore quite difficult, but I think it involves skills that can be developed and sharpened. The following analysis of the Starship investment decision process tries to give a sense of the process of diagnosis while suggesting some of the uses of a decisional imagination.

A first pass   In a quick review of the investment decision process two features might attract your attention. First, the overall decision process (particularly in the final phase prior to the board meeting) appears to compare favorably with decision making in organizations in general (see Table 10.2). Several decision alternatives were considered (*cf.* local rationality), the implications of several uncertain developments were explored (*cf.* uncertainty avoidance), and information was assembled from a wide variety of sources and decision aids (*cf.* local information search). Second, and in contrast, the decision aids used to evaluate the economic consequences of the alternative fuel saving schemes were quite cumbersome (Fig. 10.3). A proportionally large amount of time was spent entering alternatives, manually transferring data among the three different programs (calculators), and manually assembling the summary reports across alternatives and across the different scenarios considered. The IA program was in fact a first-generation, terminal-based system with limited facilities for interactive analysis. The program was essentially a remote-job-entry version of a batch program rather than a truly interactive program.

Based on these two observations, diagnosis is straightforward: inefficient tools are used for what appears to be a relatively effective decision process. The diagnosis points toward (is based on the assumption that it is relatively straightforward to build) a single, interactive support system that integrates the functions available in the current set of programs/calculators, with support for the assembly of summary evaluation reports (Table 10.5) as add-on features.

Although the preliminary diagnosis has probably identified a good starting platform, it does not provide any guide for evolution. If what has been outlined is where the DSS effort is to end, then shopping for a suitable standard off-the-shelf DSS product is probably the appropriate strategy. If, however, the DSS outlined is to be the first step in the evolution of the decision process, then the diagnosis has to probe much further.

A second pass   The diagnosis can be extended in two major ways: (1) by broadening the scope of the process reviewed, and (2) by taking a more detailed look at those aspects of the process that have already been considered. A key postulate for diagnosis is that it is always possible to find elements of the decision process that can be improved, if we ignore some constraints in the current decision situation.

The major evaluation dimensions (see Table 10.2) have been used as a check list to help generate an overview of possible weaknesses in the current decision process. The corresponding dimensions of the check list have been noted in parentheses after the elements of the diagnosis.

Broadening the Scope   Consider problem finding. The decision process does not indicate any explicit link to the analysis of the portfolio of projects in the firm. There is apparently little attention to overall risk (local rationality).

Consider implementation and post-decision follow-up. Although the case does not cover these phases, we note that key assumptions were not made explicit (simple learning) and that key contingencies were not identified explicitly (uncertainty avoidance). In addition, in the decision activities sampled, there was apparently no explicit review of similar earlier decisions (simple learning).

A Closer Look   The analysis proceeded as if the development of fuel costs and crude carrier spot market rates were independent, but there are good reasons to believe that they are interdependent (uncertainty avoidance). The sensitivity analysis performed therefore gave a false sense of having explored a large number of contingencies while in fact the realistic set considered was perhaps quite small.

The analysis was performed with constant fuel, cost, and market rates over the planning horizon (uncertainty avoidance). Relatively familiar variables—for example, spot rates—were analyzed in great depth, but there was no sensitivity analysis of estimated fuel savings produced by the engineering department (local search).

Competitive developments were not explicitly considered (local search, uncertainty avoidance). The decision problem should perhaps instead have been formulated as an issue of how fuel consumption affects ability to obtain time charters. In general, developments external to the firm were not translated into terms relevant to the investment decision.

In short, a closer look suggests that the decision process was characterized by a lot of numbers and only a very limited analysis. There were few insights gained from the analysis. Part of the problem might be that inefficient tools consumed too much attention. However, apparently there is an opportunity for improving the decision process.

Some Concluding Comments

The two-pass diagnosis illustrates the dangers of an "approche evolutive" that short-circuits analysis and diagnosis. The DSS development effort might never get beyond the goal of making sure the system is used. A key development activity not covered here is having an early discussion with the manager and others in the organization on what it means to make good decisions.

The use of a decisional imagination points to the role in DSS development of a broad understanding of decision making in organizations. However, there is also a need for methods and skills to operationalize this understanding in a specific decision situation. Furthermore, it is not sufficient to be able to recite and recognize general patterns of managerial decision behavior—for example, that managers satisfice. For an effort to be successful it is also necessary to understand *why* managers satisfice—in the sense that it might be a perfectly rational behavior given their current decision situation and the decision aids at their disposal.

PRINCIPLES AND GUIDELINES FOR
A DECISION-ORIENTED DESIGN

In this section we focus on principles and guidelines for those activities that translate and transform the description and diagnosis of current decision behavior into a decision-oriented functional specification and design for a computer-based DSS (see Fig. 10.1). Suggestions for the design of human-computer interfaces in general (see, for example, Shneiderman, 1980) are not covered explicitly. If general guidelines, such as keeping the interface simple, responsive, user-controlled, flexible, stable, protective, self-documenting, and reliable (Cheriton, 1976), are violated, the system will most likely not be used. However, respecting such guidelines will not necessarily secure an effective system for decision support.

I argued earlier that the predesign description and diagnosis of decision making is the key to securing a decision-oriented approach to DSS development. As an introduction to this section it is useful to review why we might also need principles and guidelines for the design of the computer-based system. Or, stated differently, does diagnosis provide a necessary and sufficient basis for the specification of the DSS? Translating the diagnosis of behavior in the current decision situation into a DSS is not a trivial mechanical activity. In most cases there is a many-to-many mapping between elements of the diagnosis and system functions intended to support decisions. A single system function can be aimed at several problems in the current decision behavior; one aspect of the diagnosis can motivate several system capabilities.

Design involves several difficult trade-offs. One important trade-off follows from the need to perform two rather different and conflicting functions at the same time. On the one hand the DSS must support the existing decision-making process, and on the other hand it must assist a move toward (and support) the more effective decision process that is implied by the predesign diagnosis. As a result, there is not likely to be a simple mapping from the current decision process to system functions. Using the language of a representation-centered (or verb-

FIGURE 10.4   Scope versus Depth of System Capabilities

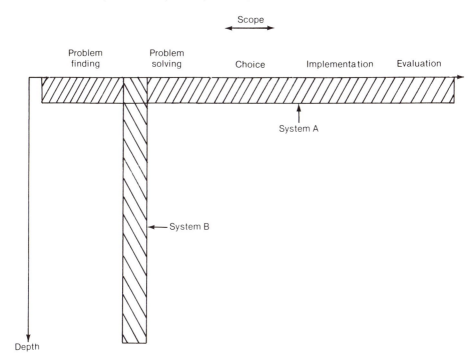

oriented) design, an effective system will involve a combination of familiar and relatively novel representations (or verbs).

There is also a trade-off between (1) the depth of the capabilities that a system might bring to bear on any single phase of the decision process and (2) the scope of the process that the system is designed to support. Figure 10.4 illustrates the scope versus depth trade-off. System A provides simple capabilities (for example, equivalent to the computations performed by current hand calculators) but is designed to be used in all phases of the decision process. System B, on the other hand, provides great depth (for example, an elaborate mathematical programming algorithm) but is only of use for the evaluation of alternatives in the problem-solving phase of the decision process. System scope also needs to be considered in terms of to what extent the system deals with the whole or with only a part of the decision problem. For example, a system to support the marketing decisions of brand managers that only deals with pricing decisions is of narrower scope than a system that also supports advertising budget decisions and media choice.

The guidelines developed in the remainder of this section deal with the design trade-offs identified above. The discussion addresses: (1) the issue of depth *versus* scope, and (2) the concept of decision channeling as a design approach to the trade-off between support of the current decision process and evolution toward more effective decision making. An example is outlined using the case of investment decision making presented in the second section of this chapter.

Scope versus Depth of System Capabilities

The DSS should be designed to support the whole process of decision making, including problem finding, problem solving, choice, implementation, and evaluation. This means emphasizing scope over depth. This design principle follows from a desire to keep the system simple but at the same time usable and useful. It is important to address the whole decision cycle for substantive and procedural learning. In terms of actual system use the transition between system-supported phases and nonsupported phases is a bottleneck that might limit system use and system usefulness.

It is seldom feasible to start with a system that does everything at once. The principle that scope should be given priority at the expense of depth is to be viewed as a long-term objective for what necessarily needs to be an evolutionary system development process. The principle is meant to counter the natural tendency to refine what exists.

In order to ensure that focus remains on the decision situation, it is important that system use be explicitly linked to the choice point in the decision process (see the following discussion of decision channeling). In practice this implies that systems will start by (and evolve from) providing support for the alternative evaluation and comparison phases of the decision process.

As a means to implement the principle of a complete system, the system specification should also include a statement of what phases of the decision process are not supported, of why the current version of the system does not support these phases, and of how the system might be extended to support the phases not currently covered.

We need to distinguish between an organizational and a cognitive time frame in the decision process. The organizational time frame involves the whole cycle from problem finding through implementation to evaluation and control. In an unstructured task this process will typically require several weeks, months, or perhaps years (Mintzberg, Raisinghani, and Théorêt, 1976). The cognitive time frame of the decision process is primarily linked to the disjoint phases of problem finding, problem solving, choice, and evaluation/control interspersed as intense bursts of activity within the organizational time frame. The cognitive time frame is typically on the order of seconds, minutes, or hours.[12]

A system to support the total process will have to rely to a large extent on organizational procedures as well as on components that are embedded in a computer-based system. This reminds us that system development and use is not an end in itself but should be viewed as one means toward more effective decision making.

Decision Channeling

There is a need to choose an architecture for the user-system interface in terms of how it is adapted to the existing decision process and how it can direct the decision maker toward a more effective decision-making process. Adapting the DSS design to the existing decision process is essentially a matter of providing a system that conforms to the data, the representations, and the verbs (operators) currently used by the decision maker.

Let us use the term *decision channeling* to describe the general property of the interface architecture that serves to both support and shift the decision process. The term is meant to suggest that, while the user is in control, at the same time there are characteristics of the interface that have been chosen for their intended effect on how the user chooses to use the system. These features might involve the presentation form for logical data structures, the nature of system defaults, a differential ease of transition between different system functions, and the structure of memory aids.

The design should not constrain the user in terms of how the system can be used to support the decision process. In particular, the system should be able to support the current decision process. However, at the same time the architecture should explicitly focus attention and should orient the decision process in directions suggested by the diagnosis of the existing decision situation. Although the design of a DSS needs to emphasize features that follow from the diagnosis of the specific decision situation, it is possible to identify system features for decision channeling that should be applicable to a wide range of situations. The general diagnosis of decision making in organizations (Table 10.2), where quasi-resolution of goal conflicts, uncertainty avoidance, local search, and simple learning are common characteristics, suggests the need for the following system capabilities:

1. *Focus attention on the nature of the decision problem.* Make an explicit distinction between decision criteria, control variables, and noncontrollable parameters. Control variables define decision alternatives. Noncontrollables are variables that the decision maker cannot control but that affect the desired decision outcomes (decision criteria).[13]

2. *Facilitate the evaluation of alternatives.* Provide user-controlled report-formatting capabilities to facilitate comparison on the basis of multiple decision criteria.

3. *Extend the planning horizon.* Give default definitions of variables as if they were time-dependent to remind the decision-maker of possible changes.

4. *Support uncertainty exploration.* Simulate the consequences of differences in cause-effect relationships and of different states of the environment.

5. *Facilitate the integration of the user's subjective estimates (judgment).* Allow the user to modify a private copy of data inputs, and do not restrict the system to readily available and objective computer-based data.

6. *Facilitate learning.* Provide functions for recording and revisiting key deci-
    sion assumptions.

This list can be seen as a revised and extended version of Little's (1970) concept of
a decision calculus. Little's principles—that the decision calculus should be
simple, robust, complete on important issues, easy to control, adaptive, and easy
to communicate with—have been translated into terms more relevant to the
design of the user-system interface. The list of features is tentative and is weak in
features that are particularly relevant to support of the problem-finding and post-
implementation evaluation phases of decision making. Actual implementation of
decision channeling features will necessarily vary, depending on the characteristics of the decision situation and on the technological building blocks used. Each
individual feature is currently available on one or more existing systems. It is
their sum and the underlying design orientation that is important.

An Example

In order to elaborate on the guidelines for a decision-oriented design approach,
let us return to the case of supporting the tanker investment decision process
described and diagnosed in the last section. To illustrate the issue of scope and
orientation for a possible first version of a DSS for investment decision making at
Starship, we will contrast the kind of system that might arise from a decision-
oriented approach with the kind arising from an Operations Research and
Management Science (OR/MS) model-oriented approach or from an information
systems (IS) data-oriented approach. Briefly outlined, the two latter approaches
might consider the following designs.

1. OR/MS approach
    a. Develop a general model of the relationship between characteristics of
       ships, voyages, speed, and fuel consumption. The model would be de-
       signed to determine the optimal speed.
    b. Develop econometric models that provide estimates of future demand for
       tankers, spot market rates, and bunker fuel prices.

2. IS approach
    a. Develop a system that provides on-line access to the world scale rates
       for all voyages. The world scale rate is an input to the voyage analysis
       program.
    b. Develop a data bank that contains all vital data on all ships currently
       owned.
    c. Develop a system for monitoring investment project results.

In contrast, the decision-oriented design principles suggest that a first system
should provide functions for evaluating and comparing investment alternatives
generated by the user. The functions should rely on evaluation in terms of specific
ships and specific voyages, as was done in the described decision process. It should

be possible to evaluate alternatives using the decision maker's own estimates of future market rates and future bunker fuel prices. Such a first system would not support problem-finding, alternative generation, or post-implementation evaluation. When we start describing how the system might be extended in subsequent versions, elements from the OR/MS approach and from the IS approach might be considered as a part of a balanced and coherent system architecture to support the whole process. In order to support problem finding, the system might include data on the portfolio of current investments (ships) to show how different ships are sensitive to shifts in fuel prices. Generation of alternatives might be supported by providing a model of the relationship between speed and fuel consumption, for specific ships and with user-controlled parameterization. Post-implementation evaluation might be supported by extending the system to include facilities for entering data on operating results and for generating reports that compare planned to actual investment performance.

In order to illustrate the application of the concept of decision channeling, we will consider the following examples of features from current work on an APL-based, VDU-oriented DSS architecture named D*2 (Stabell and Fuglseth, 1981):

1. The function for entry/display/alter of model inputs accesses the different pages of inputs through a menu of items grouped according to the distinction between controllables and noncontrollables (see Fig. 10.5). In addition, the

FIGURE 10.5   *Display of Input Variables Organized into Groups of Control Variables and Noncontrollables*

```
SHIPINVEST: ENTER/ALTER                                          PAGE 5/6
COMMANDS: /F /I /N /P /O /C /FGND /Q

NON-CONTROLLABLES - MARKET

                      1981      1982      1983      1984      1985
PRICE HVFUEL           175       175       175       175       175
PRICE DIESEL           350       350       350       350       350
WORLDSCALE RATE      17.82     17.82     17.82     17.82     17.82
RATE LEVEL              60        60        60        60        60

PRICE HVFUEL    >
```

FIGURE 10.6   All Noncontrollable Variables Assumed to
Be Time-Varying Even When User Treats Them as Constant

```
SHIPINVEST: ENTER/ALTER
COMMANDS: /F /L /N /P /O /C /PGNO /Q


CONTENTS: GROUPS OF VARIABLES

PAGE    1    DECISION VARIABLES  - PROJECT
        2                        - INVESTMENT
        3                        - SHIP
        4                        - TRADE
        5    NON-CONTROLLABLES   - MARKET
        6                        - OPERATING COSTS



SELECT GROUP BY ENTERING '/PAGE NUMBER'> /5
```

same distinction is used as an element in the title of each page of input data
(see Fig. 10.6).

2. All noncontrollable variables are assumed to be time-varying. If the user explicitly chooses to define the noncontrollables as constants (and thus ignore
   uncertainty about current and future values), they are still displayed as a
   time-dependent series (constants) (see Fig. 10.6).

3. The system is designed to facilitate the pairwise comparison of alternatives
   by providing a data structure composed of a working set and a reference set.
   Both sets contain a full copy of input variables. The user can alter the working set and can then "freeze" the working set by transferring it to the reference
   set. The reference set can then be used as a basis (a base case) for comparison
   as the user continues to explore changes in the working set (by changing both
   decision variables and assumptions concerning noncontrollables). Figure 10.7
   provides an example of a report which shows working set results. The
   percent change relative to each corresponding reference set value is given in
   bold-face.

4. The menu of system functions is organized for ease of navigation according
   to the phases of the decision process. The hierarchy of functions is "shallow"
   where quick movement between functions is important.

FIGURE 10.7   Changes Relative to Reference Set (Base Case)
Displayed Together with Results for Current Working Set Values

```
SHIPINVEST: PRINT                                                PAGE 1/5
COMMANDS: /P /L /N /P /O /C /PGNO /Q

SOLAR NICHU - TUB-PG - REVSPEED RL60
WS & REL CHANGES BC
                     1981         1982         1983         1984         1985
INVESTMENT          -24 000
T/C-REVENUES       4 517 710    4 517 710    4 517 710    4 517 710    4 517 710
                      +31%         +31%         +31%         +31%         +31%
RUNNING COSTS     -2 772 480   -2 772 480   -2 772 480   -2 772 480   -2 772 480
FINANCING EXP        12 000       -3 320       -3 100       -2 880       -2 660

CASH FLOW          1 733 230    1 741 910    1 742 130    1 742 350    1 742 570
                     +160%        +158%        +158%        +158%        +158%

NPV EQUITY        10 618 447
                     +138%
NPV TOT CAP       11 342 917
                     +137%
```

Each feature of the system is relatively trivial and often found on other systems. The challenge for a decision-oriented design is to put together a large number of such features into a coherent architecture.

SUMMARY: ALTERNATIVE APPROACHES TO THE DEVELOPMENT OF DSS?

Most proposals for how to build DSS can be seen as combinations of two fundamentally different strategies.

Strategy 1 is a nondirected approach based on computer-based technology developed as a simple, easy-to-use personal aid—an extended hand calculator. It is primarily up to the user to decide when and how to use the system. The total costs of the system are sufficiently low that it does not matter whether the system is used or not. The potential value might be great, but it remains unspecified. This strategy will most likely dominate as the market (that is, external supply) for support system products grows (see Keen, 1981).

Strategy 2 is a directed approach based on improving decision-making effectiveness. It is a costly, long-term effort where the development of a computer-based DSS is viewed as one among several means to increase effectiveness. It is based on an organized effort to diagnose current decision making prior to the development of DSS, requires a clear idea of what kind of changes are sought, and results in changes that are explicitly anchored in the view of the user as a decision maker. However, in Strategy 2 the computer technology also needs to be kept simple, easy to use, and adaptable. The technology should not dominate the change process. A key difference from the simple technology of Strategy 1 is that here the simplicity is consciously chosen in order to provide the desired decision channeling.

Contrasting the two strategies suggests that the ideas developed in this chapter are primarily extensions of the work of other authors in this book. However, the notion of a decision-oriented approach embodied in the concepts of a decisional imagination and of decision channeling is clearly different.

It is not necessarily an issue of being right or wrong, but one of different approaches to the development of DSS that reflect fundamental differences in both the objectives for DSS development and beliefs about what it is possible to achieve. Simply stated, the decision-oriented approach outlined here reflects a less sanguine view of past achievements, or perhaps a perspective that emphasizes the failures. In part the issue is one of a different emphasis on improvements through substantive and procedural learning. The decision-oriented approach that I have outlined is heavily oriented toward procedural learning—improving how decisions are made.

ENDNOTES

1. In the emerging DSS industry we also observe an attempt to capitalize on the reverse association. Managers are decision makers, and DSS should therefore be particularly important to managers. Or as this is put in a recent advertisement: "DSS—power in the hands of the people who need it most." We might thus be reliving our earlier experience with the concept of management information systems (MIS), where it often appeared that the only purpose of the label was to capture the interest of management in the application of computers (although the computers were essentially used for transaction processing). Similarly, the word *decision* in DSS might end up primarily serving as a means to catch the attention of management (while the tool is essentially used by their staff).

2. The adaptability of a given system for different uses (the external adaptability) should be distinguished from the kinds of adaptation that involve changing and extending the system design by adding (or modifying) functions, variables, models, or reports (the internal adaptability).

3. These five chapters deal explicitly with the actual design and implementation of whole systems. Other chapters—by Carlson (Chapter 4), Dyer and Mulvey (Chapter 5), Gorry and Krumland (Chapter 9)—review alternative technological and conceptual building blocks for DSS. As I see it, these chapters are therefore primarily relevant to the choice among building blocks. The decision-oriented approach provides the context for this choice among alternative building blocks.

4. The discussion could perhaps suggest that the design of the system was inadequate because it did not support a complete decision cycle at the level of aggregates. The decision process would seem to require alternative levels of aggregation for different planning horizons.

5. The focus is on individual decision making in an organizational context. Keen and Hackathorn (1979) have suggested a distinction between decision support at the personal, group, and organizational levels. They are raising an important issue that needs to be clarified. However, their framework is largely based on alternative forms of resource interdependence. I personally think that alternative structures of objectives provide a more useful basis for distinguishing different types of decision support. We want to distinguish between support of decision making in terms of the personal (private) objectives of the manager and support in terms of the objectives of the organization in which the managerial task is performed.

6. Marketing research (see, for example, Green and Tull, 1973) and decision research should have a lot in common in terms of both analysis models and measurement methods. Both are involved in the study of human behavior. However, as an activity in a firm, marketing research considers the behavior of consumers—"them"—while decision research is concerned about the behavior of managers—"us." Marketing research is typically interested in describing the relatively simple behavior of a large number of actors in order to predict and affect behavior. In decision research we are interested in describing the apparently complex behavior of a small number of actors (a single manager) in order to understand and improve performance.

7. The following set of references provides a starting point for further study of the models and methods of decision research that are outlined in Table 10.1: Cyert and March (1963), Wilcox (1972), Mintzberg (1973, particularly Appendixes B and C), and Farace, Monge, and Russell (1977, particularly Chapters 9 and 10). Wilcox provides a cognitive perspective; that of Cyert and March is both cognitive and organizational; while both Mintzberg and Farace, Monge, and Russell provide primarily a basis for describing and diagnosing individual decision-making behavior in an organizational context.

8. This requirement excludes the use of measures of cognitive style (see McKenney and Keen, 1977). A key concept for cognitive style measures is precisely that they are intended to measure characteristics of behavior that are general and thus are not bound to any specific decision situation (that is, the behavior is independent of the cognitive domain). However, it does not seem very useful for specifying the actual design of a production planning system to know that a decision maker has a "heuristic" decision style. I would rather know what variables the decision maker considers, what relationships between variables are considered and how they are viewed, when and why the inputs from the marketing managers are ignored, etc.

9. For additional background information on planning and decision situations in shipping, consult the Gotaas-Larsen Case in Alter (1980, pp. 47–70).

10. Recent decisions are sampled in order to avoid the tendency for a manager to make very broad and general statements when asked to describe how decisions are made. A more representative view is obtained by probing for unusual features of the specific decision cases considered.

11. There might be an opportunity for improving a manager's ability to communicate the assumptions and conclusions of the analysis.

12. Understanding the cognitive dimension of the decision process is key to the design of the interface in a computer-based DSS. Understanding the organizational dimension of the decision process is important for defining the setting, current problems with and opportunities for improving organizational support systems, limits to improvements in decision-making effectiveness, and implementation problems.

13. The effect of a decision-oriented organization of the DSS inputs can be increased by deliberately focusing the user's attention on the distinction during the introduction of the system. The design of computer-based functions and the design of user training are two interdependent aspects of DSS design. It is also important to recognize the need for training in active system use—how to use the system in support of decision making, how the system relates to the decision situation, and how the perspective on the decision situation is embodied in the system design. User training is not merely training in the mechanics of system use.

REFERENCES

Ackoff, R. L. (1967). "Management Misinformation Systems," *Management Science*, 14(4), 147–56.

Alter, S. L. (1980). *Decision Support Systems: Current Practice and Continuing Challenges*. Reading, Mass.: Addison-Wesley.

Bachrach, P., and M. S. Baratz (1962). "The Two Faces of Power," *American Politcal Science Review*, 56, 947–52.

Braybrooke, D. (1963). "The Mystery of Executive Success Re-examined," *Administrative Science Quarterly*, 8(4), 533–60.

Brooks, F. P., Jr. (1975). *The Mythical Man-Month*. Reading, Mass.: Addison-Wesley.

Cheriton, D. R. (1976). "Man-Machine Interface Design for Time-Sharing Systems," in *Proceedings of the Association for Computing Machinery National Conference*, New York, 362–80.

Clarkson, G. P. E. (1962). *Portfolio Selection: A Simulation of Trust Investment*. Englewood Cliffs, N.J.: Prentice-Hall.

Cyert, R. M., and J. G. March (1963). *A Behavioral Theory of the Firm*. Englewood Cliffs, N.J.: Prentice-Hall.

Farace, R. V., P. R. Monge, and H. M. Russell (1977). *Communicating and Organizing*. Reading, Mass.: Addison-Wesley.

Fick, G., and R. H. Sprague, Jr. (eds.) (1980). *Decision Support Systems: Issues and Challenges*. London: Pergamon Press.

Gerrity, T. P., Jr. (1971). "Design of Man-Machine Decision Systems: An Application to Portfolio Management," *Sloan Management Review*, 12(2), 59–75.

Green, P. E., and D. S. Tull (1972). *Research for Marketing Decisions*. Englewood Cliffs, N.J.: Prentice-Hall.

Guedj, R. A., P. J. W. tenHagen, F. R. A. Hopwood, H. A. Tucker, and D. A. Tuce (eds.) (1980). *Methodology of Interaction*. Amsterdam: North Holland.

Keen, P. G. W. (1976). "Computer Systems for Top Managers: A Modest Proposal," *Sloan Management Review*, 18(1), 1–17.

Keen, P. G. W. (1980). "Decision Support Systems: A Research Perspective," in G. Fick and R. H. Sprague, Jr. (eds.), *Decision Support Systems: Issues and Challenges*. London: Pergamon Press.

Keen, P. G. W., and R. D. Hackathorn (1979). "Decision Support Systems and Personal Computing," Working Paper 79-91-03. Philadelphia: Department of Decision Sciences, The Wharton School, University of Pennsylvania.

Keen, P. G. W., and M. S. Scott Morton (1978). *Decision Support Systems: An Organizational Perspective*. Reading, Mass.: Addison-Wesley.

Little, J. D. C. (1970). "Models and Managers: The Concept of a Decision Calculus," *Management Science*, 16(8), 466–85.

March, J., and H. A. Simon (1958). *Organizations*. New York: Wiley.

Mason, R. O., and I. I. Mitroff (1973). "A Program for Research on Management Information Systems," *Management Science*, 19(5), 475–87.

McKenney, J. L., and P. G. W. Keen (1977). "How Managers' Minds Work," *Harvard Business Review*, 52(3), 79–90.

Meador, C. L., and D. N. Ness (1974). "Decision Support Systems: An Application to Corporate Planning," *Sloan Management Review*, 15(2), 51–68.

Mintzberg, H. (1973). *The Nature of Managerial Work*. New York: Harper & Row.

Mintzberg, H., D. Raisinghani, and A. Théorêt (1976). "The Structure of Unstructured Decision Processes," *Administrative Science Quarterly*, 21, 246–75.

Rockart, J., and M. Treacy (1980). "Executive Information Support Systems," Report No. 65. Cambridge, Mass.: Center for Information Systems Research, Sloan School of Management, M.I.T.

Scott Morton, M. S. (1971). *Management Decision Systems: Computer-Based Support for Decision Making*. Cambridge, Mass.: Division of Research, Graduate School of Business Administration, Harvard University.

Shneiderman, B. (1980). *Software Psychology: Human Factors in Computer and Information Systems*. Cambridge, Mass.: Winthrop.

Simon, H. A. (1977). *The New Science of Management Decisions*, 2nd ed. Englewood Cliffs, N.J.: Prentice-Hall.

Simon, H. A. (1981). *The Sciences of the Artificial*, 2nd ed. Cambridge, Mass.: MIT Press.

Smith, H. T., and T. R. G. Green (eds.) (1980). *Human Interaction with Computers*. New York: Academic Press.

Sprague, R. H., Jr. (1980). "A Framework for Research on Decision Support Systems," in G. Fick and R. H. Sprague, Jr. (eds), *Decision Support Systems: Issues and Challenges*. London: Pergamon Press.

Stabell, C. B. (1974). "On the Development of Decision Support Systems as a Marketing Problem," in *Proceedings of IFIP 1974*. Amsterdam: North Holland.

Stabell, C. B. (1975). "Design and Implementation of Decision Support Systems: Some Implications of a Recent Study," in P. G. W. Keen (ed.), *The Implementation of Computer-Based Decision Aids*, Proceedings of a Conference Sponsored by the Center for Information Systems Research, April 3–5. Cambridge, Mass.: M.I.T.

Stabell, C. B. (1978). "On Defining and Improving Decision Making Effectiveness," Research Paper No. 287. Palo Alto, Calif.: Graduate School of Business, Stanford University.

Stabell, C. B. (1979). "Decision Research: Description and Diagnosis of Decision Making in Organizations," Working Paper No. 79.006. Bergen: Institute for Information Systems Research, Norwegian School of Economics and Business Administration.

Stabell, C. B., and A. M. Fuglseth (1981). "The D*2 Approach to Decision Support," Working Paper No. 81.002. Bergen: Institute for Information Systems Research, Norwegian School of Economics and Business Administration.

Uhlig, R. P., D. J. Farber, and J. H. Bair (1979). *The Office of the Future*. Amsterdam: North Holland.

Wagner, G. R. (1981). "DSS: Dealing with Executive Assumptions in the Office of the Future," in D. Young and P. G. W. Keen (eds.), *Transactions of DSS-81*. Austin, Tex.: Execucom Systems Corporation.

Wilcox, J. W. (1972). *A Method for Measuring Decision Assumptions*. Cambridge, Mass.: MIT Press.

Young, D., and P. G. W. Keen (eds.) (1981). *Transactions of DSS-81*. Austin, Tex.: Execucom Systems Corporation.

INDEX

THE AUTHOR TEAMS

Though the first four chapters were written separately by John Bennett and Eric Carlson, the themes developed represent their close work together at the IBM Research Laboratory, San Jose.

John has been a Research Staff Member since 1961. He received a BS in Engineering Science from Stanford and an MS in Electrical Engineering from MIT (1961). While at MIT he worked on implementation of the COMIT language, used in string manipulation for mechanical translation research. At San Jose he worked on information retrieval techniques, the Geodata Analysis and Display System (GADS), and usability requirements for terminal-based interactive systems. He has been manager of Geographic Data Systems and of Interactive Problem-Solving Systems at the Research Laboratory. Recently he has worked with other IBM Divisions on integration of measurable, testable usability objectives into the development cycle for software products.

Eric's degrees underline the breadth of his studies: his undergraduate degree was in Economics, his Masters degree was in City Planning, and his Ph.D. was in Computer Science from the University of North Carolina at Chapel Hill (1972). Since joining the IBM Research Laboratory at San Jose in 1972 he has been involved in research on improved hardware and software for interactive computer applications. He was a member of the team that developed GADS, one of the first DSS to make extensive use of computer graphics. From 1974 to 1976 he managed the DSS research group at IBM, San Jose. He was Chairman of the ACM/MIT/ Wharton/IBM Conference on Decision Support Systems in 1977 and edited the Proceedings published in *DATABASE*. He currently manages a group of thirty computer scientists working on advanced application systems at the Research Laboratory.

Chapter 5 is a good example of team collaboration. Jim Dyer and John Mulvey began their work on the faculty course-scheduling model while Dyer was Vice-Chairman of the Graduate School of Management at the University of California at Los Angeles (UCLA) and Mulvey was a doctoral student. The task began as an implementation of a state-of-the-art optimization model. It soon became apparent that usability was more important than algorithmic sophistication in determining the success of their project. They came to view their final product as an optimization problem imbedded within a DSS.

Jim obtained both his BA in Physics and his Ph.D. in Business Administration from the University of Texas (1969). He is currently Jack G. Taylor Professor of Business at the Graduate School of Business, University of Texas.

John completed his Ph.D. in Management Science at UCLA (1975). His BS is in General Engineering and his MS is in Computer Science. During the time he was in the program at UCLA he was a manager of various Management Science projects at TRW, Inc. (1969–75). He is currently an Associate Professor in Engineering Management Systems at Princeton University. He teaches courses in Corporate Planning, Applications of Linear Programming, and Decision Analysis for Public Policy.

Gerry Hurst was the driving force behind Chapter 6. He organized the collection of observations that might be called "the Wharton experience." His BS in Civil Engineering, MS in Operations Research, and Ph.D. in Management (1967) are all from MIT. He has taught courses in Production and Operations Management, Information Systems, and Multinational Enterprise Management. He is currently Associate Professor of Decision Sciences at The Wharton School, University of Pennsylvania.

David Ness gained much of his experience in DSS as consulting associate and co-founder of Interactive Market Systems of New York. His academic work was in Management at MIT and Economics and Philosophy at Oxford, where he was a Rhodes Scholar (1961). Prior to joining the Wharton faculty, he was Associate Professor of Management Science at the Sloan School, MIT, and a member of the research staff at Project MAC. He is currently Vice Dean and Associate Professor of Decision Sciences at The Wharton School, University of Pennsylvania, where he teaches courses in Business Policy and Strategy, Computers, and Decision Support.

Tom Gambino has been building systems to provide decision support services for over ten years. He has a BS in Economics from the University of Pennsylvania and an MBA from The Wharton School (1976). Between 1976 and 1979 he was a lecturer at The Wharton School, where he taught introductory courses in Information Systems and Decision Support Systems. He has consulted for a large number of private and public institutions. He is currently an editor for the Addison-Wesley Series on Practical Computing, and he is the author of Micro-DSS*/Analysis, a product that is the outgrowth of the work reported in Chapter 7.

Tom Johnson started working in DSS as Director of Corporate MIS for IU International, where he managed the development and use of corporate-strategy

*Trademark.

decision support systems for this $2.5 billion conglomerate (1969–73). He was Chairman of the Department of Information Systems Applied to Management at the University of Grenoble from 1976 to 1978. While in France he started a research program with twelve corporations that led to the thesis by Grajew and Tolovi referenced in the chapter. At Nolan, Norton & Company he continues research and consulting in DSS as a Director of Research and Manager of Advanced Consulting Services. He has a BS in Electrical Engineering from Carnegie-Mellon University and an MS in Computer and Information Sciences from the University of Pennsylvania (1967).

The work reported in Chapter 7 grew out of a mutual interest in effective support for public policy analysis in school funding. Peter Keen and Tom Gambino collaborated while Peter was visiting at The Wharton School. The account of ISSPA, influenced by Peter's wide experience while teaching and consulting at Stanford and MIT, illustrates well the problems in moving from an application to a system product.

Peter's research has focused on the links between computers and people: DSS, implementation, organizational change, and the design of systems for non-technical managers and professionals. His undergraduate degree is in English Literature from Oxford, and he earned MBA and DBA degrees in Organization Behavior, Computer-Based Information Systems from Harvard (1973). He is currently Associate Professor of Management Science at the Sloan School of Management and on the staff of the Center for Information Systems Research at MIT. His book, *Decision Support Systems: An Organizational Perspective*, written with Michael Scott Morton, was the first in the Addison-Wesley Series on DSS. He is consulting editor for the Addison-Wesley Software Series on Practical Computing, which includes a microcomputer version and extension of ISSPA (Micro-DSS*/Analysis). He is also managing editor of the journal *Office: Technology and People*.

Tom's expertise in APL played a major role in the development of ISSPA. His deep understanding of user needs comes out of his skill in working one-on-one with policy analysts. He is the author of Micro-DSS*/Analysis issued by Addison-Wesley. His background is reviewed in the description of Chapter 6 authors.

Jeff Moore and Mike Chang documented the experience reported in Chapter 8 while Mike was a doctoral student at Stanford. Their analysis of their separate adventures in building DSS led to the meta-design observations they make.

Jeff has a BS in Electrical Engineering from the University of Cincinnati, an MBA and MS in Computer Science from Texas A. & M., and a Ph.D. in Business Administration from the University of California, Berkeley (1973). He has consulted for over a dozen companies in the organization of MIS, the design of DSS,

*Trademark.

and business planning for computer operations. He is currently Assistant Dean for Computer and Information Systems at the Graduate School of Business, Stanford, where he teaches courses in MIS and in Computers.

Mike gained experience in building computer systems while working for several years with commercial application development and systems programming groups in industry, using a variety of IBM, Hewlett Packard, and Digital Equipment Corporation equipment. He earned a BS in Computer Science and Engineering from MIT, an MS in Management from Sloan School of Management (MIT), an MS in Operations Research from Stanford, and his Ph.D. in Decision Sciences from the Stanford School of Business (1981). His current interests are in expert systems, use of graphics to convey information to managers, and advanced manager workstations. He is now Assistant Professor of Decision Sciences, The Wharton School, University of Pennsylvania.

Tony Gorry and Rand Krumland worked together at MIT and later at the Baylor College of Medicine, where they developed their view of the relationship of artificial intelligence research to issues in building DSS.

Tony has a BS in Chemical Engineering from Yale and an MS in Chemical Engineering from the University of California at Berkeley. His Ph.D. in Computer Science is from MIT (1967). During his seven years on the Management and Computer Science faculty at MIT he did research on management science models and decision support systems. He has been a consultant to a variety of industrial companies and educational institutions. His participation in the development of several large computer programs to assist in medical decision making made use of research in artificial intelligence. He is now Vice President of Baylor College of Medicine and Adjunct Professor of Mathematical Sciences at Rice University, Houston, Texas.

Rand received a BS in Engineering Physics from the University of California at Berkeley, an MS in Electrical Engineering from Stanford, and his Ph.D. in Management Planning and Control, with emphasis on Information Systems Technology, from the Sloan School of Management, MIT (1977). While at MIT he worked at the Laboratory for Computer Science (formerly Project MAC) on knowledge-based systems for managers and on automatic programming techniques appropriate for standard data processing applications. His thesis work was on knowledge systems designed to help a manager construct a financial model. At Baylor he was on the faculty in Health Management. He is currently manager of Information Systems Planning, Policy and Research for The El Paso Company in Houston.

Charles Stabell, along with Peter Keen, serves as a Series Editor for the Addison-Wesley Series on DSS. Charles was inspired to write his observations on the relation of building DSS to his own work on "decision research" while reviewing the chapters of his fellow authors. His chapter, therefore, makes connections among the experiences of the various authors and points to the continuing challenge we all face in an effort to be certain that the systems we build do indeed support *decisions*.

Charles has a BS in Engineering from Grenoble University, an MS in Business Administration from McGill University, and his Ph.D. in Management from The Sloan School of Management, MIT (1974). His thesis topic addressed the impact of an interactive system for portfolio management used by thirty managers in the trust department of a large bank. Before beginning his studies in North America, he gained industrial experience when he spent three years as a systems engineer with IBM Norway, where he worked on a prototype data base/data communications system for the Norwegian government. He has served on the faculty at Stanford and has had extensive experience consulting for government and industry. He is currently Associate Professor of Information Systems at the Norwegian School of Economics and Business Administration, Bergen, Norway.